REGIONAL ECONOMICS

A STUDY IN THE ECONOMIC STRUCTURE, STABILITY, AND GROWTH OF REGIONS

HUGH O. NOURSE
ASSOCIATE PROFESSOR
OF ECONOMICS
UNIVERSITY OF MISSOURI—
ST. LOUIS

McGRAW-HILL
BOOK COMPANY

NEW YORK
ST. LOUIS
SAN FRANCISCO
TORONTO
LONDON
SYDNEY

REGIONAL ECONOMICS

Library of Congress Catalog Card Number
68-11935
ISBN 07-047547-4

7890 MAMM 754321

PREFACE

This book is intended for two groups of students. It is meant to be an introduction to location theory and regional economic development for undergraduate juniors and seniors in economics. It is also meant to be an introduction to the economic analysis useful to students in geography, city planning, and urban land economics. To serve both groups of students I have tried to keep the analysis as simple as possible and to explain the techniques of economic analysis when they are introduced. Although these explanations of techniques of analysis are repetitious to students with some study of economics, it is my experience that they need to be repeated. There is no denying, however, that the material will be much easier and more understandable to those with a course in principles of economics and in intermediate economic theory. Perhaps by showing the usefulness of the struggle to students in geography, city planning, and urban land economics, this book will induce them to pursue further study in economic analysis.

I wish to thank Edgar M. Hoover, Jr. and Howard Roepke for their helpful comments on a draft of the entire manuscript. I should also like to thank the following persons who commented on various parts of the manuscript when it was in preliminary draft: George Borts, Charles Goetz, Robert Harbeson, Richard F. Muth, Charles M. Tiebout, and Harold F. Williamson, Jr.

HUGH O. NOURSE

CONTENTS

CHAPTER 1

SCOPE AND METHOD OF REGIONAL ECONOMICS

Economics is the study of social organizations formed to produce and distribute scarce goods and services. Economists, however, usually neglect the spatial arrangement of the social order, and prefer to analyze an economy as if it were located at a point. *Regional economics* is the study of the neglected spatial order of the economy. It is the study of the geographic allocation of scarce resources. Households, retail stores, wholesale outlets, manufacturing plants, corporate headquarters, research laboratories, schools, churches, banks, farms, and mines are not chaotically located in the cities and regions of the world, but show an order and pattern that can be studied and understood.

The method for studying the geographic allocation of resources will be that of traditional economic analysis. Economic models of the spatial pattern of economic activity will be constructed that fit into the traditional models of the economy. They are not meant to be exact descriptions of the actual geographic distribution of economic activity. They are models showing tendencies. Their importance is not so much that they predict where activities will be situated as that they isolate the critical variables causing change and predict how the geographic distribution of economic activity will change with changes in the critical variables. Furthermore, it is impossible to interpret the complexity of reality without theories to indicate the meaning of facts. Facts have no meaning without interpretation. Theories are needed to link facts together so that they can be interpreted. Most of the book is devoted to developing the models, but Chapter 9 is an attempt to tie them all together in order to predict locational changes resulting from population growth, increases in per capita income, and changes in technology.

This book is not an analysis of the location of individual industries, although the principles for such an analysis are included. It is an analysis of the location patterns of people and industry in general. So that you may understand more fully this point of view, a thumbnail sketch, or road map, of the study follows.

THUMBNAIL SKETCH OF REGIONAL ECONOMICS

Businesses and households locate where they can gain more than they can elsewhere. Businesses provide goods and services to households, and they profit by providing the goods people want. Business puts together resources as efficiently as possible so that profits may be greater; one aspect of efficient production of goods and services is location. Some locations will yield greater profits than others. Businesses do not locate where costs are least, or receipts greatest, but where the positive difference, profits, is greatest.

Households gain by locating where they would most like to be, but this location must also include the opportunity to earn income from ownership of resources sold to business, including labor. Households, therefore, tend to locate where employment opportunities exist. Thus, we can concentrate on the location of production, rather than on the location of individual households.

In order to concentrate on the economic factors determining location patterns of production, assume that there is a flat plain over which natural resources and population are uniformly distributed. Two factors will cause the establishment of trading areas in such a plain. One factor is that average cost decreases with increased rates of production, so that it is profitable for one firm to produce and sell to others. The producer's price will be less than the cost to individual families of producing the goods. The second factor is that the limit of the market or trading area will be determined by the transportation cost of shipping the product. Each producer of a particular good will find a site away from his rivals. Finally, there will be a honeycomb of trading areas on the plain for each product. Each will be just large enough to yield sufficient sales to keep the firms in business. Under certain conditions there will be a finite number of possible trading area sizes. Thus, many economic activities will have the same size market areas.

If we assume that each activity with the same size market area is distributed so that one of each is in the center of each area in the honeycomb of areas, a system of cities will be generated. The smallest central place might be a small town providing convenience goods through a grocery store, drugstore, barber shop, and filling station. The size of the hinterland served would depend upon the trading area for each of the businesses, which must include enough families to yield sufficient sales for a profitable operation. For each of the stores providing convenience goods in the small town, the trading area would be about the same size. The towns providing convenience goods would be equally distant from each other, the distance depending upon how far people would be willing to travel for these goods.

Other retail outlets can have larger trading areas because household buyers are willing to travel longer distances to obtain their particular kinds of goods and services and a larger market is necessary to stay in business. For example, shopping for goods such as furniture and clothing, banking facilities, and perhaps schools can be provided to a trading area including several small towns and their hinterlands. The central place providing these added functions would be larger than each of the satellite towns that it services. City size would continue to increase with added functions. The largest central place, in turn, would provide all other places with certain functions. For example, New York provides international banking services to all areas of the United States, while several regional centers provide banking and other services to their respective hinterlands. The regional centers might include Chicago and Los Angeles. If we listed the cities from the lowest order (the town providing convenience goods to surrounding farmers) to the highest order (New York), we would be tracing out a hierarchy of cities.

Although pricing policies, population density, differences in managerial talent, topography, and political boundaries cause changes in the size and shapes of trading areas, the regularity of distances between places of the same population and the hierarchical structure of these places remain undisturbed. There are, however, several other factors causing distortion between the model and reality. Not every activity with the same size trading area will find it profitable to locate in the same place. The reasons why different activities with the same market size may not locate in the same center are that resources are not uniformly distributed, that labor productivity is not uniformly distributed, and that some activities will be drawn to the same center even though they do not have the same market size. Resources may attract firms from the center of their markets if lower input prices will offset reduced revenues and thus increase profits. The same would be true for sites where labor costs per unit of output would be lower. It may also be profitable to locate a plant adjacent to other plants in the same industry because of the advantages of a common input market, or it may be profitable to locate plants adjacent to each other because they have important transactions with each other.

The order in the spatial arrangement of land use within a particular city-region can also be logically derived from the firm's attempt to maximize profits. Every activity—selling, housing, manufacturing, farming, and mining—bids for space to operate. The activities that offer the highest bid for a particular site obtain it. The bid, or land rent, offered by each activity depends upon the profit that the activity can make at alternative sites. Two factors will be mainly responsible for differences in profits at different sites within a city region, and hence for the location patterns of various activities. They are the transportation cost to send goods to the market center and the output per acre of land. Once again assume that there is a flat plain over which natural resources are uniformly distributed.

In the center is the market for goods and services. Transportation costs increase at the same rate in every direction from the center. As distance from the center is increased, the rent offered for land will decline faster for those goods for which transportation cost is greater and for which physical volume of output per acre of land is greater. These goods will have to be located nearest the market, if they are to outbid other uses for land, since the amount that they can bid for rent declines faster with increasing distance than it does for other uses. This land use model yields a concentric land use pattern surrounding the central market, which under certain variations could be the central business district of a metropolitan area. Obviously, as transportation networks, waterways, topography, and historical change are taken into account, the neat concentric pattern is demolished. Nevertheless, the principles determining location are those isolated as being important in the model. In spite of these modifications some of the predictions of the model have been shown to be true. For example, it has been found that population density does decline with distance from the central business district, as would be suggested by the land use model.

Geographic patterns of economic activity are not static, but change with time. In order to analyze the changes, one must first be able to measure them. Measurement of the economic activities in city-regions is difficult. To measure activity in a place, the place must be bounded. Thus, the first problem is to define the region of study. We shall find that most regional definitions do not define "natural" regions; the reason is that clear-cut city-regions do not exist. The second problem is that once an area is defined and income or some other economic data are measured for the area, the data are treated in current systems as though they were located at a single point. Thus, the very act of measuring hides the continuity of the spatial order of the economy. The descriptive input-output model provides a framework that integrates the various accounts of a regional economy. Although data are not available to fill the conceptual boxes of the accounting framework, the concepts are useful variables in the analysis of differential growth in income and employment and of the differential susceptibility of regions to business cycles.

Short-run changes in the location of some economic activity or in the volume of some activity in a region will have a multiple impact on all employment and income in the region. The loss of exports because of the loss of a government contract, the loss of income because coal or other products are temporarily facing a falling demand due to cyclical declines in national income, or the temporary reduction in investments based on pessimistic expectations will cause a reduction of employment and income greater than the initial loss. The reason, of course, is that employees and others incurring a loss in income will spend less and cause a decline in retail sales in the local area. The short-run loss in income will vary between regions, depending upon the nature of exports, imports, and the structure of local industry. The same factors will also determine the effect of change in income of one region on that of other regions.

Long-run changes in the location of economic activity or its volume cause the growth and decline of regions. Such changes might include the shift of a specific manufacturing activity caused by changes in local production costs, market accessibility, or transportation costs in that area or elsewhere. Changes in the demand for local resources or products most profitably produced in the area are also in this category. For example, demand may increase, as it has in the last thirty years in the case of petroleum and natural gas, or decrease, as in the case of coal. These shifts in the growth of industry, or in the growth of industry in a particular place, may span a decade or more. The term "shift" as applied to industry does not necessarily mean the migration of workers, plant, and equipment; it can also be applied to the growth of new firms in a new area, as the old ones die in older areas.

The short-run and long-run impacts on regions of changes in the volume and location of economic activity are fundamentally different. In the short run, prices and wages do not have a chance to respond: the impact of a reduction in exports thus falls directly on the volume of employment and income in the region. In the long run, however, prices and wages would change in the region. As prices and wages fell as a result of a decline in exports, the region would be a more attractive place to locate industries attracted by low-wage labor. At the same time, some workers would migrate to other areas in which wages were higher. Of course, the size of the labor force might continue to grow as children reached working age, so that wages might remain depressed until new employment opportunities grew faster than the labor force. Thus, in the long run, prices and wages would change so that a region could adjust to a shift of economic activity.

The smooth working of the adjustment process may be hindered by certain factors. Uniform minimum wage laws throughout the whole nation may prevent further reduction of wages in some depressed areas. The lack of knowledge of employment opportunities in other areas, the lack of capital to retrain for new jobs, and the lack of capital to move a family to new locations may prevent workers from migrating from depressed areas. The shortage of skilled workers and transportation facilities and the lack of knowledge of investment possibilities prevent businesses from developing in depressed areas. These hindrances to the smooth working of the market mechanism create problem areas when there is a reduction of demand for a region's resources, when resources are depleted, or when industry shifts to other regions.

Moreover, the adjustment process might not take place, even if the market mechanism were working smoothly. If the migration decision is considered as if it were an investment decision, differences between regions in wages and rates of return on investment could persist because the rate of return on alternative investments could be greater than that on migration. In particular the return on investment in migration would be less for older workers because they have a shorter remaining working life and less for workers whose alternative opportunities for higher wages are farther from the worker's current location.

Local, state, and national policies may initiate depressed areas, have no effect, or help to bring readjustment. Taxation and expenditure policies channel funds from one region to another, but they can be channeled away from as well as toward depressed areas. Information concerning investment opportunities in depressed areas and employment opportunities for unemployed workers can be helpful if published. Subsidies to households for moving to places where job opportunities exist and for retraining assist in bringing about readjustment. Income transfers to the poor would also help.

Finally, many of the factors of economic growth cause changes in the geographic structure of the economy. Changes in population, per capita income, and technology affect the number, size, and spacing of cities, as well as land use patterns within and around them. The causal relation, however, is not one way. There is evidence that economic growth progresses more rapidly in regions adjacent to highly developed urban-industrial centers.

Thus, regional economics covers a broad range of topics. As we have seen, it includes a discussion of such questions as the following: What factors cause cities to arise at regular intervals? What factors cause systematic differences in size of cities? What factors lie behind the concentration and dispersion of industry? What factors are important in determining land use patterns within city-regions? What is the impact of the loss of exports from a region on income and employment in the short run? What causes depressed areas? What is the impact of increases in per capita income and population on the location and size of cities and the land use pattern within cities? What is the impact of the system of cities on the process of development? What is the scope for public policy with such regional problems as depressed areas and urban blight?

In spite of the breadth of these topics there is a connecting link among all of them. In finding answers to each question the solution appears to hinge on the determinants of the location of business. Recall that city size and location depend on the functions of the place, which in turn depends upon profitable locations for sellers. Land use patterns depend upon who can pay the highest rent, which is also dependent on the profitability of sites to firms. Short-run and long-run changes in income and employment depend upon why exports fall off. But this can be asked another way. Why is this region no longer a profitable location for the production of the particular export? The depressed area problem can also be viewed as a location problem. Why do families persist in locating where economic enterprise is unprofitable, and why do firms find such places unprofitable sites for investment since there are unemployed workers? Since locational analysis of the individual producer is central to an understanding of the economic structure, stabilization, and growth of regions, we shall begin in the next chapter with a detailed study of the location of production.

CHAPTER 2

LOCATION OF THE INDIVIDUAL PRODUCER

The profits of the individual producer are his receipts minus his costs. Consumer tastes, income, and the prices of substitute products affect the receipts of an industry and the individual producer. Improved organization, new technology, and a more skilled work force affect costs. Changes in location, however, may also affect the receipts and costs of the producer. Since the producer's primary goal is to maximize his profits, and since some places will yield greater profits than others, his location is as important as his price and output. After a brief discussion of the profit motive in location decisions, this chapter will attempt to explain how various factors affect the profitability of sites through use of the theory of the firm. Although the theory may appear extremely abstract and unnecessary at this juncture, its usefulness for developing the underlying logic of regional structure will be clear in the next chapter.[1] Chapter 4 will specifically use the framework developed in this chapter to discuss the way in which agglomeration, transportation, and labor can influence the profitability of sites.

MAXIMIZING PROFIT

The producer can be viewed as a rational man seeking out the most profitable location by economic analysis of alternative sites, prices, and output. Surveys of manufacturers seeking the reasons for the location of new plants, however, have revealed that personal reasons rather than economic factors are important in a large number of cases. This would seem to contradict the assumption that the firm primarily attempts to maximize profits. For example, the results of one recent survey of manufacturers in Michigan, reported in Table 2-1, indicate that personal reasons were an important factor in location decisions.

The importance of personal reasons in the location decision may be stated too strongly in these surveys. For example, a man living in a particular community and wanting to continue to live there may decide to go into business for himself. The business that he establishes will be one that he

---

[1] Persons already familiar with the theory of the firm may wish to skip to the last section of this chapter, the conditions for optimum location. Nevertheless, those unfamiliar with the theory in a spatial setting will find enough new to at least skim this chapter. Those for whom the discussion in this chapter is too brief should consult a good intermediate text in economic theory, such as Richard H. Leftwich, *The Price System and Resource Allocation*, 3d ed. (New York: Holt, Rinehart, and Winston, Inc., 1966).

thinks will be profitable in that place. Nevertheless, the reasons that he would give in the interview would be personal reasons. This decision is not less economic than that of the individual who moves a business into a particular place because of some economic factor.[2]

The survey results also indicate that personal reasons are more important for small firms than for large firms, and are more important for new than for old firms. Large firms locating a new branch would be expected to rely more on cost and receipt information than on personal preference for

[2] Charles M. Tiebout, "Location Theory, Empirical Evidence, and Economic Evolution," *Papers and Proceedings of the Regional Science Association,* vol. 3 (1957); pp. 80–82.

TABLE 2-1 EXPLANATIONS GIVEN FOR LOCATION OF PLANT BY NUMBER OF PLANTS OPERATED BY FIRM

	Number of plants operated by firm			
	All Michigan	1 plant	2–4 plants	5 or more plants
Main reasons for locating plant in Michigan*	Percentage of employment represented			
Personal reasons; chance	50	63	52	32
Opportunity—found good site, etc.	19	23	20	14
Proximity to customers; central location	15	17	20	4
Proximity to auto industry	8	14	4	4
Labor advantages	7	†	12	14
Proximity to materials	6	3	8	9
Local concessions and inducements; encouragement by groups or persons	2	†	†	4
Better tax situation	1	†	†	4
State already established as a center for the industry	1	†	4	†
Total	‡	‡	‡	‡

* Asked only at plants that started operating at present locations after 1940. The question was: "What were the main reasons for locating the plant in Michigan?"
† Less than one-half of 1 percent.
‡ Totals differ from 100 percent because some respondents mentioned more than one reason, and for some others the reasons were not ascertained.

SOURCE: By permission from Eva Mueller, Arnold Wilken, and Margaret Wood, *Location Decisions and Industrial Mobility in Michigan, 1961* (Ann Arbor, Mich.: Institute of Social Research, The University of Michigan, 1961), p. 16.

particular towns. As it happens, new firms are also small firms. Their location is more likely to be based on personal preferences.

Obviously, if a producer sacrifices monetary profit in order to reap the nonpecuniary gain of a particular place, he is being rational. His decision would conform to a broader definition of profit that would include both pecuniary and nonpecuniary gain. Nevertheless, if the nonpecuniary influences dominated location decisions, location patterns based on economic analysis would not usefully describe reality.

Chance is associated with personal reasons in Table 2-1 as a reason for a Michigan site. In the uncertain world that we live in, producers do not have the information to select a site that would maximize profits. Even if plants were established randomly by choice or chance, competition would cause a pattern of locations to emerge. The pattern that emerges is the one predicted by assuming that firms acted as if they maximized profits.[3] The analysis that follows is useful for predicting patterns of location, but may not predict the location decision of a particular producer.[4] Thus, the test of the usefulness of the following analysis will be the locational patterns of economic activity that it explains.

To maximize profits the producer selects the product and the rate of production that will yield the maximum excess of receipts over cost. Cost will increase with increases in the rate of production. But cost may vary for a particular rate of production because of the production method— the combination of inputs used. Obviously, the producer will combine inputs in the most efficient way for the rate of production that is selected. For exposition purposes it is assumed that the choice of product has been made. The minimum-cost combination of inputs will be explained first. Then the relationship of cost and receipts to rate of production will be analyzed in separate sections. Minimum cost, rate of production, and receipts will be integrated in the final section on the conditions for the optimal (most profitable) location.

MINIMIZING COST

A labor force equipped with different skills is combined with other resources such as materials, equipment, buildings, land, and management to yield

[3] This is the "survival argument" found in Edgar M. Hoover, *The Location of Economic Activity* (New York: McGraw-Hill Book Company, 1948), pp. 9–10; Armen Alchian, "Uncertainty, Evolution, and Economic Theory," *Journal of Political Economy*, vol. 58 (June, 1950), pp. 211–221; and Tiebout, *op. cit.*, pp. 83–86.
[4] One mistaken argument against the "survival argument" states that the theory of the firm must select the characteristics of the surviving firm to be correct. See Sidney G. Winter, "Economic 'Natural Selection' and the Theory of the Firm," *Yale Economic Essays*, vol. 4, no. 1 (Spring, 1964), p. 240. The point is that the theory is not a theory of the behavior of individual entrepreneurs or corporations.

an output. For example, a producer can use many semiskilled workers and a large amount of machinery in an assembly-line process, or he can hire highly skilled workers and use less machinery. The economist calls this relationship between the inputs and the rate of production the production function. The *production function,* thus, describes the possible combinations of resources for producing any particular output per hour, day, week, or other unit of time.

The particular combination chosen depends upon the relative prices of each of the inputs. Usually, no one producer is sufficiently large to effect changes in prices of resources that he must purchase. Thus, prices of inputs are thought of as being fixed to the producer. Nevertheless, they are fixed in particular places, and he may be able to reduce the price paid for land, labor, or materials by considering alternative locations. Therefore, to find the least-cost combination for any rate of production, the producer must calculate the minimum-cost combination at each alternative site.

These concepts and relationships can be made more explicit by the following graphical analysis. In Figure 2-1, physical quantities of one input are measured along the vertical axis, and physical quantities of another input are measured along the horizontal axis. Assume that only two inputs

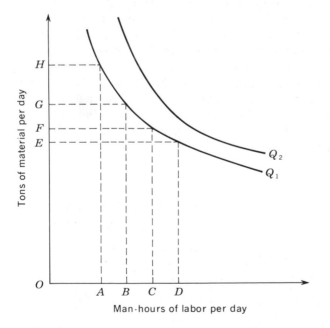

FIGURE 2-1

are required in the production process. One might be tons of material; the other might be man-hours of labor. Assume also that the state of technological knowledge allows the producer to make the product, perhaps some kind of toy, in many ways, so that continuous infinitesimal changes, substituting labor for materials or materials for labor, can be made while maintaining the same rate of production. The curve Q_1 represents all combinations of labor and material that will produce a particular rate of production. Such a curve is an *isoquant.* The figure illustrates that the rate of production Q_1 can be achieved using OA man-hours and OH tons of material, or OB man-hours and OG tons of material, or one of the many other combinations traced out by the isoquant Q_1. Isoquant Q_2 represents the possible combinations of labor and material to produce a greater rate of production.

Both isoquants are convex to the origin. Over the relevant range of possibilities a reduction in man-hours of labor requires an increase in tons of material to maintain the same rate of production. Furthermore, while labor and materials may be substitutes, they are not perfect substitutes. As fewer man-hours and more tons of material are used, it becomes more difficult to substitute additional material for man-hours. Therefore, equal reductions in man-hours from OD to OC, from OC to OB, and from OB to OA require increasing increments of tons of material, EF, FG, and GH, to maintain the same rate of production.

The least-cost combination depends upon the prices per ton of material and per man-hour of labor. Suppose prices are given for one of the alternative sites. If the prices were $2 per man-hour and $1 per ton of material, $1,000 could buy either 500 man-hours or 1,000 tons of material. It would also be possible to buy 800 tons of material and 100 man-hours, or any other combination of material and labor the cost of which sums to $1,000. In Figure 2-2, the line XY shows the combinations of material and man-hours that could be bought with a constant sum of money, given prices. Such a line is an *isocost* line. OY shows the tons of material that could be purchased if the whole sum were used to buy materials. OX shows the man-hours that could be bought if the whole sum were used to buy man-hours. The line XY traces out the combinations of purchases of both inputs that could be made with this sum.

If the price per man-hour of labor should be higher at a second site, say $2.50 per man-hour, fewer man-hours (only 400) could be purchased with the $1,000 if it were all spent on labor. Suppose the price per ton of material is the same at the second site, so that 1,000 tons could still be purchased if the sum were all spent on material. If $800 were spent on 800 tons of material, 100 man-hours of labor could be bought at the first site with the

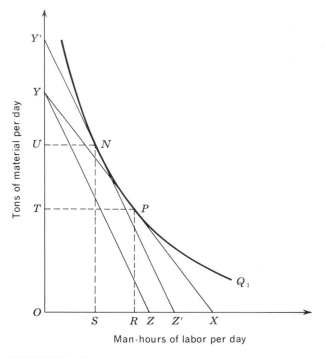

FIGURE 2-2

remaining $200, but only 80 man-hours could be bought at the second site. The possible quantities of inputs that could be purchased at the second site with an outlay equal to that of XY are shown in Figure 2-2 by the iso-cost line YZ. The vertical intercept OY is unchanged since the price of material is the same. The horizontal intercept OZ is less than OX since fewer man-hours can be purchased with the outlay at the second site.

Parallel shifts of the isocost line represent changes in the total outlay without changes in the relative prices of the inputs. A shift away from the origin, as from YZ to $Y'Z'$, represents an increase in total outlay. The line $Y'Z'$ shows the quantities of material and man-hours that could be purchased at the second site with a greater outlay. Similarly, parallel shifts toward the origin represent lower total outlays. Since XY and YZ represent the same outlay with different sets of prices, and $Y'Z'$ represents a greater outlay than YZ, $Y'Z'$ also represents a greater outlay than XY.

Given the prices of inputs, say as they are at the first site, the isocost line XY bounds a triangular area OXY that includes all the combinations that It Is possible to buy with the given outlay or less outlay. The question of finding the least-cost combination of inputs to produce an output is the same as asking which combination of inputs with a given outlay will produce the largest output. For the outlay represented by XY in Figure 2-2, the highest output obtainable is Q_1. This is the highest isoquant that XY touches. XY is tangent to Q_1 at P. Higher outputs are represented by isoquants farther from the origin than Q_1. Higher outputs would require combinations of inputs represented by points outside the triangle OXY, and thus could not be obtained with the given outlay and prices. This also means that XY represents the least cost for which output Q_1 could be produced. Greater outlays could be used to produce Q_1, but lower outlays could not purchase enough inputs for producing output Q_1.

In Figure 2-2, the least-cost combination of man-hours and material to produce output Q_1 at the first site is OR man-hours of labor and OT tons of material, as shown by point P. The least-cost combination of man-hours and material to produce Q_1 at the second site is OS man-hours of labor and OU tons of material, as shown by the point N. At N, the isocost line $Y'Z'$ is just tangent to the isoquant Q_1. The first site requires less cost to produce output Q_1 than the second site since, as noted above, $Y'Z'$ represents a higher outlay than XY.

COST AND SCALE OF OUTPUT

So far, we have held the rate of production constant. The next step is to vary the rate of production and relate it to the changes in cost that are incurred. In Figure 2-3 we can trace the least-cost combinations of man-hours and material at the first site given the input prices described in the previous section.

The points A through F represent the least-cost combinations for each of the rates of production Q_1 through Q_6 respectively. The line connecting these points, OF in Figure 2-3, is an expansion path. The cost of producing a level of output is determined by the value represented by the isocost line tangent to the appropriate isoquant. In Figure 2-4 the total cost at each rate of production is shown as the height of the curve at a given output. For example, the total cost for the rate of production Q_3 is Q_3C. The curve OF in Figure 2-4 traces the total costs at all the alternative rates of production.

In Figure 2-4, total cost is zero when the rate of production is zero. This would not always be the case. If the planning horizon of the firm is only a

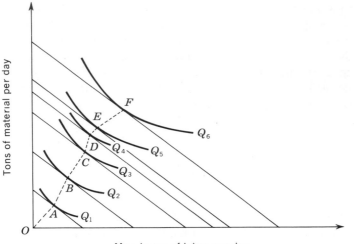

FIGURE 2-3

few years, and the questions being asked are only about output and pricing, there would be no question of building another plant. During such a period, the firm incurs fixed costs, costs incurred whether it produces or not. Economists describe this situation as the "short run." For a longer planning horizon, however, there may be a question whether the plant should be producing at all, or whether it should be producing in another place. Economists describe this situation as the "long run." The location

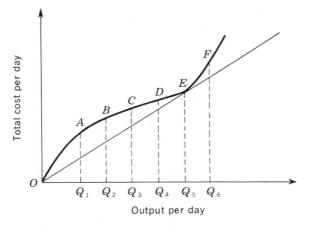

FIGURE 2-4

decision is a long-run decision in which all costs are variable costs. There are no fixed costs incurred if production is completely stopped and the investment is sold. The long-run total cost curve, such as OF in Figure 2-4, shows the least cost for achieving each rate of production with the most efficient size of plant. There would be a separate long-run total cost curve for each alternative site.

Total cost divided by the rate of production yields average cost. In Figure 2-4, the slope of OE is Q_5E divided by OQ_5. Since Q_5E is total cost and OQ_5 is the rate of production, the slope of OE is the average cost of producing OQ_5. In Figure 2-4, the slopes of lines from the origin to points on the cost curve decrease until OE is reached. After point OE the slopes increase. Thus, as the rate of production increases to OQ_5, average cost decreases. As the rate of production increases to rates greater than OQ_5, average cost increases.

Up to OQ_5 units, the more that is produced, the less the cost is per unit. This condition of decreasing average cost is called *economies of scale.* Economies of scale may be the result of a number of factors. Purchases of some inputs in large quantities often reduce input prices by quantity discounts. The fuller use of some inputs with a large fixed capacity will reduce the average cost of using such inputs. The less than proportionate increase in reserves required for unexpected interruptions in supply, increases in demand, or production breakdowns by large plants will reduce the average cost of inventories. A greater rate of production also allows more specialization of functions with its attendant greater efficiency.[5]

Long-run average costs may increase with increased rates of production, as they do in Figure 2-4 for rates of production greater than OQ_5, mainly because of limitations in flexibility, adaptability, and managerial capacity. Flexibility and adaptability are lost in very large operations. Furthermore, some operations require rapid changes in rates of production or in product (to meet changes in seasonal demand and in tastes of the consumer), so that these diseconomies occur with relatively small size. For example, high-style clothing could not be mass-produced. On the other hand, the production of cloth can utilize larger and less flexible facilities because the demands for the basic product do not change rapidly either in kind or in quantity. In any operation managerial capacity becomes less efficient with greater rates of production because the coordination of all activities becomes more difficult. The elaborate forms of coordination required may cause average costs to rise.

[5] For further elaboration on economies of scale and the diseconomies of the next paragraph, see E. A. G. Robinson, *The Structure of Competitive Industry* (Chicago: The University of Chicago Press, 1958).

RECEIPTS AND LOCATION

Cost information is insufficient to determine the most profitable rate of production or the most profitable site. The potential receipts of the plant at each site and for each rate of production are needed. Total receipts are price per unit times the total quantity sold. The total quantity sold depends on the number of customers and the quantity each customer purchases. The number of customers and the quantity each customer purchases depend on their incomes and taste, the prices of other commodities and the price of the product in question, and the distance between the cus-tomer and the seller.

Consider the quantity of a product one consumer will purchase as its price varies. None of the other factors are assumed to vary. During any specified time period the quantity demanded by the consumer would be more if the price were lower and would be less if the price were higher. One reason is that a lower price increases the real income of the consumer. He can buy everything he had purchased before and still have income left for other expenditures. Another reason is that if the price of the product is lower and all other prices remain the same, as assumed, the product in question is more attractive and the consumer will reduce purchases of some other items in his budget in order to buy more of the product. This relation between the quantity demanded and the price of a good is the demand for a product. An illustrative demand curve XY is drawn in Figure 2-5. In this figure the curve is assumed to be linear. The line XY traces the

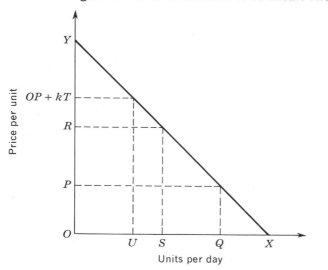

FIGURE 2-5

quantity demanded by an individual consumer per unit of time for alternative prices. For example, if the price were OP, the consumer would purchase OQ units per day; if the price were OR, the consumer would purchase OS units per day.

The farther a consumer is from the point of sale, the less he will purchase at a given price. If the price were OP, and the consumer were adjacent to the producer, he would purchase OQ units per day. If the price were OP, and he were k miles from the producer, he might only purchase OU units per day. The price to him would no longer be OP, but OP plus the transportation cost of moving the product from the producer. If the cost of transportation were T per unit per mile, the price to the consumer would be $OP + kT$, and the quantity that he would demand would be OU, as stated. On the other hand, if the producer pays the transportation cost of shipping the product to the consumer, the price he receives is $OP - kT$, and the consumer purchases OQ units of the product.

A useful distinction can be made between enterprises that sell to a geographically dispersed market and those that sell to one centrally located market.[6] Manufacturers, retailers, and local service enterprises tend to sell to consumers dispersed throughout a geographic area. Farmers and mining enterprises tend to sell their products in one central market. Those enterprises selling to consumers in a spatial market tend to have control of their price because of their isolation from other competitors. For the present assume that these enterprises establish prices at the plant and each consumer pays this price plus the transportation cost of shipping the product from seller to buyer.[7] An enterprise that sells to one central market is forced to accept the market price of its product because it is one of many sellers in the same market. The net price that it receives is the price at the market less the transportation cost of shipping the product from seller to market.

Analysis of receipts in the latter case is simpler. To the producer the net price will be the same no matter how great is the rate of production. Therefore, total receipts will increase proportionately with the rate of production. The relation between total receipts or revenues and the rate of production is the net revenue line, illustrated by line OR in Figure 2-6. If the production site were shifted to a different location, the producer's net revenue line would rotate up or down depending on whether the alternative site were

---

[6] August Lösch, *The Economics of Location* (New Haven, Conn.: Yale University Press, 1954), pp. 63–66.
[7] The student versed in price theory should wonder why the monopolist does not split the burden of the transportation cost with the consumer. Because price discrimination is complex to handle, and because it would not contribute much to the essential problem of the individual producer's location, it is left for later treatment in Chapter 3.

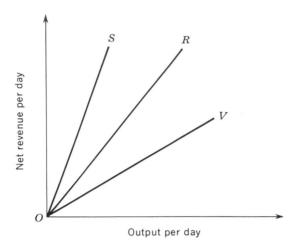

FIGURE 2-6

closer to or farther from the market. For example, a site closer to the market would cause the net price to be higher because the transportation cost to market would be less, and the net revenue line would rotate upward to OS. A site farther from the market would cause the net price to be lower because the transportation cost to market would be more, and the net revenue line would rotate downward to OV.

The relationship between revenue and the rate of production for the enterprise with a spatial market is more complicated because price and the extent of the market are also related to the rate of production. Assume that consumers are uniformly distributed spatially, say one per acre, that each consumer has the same taste and income, and that each consumer has the same demand, as represented by line XY in Figure 2-5. With these conditions, the quantity of product demanded by each consumer would depend on the price of the product at the plant and the distance the consumer was from the plant. This relation can be made more explicit. If the price at the plant were OP, the consumers adjacent to the plant would purchase OQ units per day. As demonstrated in Figure 2-5, customers farther from the plant would demand less because the transportation cost would be increased. At the distance where $OP + kT$ was equal to OY, consumers would purchase no units.

The total quantity demanded from the producer for any price, say OP, can be best illustrated by the *demand cone*, as in Figure 2-7.[8] The two lines

---

[8] Lösch, *op. cit.*, pp. 105–108.

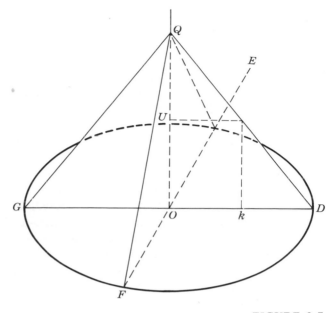

FIGURE 2-7

EF and GD intersect at O on a plane to represent the north-south and east-west directions of geographic space. OQ is the quantity of the product that is demanded by the consumer adjacent to the plant. Consumers far-ther from the plant demand less per day: OU units per day by the con-sumer k miles from the plant. At location D, the consumer would purchase none of the product. If transportation is equally difficult in every direction from the plant, the quantity demanded by consumers at alternative dis-tances from O will be the same in every direction as in the easterly direction. Thus, the triangle OQD can be revolved on the axis OQ to generate a cone. The height of the surface at any point shows the quantity demanded by the consumer at that location, given that the plant is at O, that the price at the plant is OP, and that the transportation cost is T per unit per mile. With uniform population density, the quantity of output that would be sold is the volume of the cone times the population density. The total revenue received would be price, OP, times the quantity demanded.

There is a different demand cone for every price established at the plant. If the price at the plant were greater than OP, fewer units per day would be demanded adjacent to the plant. The height and base of the cone would be smaller, and the volume would be less. Thus, with an increase in price the total quantity demanded would decrease. If the price at the plant were less than OP, more units per day would be demanded adjacent to the plant. Demand would vanish farther from the plant. The height and base of the cone would be larger, and the volume would also be greater. Thus, with a decrease in price the total quantity demanded would increase.

For each rate of production, then, there is one price at the plant at which that total output level can be sold. Assume that a price is established such that the output of each period is sold during that period, so that the number of units produced equals the number of units sold. Low rates of production are associated with high prices, and high rates of production are associated with low prices. Whether revenues will be higher as the rate of production is increased depends on whether the percentage increase in production is greater than the percentage decrease in price necessary to sell the greater output. The total revenue curve OR in Figure 2-8 shows one possible relation between revenue and rate of production. In this example, percentage decreases in price are less than percentage increases in production as the rate of production increases to OQ_6 units per day, and revenues increase. As the rate of production increases beyond OQ_6 units per day, however, percentage decreases in price are greater than percentage increases in production, and revenues decrease.

The responsiveness of changes in the quantity demanded by consumers to changes in price is measured by the *elasticity of demand*. Elasticity is simply the percentage change in demand divided by the percentage change in price causing the change in demand. Thus, if the elasticity is greater than one, revenues will rise, as from O to Q_6 in Figure 2-8. If the elasticity is one, revenues will be unchanged, as at output OQ_6 per day. If the elas-

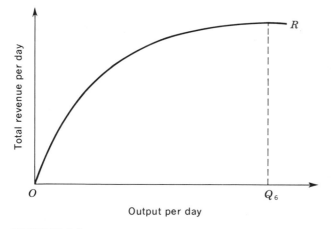

FIGURE 2-8

ticity is less than one, revenues will decrease, as for production rates beyond Q_6 in Figure 2-8.

Instead of assuming that consumers are evenly distributed over geographic space, it would be more realistic to assume that they are more densely distributed around some site O, and that their density decreases with distance from that site. If the plant should be located at O, the demand cone would be the same as in Figure 2-7. The total quantity demanded, however, would be different. The quantity demanded by each consumer must be multiplied by the number of consumers at a particular location to arrive at the total quantity demanded at each location. Summing these quantities over all locations would yield the total quantity demanded at any particular price. Total revenue would be the product of price and quantity, such as OR in Figure 2-8.

If, however, the plant should be located some distance from O, the demand cone at each price would be the same, but the total quantity demanded would be less. Consider Figure 2-9. This figure is a cross section of the situation. Site O is the center of density of population on the plain. Curve DEF plots the density of population at each place along a straight line in the plain running through O. The triangle ABC is a cross section of the demand cone (given a particular price) for a plant located at site O. The height of line AB, for example, shows the quantity demanded per person at each place along line AO. To calculate the quantity demanded from the firm at the given price it is necessary to multiply the quantity demanded per person by the number of persons at each site in the market area. As a plant site at alternative locations is considered, such as site K

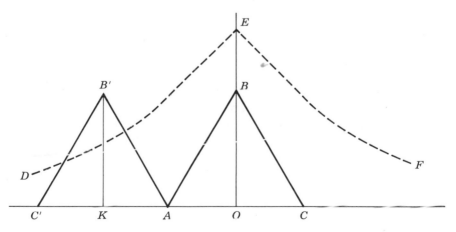

FIGURE 2-9

in Figure 2-9, the demand cone is shifted to $C'B'A$. It is the same as ABC with the same plant price. The quantity demanded per person at given distances from K is the same as at the same given distances from O. In the market around K the number of persons at each site, however, is less than in the market around O. Thus, the total quantity demanded is less than in O's market at the same price. If the plant price at K were reduced so that the demand cone was higher and included a larger area, the market would eventually be large enough that when quantity demanded per person times density was summed over the entire market the total quantity demanded from the firm would equal that of the market at O at the original price. Thus, it takes a lower price to sell a given rate of production at sites away from O than at O. If the price necessary to sell a given rate of production were lower at such sites as K, then the total revenue at each rate of production would be less, and the total revenue schedule, such as OR in Figure 2-8, would shift downward as alternative sites away from the center of density were considered.

Thus, if markets were uniformly dense and unlimited in areal extent, revenues would remain unchanged with changes in plant location, but if markets were not uniformly dense, revenues would decrease as the plant was located farther from the market center.

CONDITIONS FOR OPTIMUM LOCATION

There would be no location problem if consumers were evenly distributed over geographic space, and if input prices were invariant with location. Neither the revenue curve nor the cost curve would shift with changes in plant site. Thus, the firm's problem would simply be finding any site iso- lated from competitors and establishing the price and the rate of produc- duction that would maximize profits. In Figure 2-10, OR is the total revenue curve, and OC is the total cost curve. The firm would maximize profits at the rate of production (OQ units per day) and its associated price that would make the difference between total revenue and cost greatest.

As some variables of the analysis are allowed to vary between sites, location does become a problem. For example, if consumers were unevenly distributed over geographic space, the revenue curve would shift down as the plant site was moved from the center of density. If input prices were everywhere the same, the most profitable plant site would be at the center of density of the market, since revenues at every rate of production would be higher. The rate of production and the price at which it could be sold would be established as before.

A more complicated case will illustrate the integration of minimum cost,

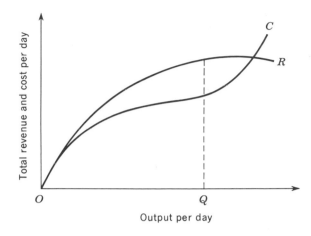

FIGURE 2-10

economies of scale, and demand in the location decision when input prices, scale, and revenues all vary between sites.[9] Assume that a production process requires two inputs: a raw material found at location M and man-hours of labor. There is an adequate number of workers and they are equally productive at both the raw material site and the center of density of the market. Nevertheless, the price of labor is less at the center because the commuting cost of workers to the plant is less. Materials cost less at the material site than at the market because the firm would not have to pay the transport cost of the material from the material site to the market.

In Figure 2-11a the isocost lines, such as UV, indicate the combinations of labor and materials that can be purchased for a given outlay at the material site. In Figure 2-11b the isocost lines, such as XY, indicate the combinations of labor and materials that can be purchased for the same given outlays at the market site. Assume that UV and XY represent the same outlay. The slopes of the two lines are different because the input prices are different at the two sites. The slope is steeper at the material site because materials cost less relative to labor than at the market center. If all a given outlay were spent on material, for example, OU tons could be purchased at the material site and only OX tons could be purchased at the market site, since the price per ton was less at the material site. In the same way, if all a given outlay were spent on labor, OV man-hours could be purchased at the material site and a greater number of man-hours, OY, could be purchased at the market. $ABCD$ shows the expansion path of

[9] The analysis for this case is essentially from Leon Moses, "Location and the Theory of Production," *Quarterly Journal of Economics* (May, 1958), pp. 259–272.

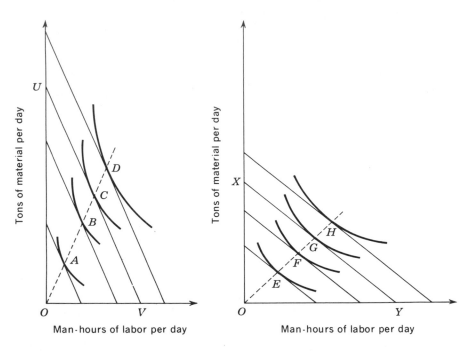

FIGURE 2-11a   FIGURE 2-11b

least-cost combinations at the material site; $EFGH$ shows the expansion path of least-cost combinations at the market site.

These two graphs, however, do not show directly which of the two sites represents the least-cost site for various rates of production. Therefore, in Figure 2-12, the isocost lines for both the material and the market site are shown. Once again, UV and XY are isocost lines for the same outlay at the material and market sites. For combinations of inputs above Z a greater rate of production can be reached along UZ than along XZ for the same outlay of money. For combinations of inputs below Z a greater rate of production can be reached along ZY than along ZV for the same outlay of money. Therefore, the relevant segments of each isocost line are UZ and ZY; XZ and ZV will be disregarded in the rest of the analysis.

The least-cost combinations of inputs are the quantities represented by the coordinates of the point at which the isoquant is just tangent to the isocost lines UZY. Since each segment of the isocost lines is associated with a particular site, the site at which a given rate of output can be produced for the least cost is simultaneously determined. In Figure 2-12, for rates of production of 300 to 500 units per day, the least-cost combinations

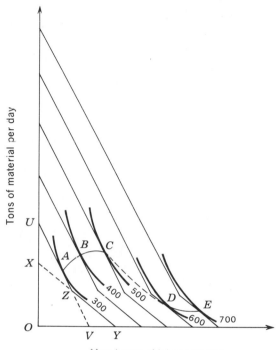

FIGURE 2-12

of inputs are located at the material site because the tangencies between the isoquants and isocost lines at A, B, and C are on the UZ segment of the isocost lines that are associated with the relative input prices at the material site. For rates of production above 500 units per day the least-cost combinations of inputs are located at the market site because the tangencies between the isoquants and isocost lines at D and E are on the ZY segment of the isocost lines that are associated with the relative input prices at the market site.

The curvature of the isoquants and the slopes of the isocost lines present two concave surfaces. When the isocost line is a straight line, only one tangency to each isoquant is possible. The similar concavity of the two lines in this case with two sites creates the possibility of two tangencies. If two tangencies should occur, one on each segment of the isocost lines, then that rate of output could be produced for the same cost at both sites. Notice, however, that the least-cost combinations of inputs would be different at the two sites. For example, if the isoquant 300 had been tangent to both UZ and ZY, production would have cost the same at both sites, but more material and less labor would have been used at the material site than at the market site. It is easy to see why. Materials cost less and labor more at the material site than at the market site.

These least-cost solutions determine the least-cost combinations of inputs for each rate of production at each site and at which site costs would be least for each rate of production. Since the actual site depends on profitability, not least cost, the next step is to combine cost with revenues.

In Figure 2-13, TR_p shows the total revenue curve for the plant, if it were located at the center of density of the market. As noted before, if the density of buyers decreases with distance from some place, the revenue curve will shift downward as the plant is moved from this center because transportation costs increase to consumers. Thus, TR_m, which shows the revenue curve for the plant if it were located at the material site, is lower than TR_p. TC_p is the total cost curve for the plant if it were located at the market; TC_m is the total cost curve for the plant if it were located at the material site. For rates of production less than 500 units, total cost is less at the material site; for rates of production greater than 500 units, total

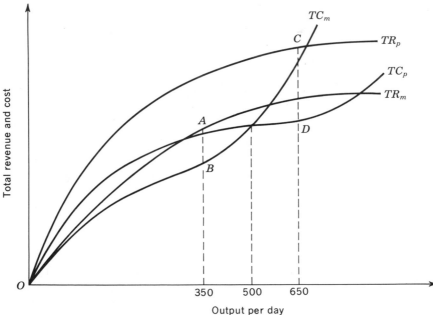

FIGURE 2-13

cost is less at the center of density of the market. This information comes from the isoquant and isocost curves in Figure 2-12.

Subtracting total cost TC_m from total revenue TR_m at the material site at each rate of production reveals that an output of 350 units per day will yield the greatest difference AB. At the market site the greatest difference CD occurs with the rate of production of 650 units per day. Since CD represents a greater profit than AB, the plant would locate at the market. The firm, of course, would have to set the price implied by the revenue curve to sell this rate of production. The most profitable site and rate of production are at the least-cost site in this case, but that would not necessarily be true for every case. The most profitable site might be one at which both costs and revenues were higher and the difference was also higher than at other sites.

So far, the integration of input price, scale, and revenues to determine maximum-profit sites and rates of production has been illustrated with the spatial monopoly case. The same analytical tools can be used to show the most profitable location for a competitive firm selling in a single central market. There are, however, a few differences. The firm must accept the market price since it is unable to influence it, so that revenues are proportional to the rate of production and the revenue curve is a straight line. The net revenue line would rotate down as sites farther from the market were considered because the firm would have to pay greater transportation costs to ship the product to market. The input prices that would differ at alternative sites would more likely be rents for land than either wages or material prices. Otherwise, the analysis of costs and revenues would proceed in the same way and the maximum-profit site and rate of production would be determined in the same way as in the spatial monopoly case.

UNCERTAINTY

As has already been noted, the plant location decision is a long-run decision, an investment decision. The theoretical determination of the profit-maximizing site assumes that the entrepreneur has perfect foresight: that he can predict the future receipts and costs at each site. The revenues and costs in the previous analysis are the expected receipts and costs that would change in each time period. The receipts and costs have been translated into the equivalent constant receipts and costs per unit time. Nevertheless, the future is so much an unknown that in this case it cannot be treated using probability theory.[10] Thus, the analysis, as stated

[10] Frank Knight, *Risk, Uncertainty, and Profit* (New York: Harper & Row, Publishers, Incorporated, 1965, copyright 1921), pp. 197–232.

under the maximizing-profit section, is a tool to use in predicting location patterns, not the behavior of a particular entrepreneur, who may have different goals, or a different assessment of the future course of events.

SUMMARY

By reviewing the analysis to see what factors might change the optimum location, we can find those which are important in determining the site at which the plant maximizes profits. The prices of the inputs and the transportation cost of the inputs to the site of production determine the position of the isocost lines. The least-cost combination depends upon the isocost lines and the production function. Total revenues depend upon the individual consumer demands, transportation costs, and the distance of the plant from the market. These are the basic determinants of the optimum location. No one factor alone is responsible for a particular location, but the combination of all factors determines the location of each plant.

PART ONE

**REGIONAL
STRUCTURE**

Population density is unequally distributed geographically. For example, population density in states in the United States is as low as 0.4 persons per square mile in Alaska and as high as 812.4 persons per square mile in Rhode Island. Population density in cities over 100,000 population in the United States varies from 1,009 persons per square mile in Oklahoma City to 76,156 persons per square mile in the borough of Manhattan in New York City. The average density of population in the United States is 50.5 persons per square mile.[1] If densities were available by county the variation would be even greater. Although variation in the resource endowment of each state is responsible for much of the variation in population density, population density would vary greatly for economic reasons even if the earth were a flat homogeneous plain in which resources were evenly and uniformly distributed over the surface. In particular, cities of various sizes would be established at regular intervals. If resources were evenly distributed, economies of scale and shipping costs would be sufficient to cause the creation of central places. The theory of these central places will be developed in this chapter. The chapter will begin with the competitive interaction of firms trying to carve spatially isolated trading areas in a homogeneous plain. These trading areas will then be linked to a system of central places which will be shown to be also equivalent to the rank-size rule for city-size distributions. The last part of the chapter will also attempt to show how the theoretical distribution compares to actual distributions of cities and will indicate some of the factors causing the actual distribution to differ from the theoretical one. The next chapter will deal in more detail with the impact of agglomeration economies and resource endowment on the distribution of economic activity.

TRADING AREAS ON A HOMOGENEOUS PLAIN[2]

Assume a flat plain over which natural resources are uniformly distributed. Population is uniformly distributed in that self-sufficient farms of equal size are scattered uniformly over the plain. Transportation costs are equal in every direction and are proportional to distance. In this situation why should any family trade with any other? What would be the boundary for the trading of any product from a particular place? Economies of scale

---

[1] U.S. Bureau of the Census, *Statistical Abstract of the United States: 1965*, 86th ed. (1965), pp. 13, 19–20.
[2] This section relies basically on August Lösch, *The Economics of Location* (New Haven, Conn.: Yale University Press, 1954), pp. 105–120.

cause trading because one family can produce a product for less cost than other families by producing more than needed by one family. The trading area for the product is bounded by the cost of shipping. At some point transport costs are so high that the quantity demanded is zero.

Assume that every family has the same income and tastes, that the quantity demanded of each product depends upon price, and that this demand schedule is the same for every family. Thus, for any price established at a production site there is a related demand cone, as described in Chapter 2. Since population density is uniform, the total quantity demanded from a producer at a particular price will be equal to the population density times the volume of the demand cone. Assuming that the rate of production will equal the quantity demanded during each time period, total revenue for each rate of production will be equal to the rate of production times the price that will cause that amount to be sold. Curve TR in Figure 3-1 shows total revenue for each rate of production. Curve TC shows the total cost at each rate of production. Since resources and population are uniformly distributed over the plain, changes in the production site will not cause shifts in either the cost or revenue schedules. There is nothing to cause input prices to vary between different sites. OC is the rate of production at which total revenue is greater than total cost by the widest margin. AB is the maximum profit. By referring to the demand cone

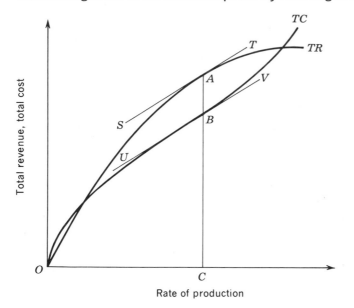

FIGURE 3-1

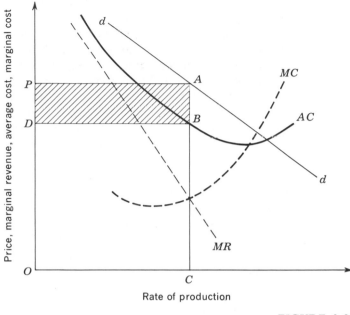

Price, marginal revenue, average cost, marginal cost

Rate of production

FIGURE 3-2

associated with this rate of production, the extent of the circular market could be determined so long as there was no competition.

There is, however, another way to look at the firm that will help in our analysis of the impact of competition on the trading area of a plant. In Figure 3-2, the horizontal axis measures the rate of production. In fact the rate of production OC in Figure 3-2 is the same as OC in Figure 3-1. The vertical axis measures the price, marginal revenue, average cost, and marginal cost. Instead of showing the total revenue, this figure shows the total quantity demanded of the plant for each price that might be set. If the price were OP, the quantity demanded would be OC, as determined by the product of population density and the volume of the demand cone. The market demand curve facing the firm, dd, shows the relation between price and quantity demanded. Instead of showing total cost, Figure 3-2 shows the average cost of production AC.

In this figure, the maximum profit rate of production and price can be determined by using two new concepts: marginal revenue and marginal cost. *Marginal revenue* is the increment of revenue brought into the firm by a small increase in the rate of production. *Marginal cost* is the incremental increase in total cost caused by the same small increase in the rate of production. The slope of the tangent to the total revenue curve at any rate of production, such as ST at A in Figure 3-1, is the marginal revenue at that rate of production, OC. The slope of the tangent to the total cost curve at any rate of production, such as UV at B in Figure 3-1, is the marginal cost at that production rate, OC. Marginal cost and marginal revenue are the rate of change of total cost and total revenue.

So long as marginal revenue is greater than marginal cost, the incremental additions to revenues are greater than the incremental additions to cost incurred by the increased rate of production, and profits will increase. Profits will continue to increase with increasing output until marginal revenue is just equal to marginal cost. Increases in the rate of production above the rate at which marginal revenue is equal to marginal cost will lower profits. As the rate of production is increased, marginal revenue is less than marginal cost so that incremental additions to revenues are less than the incremental increases in cost incurred by the increased rate of production, and profits, therefore, will decrease. When the producer establishes the rate of production to maximize profits, marginal revenue will be equal to marginal cost.

In Figure 3-2, the line MR shows the marginal revenue associated with each rate of production. It is the same as the slope of the tangent to TR in Figure 3-1 at each rate of output. The curve MC is the marginal cost associated with each rate of output. It is the same as the slope of the total cost TC in Figure 3-1, at each rate of production. Thus, OC is the rate of production that will maximize profits, since it is the output at which marginal cost will equal marginal revenue. But from Figure 3-2, the price OP that must be set to sell the rate of production OC can be determined. Total profits are equal to the difference between the price and the average cost times the number of units sold. This is shown by the area of the rectangle $ABDP$. So far the seller has been assumed to have no competition so that his market area is the circular base of the demand cone generated when the plant price is OP.

Sellers of the same commodity, unless influenced by agglomeration economies which will be discussed later, tend to find sites away from competition. Therefore, each seller will move so as to keep his circular market to himself, or a family in the homogeneous plain will produce only goods for which there is no competition. The homogeneous plain would then be filled with circular markets for the product until the markets were so crowded that they were touching each other. In Figure 3-3, the circular markets that maximize profits to each seller are all touching. Since all sellers of the same product had the same demand and cost curves, their market areas are all the same size. There are still unserved areas, however, where new sellers

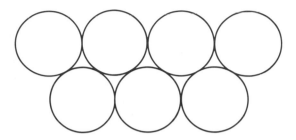

FIGURE 3-3

can crowd in. As they crowd in, they will encroach upon the market areas of the other firms.

The demand schedule facing the firm will begin to change as its monopolistic market area is encroached upon. For example, in Figure 3-4, a seller located at P before competition and found he could maximize his profits by setting a price causing his market area to have a radius of PB. A competitor finding a site among several such market areas could establish at site P' and, by setting the same price as P, take away part of the market from P. If the price at both plants is the same, and transport costs are the same, the line EF in Figure 3-4 is the locus of all consumers equally distant from P and P' in P's market. Since they are equally distant from P and P', the price of the product plus shipping costs is the same from either place. The consumers would be indifferent about the seller from whom they bought. The rest of the consumers in the previous market area of P would still find it cheaper to buy from P. The consumers in the shaded area $AFBE$, however, would find it cheaper to purchase from P'. The demand

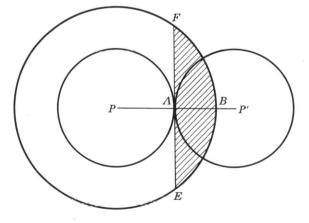

FIGURE 3-4

curve facing the firm, dd in Figure 3-5, is now changed. With the arc section $AFBE$ taken over by P' the quantity demanded falls, as from OC to OB in Figure 3-5.

So long as the price at P' is unchanged, the quantity demanded from the seller at P will be less than without competition at most prices it might establish. The demand curve would shift left to $d'd'$ in Figure 3-5. If the seller at P should raise his price, the line along which consumers would pay the same price to obtain the product from P or P', line EF in Figure 3-4, would move closer to P; the extent of the market in other directions would decrease; and the quantity demanded would be less than it was without competition. If the seller at P should lower his price, the line EF would move closer to P', the extent of the market in other directions would increase, and eventually competition from P' would be eliminated. So far P' has been assumed to maintain his price, while P changed his. In reality there would be corresponding changes so that neither seller could be eliminated.

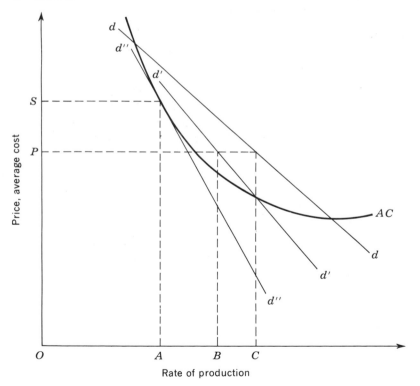

FIGURE 3-5

The number of sellers could continue to multiply and encroach upon each others' market areas until the demand curve shifted so far to the left that it was tangent to the average cost curve, as $d''d''$ in Figure 3-5. Price would then equal average cost, such as OS. OA would be the quantity of product sold. Since it is assumed that the costs of the firm include the "normal" rate of return that could be earned in alternative investments, the seller will stay in business, but will not make excess profits. The rate of production at which the demand curve is tangent to average cost is the minimum size that is possible for sellers in this industry. If the number of firms continued to multiply, the demand curve would shift farther left and would be everywhere below the average cost of production. Thus, prices would never exceed or equal average cost no matter what tne rate of production, and sellers would be unable to meet their costs. Sellers would go out of business. This minimum size is the threshold size of the firm.

The shape of this minimum-size market was first thought to be hexagonal. It was thought that circular market areas would be unstable, since the unserved but populated areas would invite new competitors. Triangles, squares, and hexagons would completely fill the space. If the demand curves for each individual were linear, it was thought that hexagons would be the market shape resulting from competition. If we compare the demand cone for polygons of equal base areas, the hexagonal shape compared to square or triangular shapes will in most cases yield the greatest final demand. Nevertheless, it has recently been pointed out that circular or dodecagonal shaped areas would also be possible. If the demand curve facing the firm for a circular area was tangent to or to the right of average cost, while the demand for the hexagonal area inscribed in that circle was nowhere above average cost, the circular area would exist, while the hexagonal areas could not. The circular areas would exist in spite of unserved areas. Under certain conditions it is also possible for more firms with a circular market to be crowded into an area than if the firms had hexagonal market areas when both shapes of markets could yield profits.[3]

Thus, each commodity or service will have a uniform network of markets, or trading areas. The market for each plant in the same industry will be the same size. This size will be the threshold size—the market area generating a demand curve tangent to average cost. If continuous variations from one market size class to the next larger are not possible, some threshold sizes may allow excess profits because the next smaller market area will not generate a demand curve that will be tangent to or above average cost.

---

[3] E. S. Mills and Michael R. Lav, "A Model of Market Areas with Free Entry," *Journal of Political Economy*, vol. 72, no. 3 (June, 1964), pp. 278–288.

A SIMPLE MODEL OF A SYSTEM OF CITIES[4]

Again assume a homogeneous plain with population and resources uniformly distributed over it, and transportation costs equal in every direction. Each commodity and service will have a uniform network of markets or trading areas. Many commodities and services, however, will have the same market sizes. Therefore, there will not be as many market networks as there are commodities and services. Each commodity or service with the same threshold size will be assumed to locate in the centers of the same network of markets. The market sizes will range from small areas for convenience items found in drugstores, groceries, barber shops, laundries and cleaners, etc., to markets that encompass the entire nation as for some manufactured products.

If all the networks are centered on one of the original self-sufficent farms, and are so adjusted that their other market centers coincide with original farms, central places will appear. Central places are the centers at which the market centers of one, two, or more networks locate. In particular if the networks are adjusted so that a cogwheel pattern of six sectors in which many centers coincide and six sectors in which there are few central places, there will be an efficient arrangement of central places. With this arrangement the greatest number of market centers will coincide, the sum of minimum distances between centers will be least, and shipments will be minimized. Since all the networks center on one great metropolis, all goods and services will have sales sites in it, and prices will tend to be lower on the average in this place than in places toward the edge of the system. There will, of course, be fluctuations as larger towns arise. Prices will rise more sharply in the sectors with few places.

A special and less general arrangement may be developed if a further assumption is made. If only networks are possible which fit together so that each market area includes exactly s areas of the next smaller size, many of the networks will be eliminated as not being possible. For example, if s equaled 3, three of the smallest trading areas would have to fit into the next largest market size. Networks with market sizes intermediate between these two sizes would be eliminated because they would not fit the scheme. This assumption also means that each place with the same number of market centers coinciding will have the same commodities and services (sometimes called functions). In the previous, more general scheme, places with the same number of functions might not have the same services and commodities.

So far, nothing about the population of the central places has been dis-

[4] Lösch, *op. cit.*, pp. 124–137, 431–438, provides the basic approach to this section.

cussed. Population is uniformly distributed, but at the same time central places of different importance have been generated on the plain. This is one of the major difficulties with the theory and will be discussed later. The importance of each place has been determined by the number of market centers coinciding in the place. If an additional assumption is made that the population of each central place is proportional to the population it serves, it can be shown that the city-size distribution will fit the rank-size rule. That is, the rank of the city or central place times its population will equal a constant for all places within the region.[5]

The smallest central places will each provide services to the same number of rural people, r, and each will be the same size in population. The population of each of these smallest places will be some proportion, k, of the rural and central place population served. The next larger place will include s number of the smallest places and its population will be the same proportion k of the population served. The population served includes the s smaller central places and the r rural populations served by each plus the population of this higher central place. The smallest places will be called first-order places, and the next largest will be called second-order places. The places serving s second-order places will be called third-order places, etc. Whereas it was assumed in the previous paragraphs that the location of the second-order place was coincident with one of the three first-order places, it is now assumed that the second-order place is located at a different site.

An illustration of one possible system is shown in Table 3-1. In this case

[5] This extension of the Lösch theory relies on Martin J. Beckmann, "City Hierarchies and the Distribution of City Size," *Economic Development and Cultural Change*, vol. 6 (April, 1958), pp. 243–248. In addition to explaining the relationship among the concepts of trade areas, systems of cities, and the rank-size rule, Beckmann in this article shows an alternative explanation for the rank-size rule derived from the biological law of allometric growth.

TABLE 3-1 HYPOTHETICAL SYSTEM OF CITIES

Order	Population of centers in order	Population served by each center	Number of centers in each order
1	1,000	2,000	243
2	6,000	12,000	81
3	36,000	72,000	27
4	216,000	432,000	9
5	1,296,000	2,592,000	3
6	7,776,000	15,552,000	1

the rural population r served by the first-order places is 1,000; each place has a population equal to one-half the total population served; and each place serves three places of the next smaller order and the population served by these smaller places.

It can be shown that the population of each order place is a multiple of $s/(1 - k)$ (equal to 6 in Table 3-1) of the next-lower-order place.[6] If

[6] Let
$$m = \text{order of a place}$$
$$P_m = \text{population served by a place of the } m\text{th order}$$
$$C_m = \text{population of places of the } m\text{th order}$$
$$k = \text{proportion of population served located in central place}$$
$$s = \text{number of places in the } m - 1\text{st order served by places in the } m\text{th order}$$
$$r = \text{rural population served by first-order place}$$

Then,

$$(1) \quad C_m = kP_m$$
$$(2) \quad P_m = C_m + sP_{m-1}$$

Substituting (1) into (2),

$$(3) \quad P_m = kP_m + sP_{m-1}$$

Solving for P_m,

$$P_m - kP_m = sP_{m-1}$$
$$(4) \quad P_m = \frac{s}{1-k} P_{m-1}$$

But

$$(5) \quad P_{m-1} = kP_{m-1} + sP_{m-2} = \frac{s}{1-k} P_{m-2}$$

Therefore,

$$(6) \quad P_m = \frac{s}{1-k} P_{m-1} = \left(\frac{s}{1-k}\right)^2 P_{m-2} = \cdots = \left(\frac{s}{1-k}\right)^{m-1} P_1$$

Now,

$$(7) \quad P_1 = r + C_1$$

and

$$(8) \quad C_1 = k(r + C_1)$$
$$C_1 = kr/(1-k)$$

So that

$$(9) \quad P_1 = r + \frac{kr}{1-k} = \frac{r - kr + kr}{1-k} = \frac{r}{1-k}$$

Substituting into (6),

$$(10) \quad P_m = \left(\frac{s}{1-k}\right)^{m-1} \frac{r}{1-k} = \frac{rs^{m-1}}{(1-k)^m}$$

Substituting (10) into (1),

$$(11) \quad C_m = \frac{krs^{m-1}}{(1-k)^m}$$

Thus, first-order place has population equal to $kr/(1-k)$. Each order place m has a population equal to $s/(1-k)$ times the population of the $m - 1$st place.

$s/(1 - k)$ were really a random variable with a mean equal to $s/(1 - k)$, instead of a constant, each city in the second and higher orders would not have the same population as all other cities in the same order. The population of each of the eighty-one second-order cities would be a different multiple of the population (1,000) of the first-order place. The average multiple would be $s/(1 - k)$, but some would be higher and others lower. Instead of all second-order places having the same population of 6,000, they would vary around a mean of 6,000. The third-order cities would be multiples of the second-order cities, or $[s/(1 - k)]^2$ times the size of the first-order places (1,000). Since $s/(1 - k)$ is still a random variable, the multiplier for third-order places will have greater variations than for the second order. Furthermore, second- and third-order places will overlap in size and begin to present one continuum of different-sized places. The more orders in the system the closer city sizes will be to a continuous distribution.

Furthermore, if k is small relative to 1, the rank of a place times its population size is approximately a constant. The rank of the city can be noted in terms of the order of the place and the s satellites. For example, the city halfway in the fourth order would have one city in the sixth order, three cities in the fifth order, and four cities in the fourth order greater in rank. The size of the city decreases as rank increases. Thus, as rank increases from order to order, the rank is increasing in multiples of s as each lower order is reached. The rank halfway in the fourth order (where order is numbered from the smallest) is $1 + s + s^2/2$. The rank halfway in the third order is $1 + s + s^2 + s^3/2$. As rank increases from order to order, city size is decreasing by multiples of $s/(1 - k)$. In our previous example with six orders, the sixth-order place had a population of $krs^5/(1 - k)^6$. The fifth-order place had a smaller population, only $krs^4/(1 - k)^5$. As lower-order cities are considered, the ranks increase by a multiple of s and the population decreases by a multiple of $s/(1 - k)$. Thus, if k is small relative to 1, city size will decrease by approximately the same multiple as ranks increase. As we introduce the random $s/(1 - k)$ rather than a constant, each city has a unique size class.[7]

---

[7] In this simple model of a system of cities there will be one largest city, s cities of the next largest size class, s^2 cities of the third largest size class, and so on. To rank the cities we would start with number 1 for the largest, number 2 for the second largest, and so on down to the smallest city. There is some difficulty in ranking the cities in any size class n. The first ranking city in a size class n is ranked $1 + s^2 + \ldots + s^{n-1} + 1$. The sum of the first n terms is $(s^n - 1)/(s - 1)$. Thus, the rank of the first city in the nth class is $[(s^n - 1)/(s - 1)] + 1$. The rank of the city halfway in the nth size class is $[(s^n - 1)/(s - 1)] + s^n/2$, or the nearest integer. This is approximated by $s^n[(1/2) + 1/(s - 1)]$.

The size of the city halfway in the nth size class is the same as for all other cities of that class, and is determined by k, s, r, and m. The mth order in this case is equal to the total number of orders, N, less the n orders ranking from the top. Thus, the city size for the nth order is as follows:

Thus, we have outlined a simple model of a system of cities that would explain an observed relationship between the rank and size of cities in a region: rank times city size is approximately equal to a constant. The model begins with a threshold-size market for each economic activity. The threshold size is determined by the tangency between the average cost and demand schedules. (Nevertheless, it may be possible for some surplus profits to exist if there are insufficient sales for an additional firm to compete in the region.) Since many activities will have the same threshold market size, they are assumed to locate in the center of the same markets. Each threshold market, except for the smallest, includes exactly s of the next smaller threshold sizes. The centers of the markets form central places. Their population is dependent on the size of the market. In fact each city is assumed to require k people in the center to serve one person in the market area (which includes the place itself), where k is a fraction between 0 and 1. Allowing k to approach 0, and allowing the population multiplier of $s/(1 - k)$ to be a random variable, causes the product of the rank times the size of each place in the region to approximate a constant.

The theory just outlined is one explanation for the development of systems of cities even when population and resources are originally uniformly distributed. The difficulty with the theory is that the initial assumption of uniform population distribution is nullified by the development of central places or towns. Since population density varies, trading area sizes will also change in more densely populated areas. The threshold sizes will be smaller geographic areas. Thus, the threshold size of markets in the same industry would vary rather than be uniform in size. Markets would be smaller in cities and larger between cities. Another problem is quite obvious. The theory takes no account of differences in resource endowments. Thus, it applies only to retailing, wholesaling, and other activities in which input prices vary relatively little between places. In addition, agglomeration econo-

---

$$C_{N-n} = \frac{krs^{N-n-1}}{(1 - k)^{N-n}} = \frac{kr}{s}\left(\frac{s}{1 - k}\right)^{N-n}$$

Therefore, the product of the rank and size of the city halfway in the nth order is as follows:

$$\begin{aligned}
\text{rank times size} &= C_{N-n}s^n\left(\frac{1}{2} + \frac{1}{s - 1}\right) \\
&= \frac{kr}{s}\left(\frac{s}{1 - k}\right)^{N-n} s^n\left(\frac{1}{2} + \frac{1}{s - 1}\right) \\
&= \frac{kr}{s}\left(\frac{1}{2} + \frac{1}{s - 1}\right)\left(\frac{s}{1 - k}\right)^{N}(1 - k)^{-n} \\
&= W(1 - k)^{-n}
\end{aligned}$$

where W is a constant. If k is small relative to 1, $(1 - k)^{-n}$ approximates 1^{-n}, and the rank of the city times its size is approximately a constant. The constant for the system of cities depends on k, r, s, and N.

mies may cause firms in the same industry to be attracted to each other rather than to seek separate sites, or may cause firms in different industries to be attracted to each other rather than to the center of their markets. These agglomeration economies and differences in resource endowments will be discussed in more detail in the next chapter.

Although no area in the world can be described by the assumptions of the theory, some places are approximately described by these assumptions. Iowa is one example. Indeed Lösch found that the central places in Iowa in 1930 did correspond with one theoretical system that could be shown to be a special case of his general framework. The correspondence of reality is, of course, statistical rather than exact because the many assumptions do not hold perfectly. In Table 3-2 is shown Lösch's comparison between the predictions of his theory and the actual system of cities or places. This table was constructed by first grouping the places into size classes such that the number of centers in each size class would be the one expected when s equals 4, but each place of orders higher than 1 would coincide in location with one of the next-lower-order places. The theoretical distribution in column 2 was based on the actual number of places in the lowest size class. These size classes are shown in column 11.

In columns 4 and 5 the theoretical and actual distances between places in the same size class are shown. Once again the theoretical distribution is based on the actual distances between settlements in the lowest size class. In the hexagonal trading system places with the same number of activities would be the same distance apart, as indicated earlier. Lösch, however, also determined what that distance would be[8]:

$$b = a \sqrt{n}$$

where

b = distance between central places of same size

a = distance between smallest settlements (in theory the distance between self-sufficient farms; in the table the distance between places in the smallest size class)

n = number of smallest settlements served by the central place.

The distances between places in the same size class are remarkably close to the theoretical distances. This is one check on the theoretical structure developed by Lösch.

In columns 7 and 8 the number of places are shown as cumulative totals starting with the sixth size class. Since s equals 4, the rank-size rule was interpreted to mean that cities in each size class would be one-fourth the

[8] Lösch, *op. cit.*, pp. 116–120, 131.

TABLE 3-2   REGIONAL SYSTEMS IN IOWA, THEORY AND REALITY

Size class of regions	Correspondence with theoretical system for $s = 4$ — Centers				Size class of regions	Correspondence with rank-size rule — Places				
	Number		Distance apart[a]			Number		Minimum size[f]		Lowest size class[f]
	Theory[b]	Reality	Theory[b]	Reality[c]		Theory[b]	Reality	Theory[b]	Reality[a]	
(1)	(2)	(3)	(4)	(5)	(6)	(7)	(8)	(9)	(10)	(11)
1	615		5.6		1	819		447		180–1,000
2	154	153	11.2	10.3	2	205	204	1,800	1,950	1,000–4,000
3	39	39	22.4	23.6	3	51	51	7,200	7,500	4,000–20,000
4[d]	10	9	44.8	49.6	4[d]	13	12	28,800	34,800	20,000–60,000
5[d]	2-3	3	89.6	94.0	5[d]	3	3	115,000	94,000	60,000–200,000
6[e]	0-1		179.2		6[e]	1		460,000		200,000–800,000

[a] In miles.

[b] The values actually obtained for class 1 were the starting point for the calculation of all theoretical values.

[c] Modal value; average value for class 5 only (because of the small number of cases). Class 1: The distances were measured first for settlements with 300–1,000 inhabitants, and the values so found were entered above in the table. A new calculation, with the inclusion of places having 180–300 inhabitants, would have taken much time, but random sampling showed that the result would not have been greatly altered.

[d] Because of the small number of settlements in these size classes, greater deviations are to be expected. If Davenport is placed in class 4 instead of in class 5, in class 4, column 10, 34,800 must be replaced by 37,600; in column 11, 20,000–60,000 must be replaced by 20,000–75,000; in class 5, column 5, 94 by 102.5; in column 8, 3 by 2; and in column 10, 94,000 by 111,000.

[e] Iowa has no city of this size class, but it lies among Minneapolis, Kansas City, Omaha, and Chicago, the first three of which fall in this class. Their average population is 490,000 and their minimum distance apart 236 miles.

[f] Population.

[g] Average size of places in the lowest size class.

SOURCE: By permission from August Lösch, *The Economics of Location* (New Haven, Conn.: Yale University Press, 1954), p. 435.

size of cities in the next higher class. The actual calculation began from the lowest size class. Cities in each class theoretically would then be four times the size of cities in the next lower class. A comparison of columns 9 and 10 shows that the actual size distribution is close to that of the theory. Nonetheless, this would be a rule where rank equaled size class, and size class would be ranked first for the largest, second for the second largest, etc. The distribution of cities by size would appear in discrete groups, unlike the more continuous distribution described by Beckmann.

The continuous distribution of city sizes has been found to fit the rank-size rule in some countries in some time periods.[9] The fit of the rule for the United States in 1960 was not particularly good. The following test is based on the method used in previous studies.[10] The general equation for the rank-size rule is as follows:

$$r \cdot s^a = C$$

where

r = rank of an urban place in population
s = population size of an urban place
a = constant that is approximately one
C = constant that is approximately equal to the population of the largest place

If this equation is transformed into logarithms, it is a linear equation of the following form:

$$\log r = \log C - a \log s$$

An estimate fitted to a tabulation of population of urban places in the United States in 1960 is as follows:

$$\log r = 7.746 - 1.134 \log s$$

or

$$r \cdot s^{1.134} = 55.72 \text{ million}$$

This estimate of the relationship between rank and size does not fit the simple form in which a equals 1. Estimates in other years have been much closer, such as 1.03 in 1920.[11] Although the particular estimate is not close to 1, perhaps the equation is still a good fit showing a linear relation be-

[9] A convenient annotated bibliography of the literature has been compiled. See Brian J. L. Berry and Allen Pred, *Central Place Studies, A Bibliography of Theory and Applications*, Bibliography Series No. 1 with supplement (Philadelphia: Regional Science Research Institute, 1965).

[10] H. W. Singer, "The 'Courbe des Populations,' A Parallel to Pareto's Law," *Economic Journal*, vol. 46 (June, 1936), pp. 254–263; and G. R. Allen, "The 'Courbe des Populations,' A Further Analysis," *Bulletin of the Oxford University Institute of Statistics*, vol. 16 (May and June, 1954), pp. 179–189.

[11] Singer, *op. cit.*, p. 255.

tween the rank and size of cities in logarithms. In Table 3-3 the observations used to obtain the above estimated equation are shown along with the ranks, estimated from the equation fitted to the data, and the percentage error of these estimates. The error ranges from 9 to 80 percent. The error is particularly high in the tails of the distribution. In estimates for previous years the percentage errors of the estimates ranged between 0 and 12 percent.[12]

One reason why rank times size does not equal a constant may be the definition of urban places. *Urban places* are incorporated places. A better definition would be Standard Metropolitan Statistical Areas (SMSAs), but in that case only places with more than 50,000 people would be included. As will be seen in Chapter 6 the SMSAs are based on county lines which may or may not be better than the legal boundaries of the incorporated places. The urban extension of cities may not conform to either of these political boundaries. Thus, the population figure may include part of the hinterland or may underestimate the population of the urbanized central place.

More important than the statistical problem of defining the city is the way in which more realistic assumptions change the predictions of an urban hierarchy. In the next two sections an attempt will be made to show the impact of more realistic assumptions on the size and shape of trading areas, and on the hierarchy of urban places.

[12] *Ibid.*

TABLE 3-3   UNITED STATES URBAN PLACES, 1960

Population size (s)	Number of places with population equal to or above (s)		Percentage error
	(r) actual	(r') estimated	
1,000,000	5	9	80
500,000	21	19	10
250,000	51	42	18
100,000	131	119	9
50,000	334	255	24
25,000	761	574	24
10,000	1,907	1,622	15
5,000	3,233	3,556	10
2,500	5,022	7,816	56

SOURCE: U.S. Bureau of the Census, *Statistical Abstract of the United States: 1966*, 87th ed. (1966), p. 15.

TRADING AREAS IN MORE COMPLEX SITUATIONS[13]

In reality trading areas are not as sharply bounded as described in the previous section. The trading areas of sellers overlap. When there is such an overlap, the buyer, the seller, or the transfer agency is absorbing part of the shipping cost. Political boundaries, such as the boundaries between states, cities, or nations, may distort the shape and size of trading or market areas. Transportation costs are not uniform in every direction, but are cheaper along established networks, so that the shapes of market areas are extended along transport routes. Topography may also affect the shape and size of market areas, as will the unequal geographic distribution of people and resources.

The transfer agency may absorb part of the transport cost by setting its rates for blocks of mileage. Because of these mileage blocks the transportation cost from two different sellers could be the same over a substantial area, and market areas would overlap.

Buyers may absorb transportation costs. They have preferences for particular brands of a particular commodity. Even though he is closer to the seller of a rival substitute, the buyer may prefer to travel farther or pay transportation costs to obtain the preferred brand. Thus, market areas may overlap because of consumer preferences.

Sellers may absorb transportation costs, or they may inflate them, although there are few examples of freight inflation. Instead of charging a price plus shipping costs, the firm might set a uniform delivered price to all customers. With uniform pricing the firm pays the transportation costs to all customers, and thus the total transportation cost of distributing the product to all customers is shared by all. The more distant customers get a break relative to the nearby customers. If the buyer should be another producer, the price of this input does not affect his location decision, since it will be the same no matter where he locates. Uniform pricing eliminates the regulator of rational use of space.[14]

Under certain conditions a seller can profit from discriminating against different buyers by charging different prices. If geographic price discrimination is practiced, the minimum size market areas will be smaller than if f.o.b. pricing (customer pays price at plant plus shipping costs) is practiced. Three conditions must exist for the seller to profit by price discrimination. First, the seller must be able to separate his markets. Otherwise buyers who have been discriminated against by being charged a high price will try to buy the product from those who have been sold the product at a

[13] The framework for this section, except where noted, is from Lösch, *op. cit.*, pp. 139–220.
[14] On market overlap, see Edgar M. Hoover, *The Location of Economic Activity* (New York: McGraw-Hill Book Company, 1948), pp. 54–59.

lower price. Second, the seller will not profit from discrimination unless the elasticities of demand are different in the separated markets. Third, the cost of separating markets must not be too large.[15] A seller may discriminate against nearby buyers relative to more distant buyers. For the nearby buyer to purchase the product from distant buyers rather than the seller, he would have to pay transport costs both ways over the distance between his location and that of the more distant buyer.

If every buyer is assumed to have the same demand for the product, and if it is assumed that the demand is linear, it will pay the seller to discriminate against the nearby buyer.[16] Assume that AB in Figure 3-6 is the demand curve for each individual wherever he should be located. If the firm sets the price at OP_1 the individual adjacent to the plant will demand the quantity OF. The buyers at some distance from the plant will have to

[15] George J. Stigler, *The Theory of Price*, 3d ed. (New York: The Macmillan Company, 1966), p. 210.
[16] Note that the price elasticity of demand for a product varies continuously along a linear demand schedule.

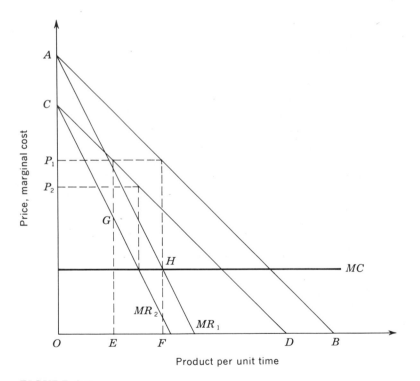

FIGURE 3-6

pay the price OP_1 plus transportation costs. Thus, these buyers will demand a smaller quantity at this plant price. Let CD be the demand curve for the more distant buyer. The vertical distance between AB and CD is the transportation cost per unit of product between the two locations. The horizontal distance shows the difference in the quantity demanded by the more distant buyer because the delivered price that he must pay is higher when the price at the plant is the same to both buyers. Thus, OE in Figure 3-6 shows the quantity that the more distant buyer will demand when the price at the plant is OP_1.

In Figure 3-2, dd is the overall demand curve facing the firm and shows the quantity demanded by all buyers for each price established at the plant. The price set is the one that maximizes profits, and the one at which marginal revenue equals marginal cost. The marginal revenue, however, is the incremental revenue when the whole market is considered. In Figure 3-6, MR_1 and MR_2 are the marginal revenue schedules for the close-in and distant buyers respectively. When the same price, OP_1, is charged to both buyers, the marginal revenue of a sale to the more distant buyer is greater than the marginal revenue to the adjacent buyer. In Figure 3-6, GE is the marginal revenue for the sales to the distant buyer, while FH is the marginal revenue for the sales to the adjacent buyer. The seller can increase his revenues and profits by lowering price for the distant buyer until the marginal revenue to the distant buyer is equal to that for the adjacent sales and both are equal to marginal cost. So long as an increment to revenue in any market is greater than in another and the cost of separating markets is small, it is profitable to discriminate until the incremental additions to revenue in each market are equal and equal to the marginal cost of production. In this case MC in Figure 3-6 is the marginal cost and is constant. The adjacent buyer would be charged OP_1 and the distant buyer would be charged a plant price of OP_2.[17]

---

[17] In general, discrimination depends on the elasticity of demand. It can be shown that the plant price is equal to the following relation:

$$(1) \quad MR = \frac{d(Pn)}{dn} - t = \frac{Pdn + ndP}{dn} - t = P - t - \frac{P}{e}$$

where
  n = quantity demanded
  p = factory price
  P = delivered price
  t = freight per unit from factory to buyer
  c = marginal cost

  e = elasticity of demand in respect to delivered price = $\left(\dfrac{dn}{dP}\right)\left(\dfrac{P}{n}\right)$

when

Thus, if the seller can raise revenues by price discrimination, for each market size total revenues will be greater to the discriminating monopolist than to the nondiscriminating monopolist. Therefore, the minimum size market can be squeezed to a smaller geographic size before surplus profits are eliminated. Hence the statement is made that price discrimination will cause market areas to be smaller and firms to be more crowded together.

If plant prices were different for sellers of the same commodity, perhaps

$$(2) \quad MR = MC, c = P - t - \frac{P}{e}$$

since

$$p = P - t$$
$$p = c + \frac{P}{e} = c + \frac{p+t}{e} = \frac{ec + p + t}{e}$$
$$(3) \quad p = \frac{ec + t}{e - 1}$$

This, of course, indicates that the factory or plant price would rise to the more distant buyers, if the elasticity of demand were constant at every price and location. Nevertheless, any such price discrimination would run into the problem of keeping the buyers from trading with each other, since the lower price is being charged the nearby buyers. This would be a case of freight inflation.

In the case of a linear demand curve the demand function might be as follows:

$$(4) \quad P = p + t = b - \left(\frac{b}{a}\right) n$$

where
  n = individual quantity demanded at delivered price
  b = delivered price at which quantity demanded equal zero
  a = quantity demanded when the delivered price is zero
  a and b are constants
The elasticity of demand can be shown to be equal to the following:

$$e = \frac{dn}{dP} \frac{P}{n} = -\frac{a}{b} \frac{p+t}{n}$$

Substitute

$$n = \left(-\frac{a}{b}\right) P + a$$
$$(5) \quad e = \frac{-(p+t)}{b - p - t}$$

Another formulation can be shown to be true with respect to the plant price to maximize profits (see equation 2):

$$(6) \quad p = c + \frac{P}{e}$$

Substituting for e (equation 5):

$$(7) \quad p = \tfrac{1}{2}(b + c - t)$$

Thus, if the demand for each individual at each location is the same straight line with respect to delivered price, the plant price will be decreased for the distant buyers by one-half the freight. For the complete proofs, see Lösch, *op. cit.*, pp. 147–157.

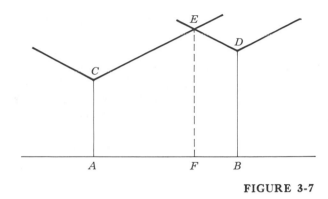

FIGURE 3-7

because managerial talents were different, market sizes would become unequal and irregular in size. The firms with the higher plant prices would have smaller market sizes; those with lower prices would have larger market sizes. In Figure 3-7, site A has a lower plant price than site B. The line AB is the straight line distance between the two sites. AC is the price at plant A; BD is the price at plant B. The delivered price to buyers along the line AB is the price at a plant plus transportation costs. CE and DE show how delivered prices might vary with distance from each plant. The boundary between the market of the two plants would be at F, where the delivered price is equal from either plant. If two-dimensional geographic space is taken into account, as in Figure 3-8, the boundary between the markets would be GH, a hyperbola. Since the price is lower at A than at B, the

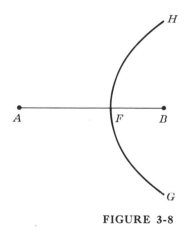

FIGURE 3-8

boundary at which delivered price is equal is more distant from A than from B.[18]

The productivity of land in different regions may be different and not uniform as assumed. One region may be extremely fertile and support a dense population. Another may not be so fertile and may support only a sparse population. Differences in population also result from the development of central places. If producer's cost curves are the same whether population is dense or sparse, market areas tend to be smaller and prices higher in the densely populated area. If plants in two such areas had the same cost curves, curve AC in Figure 3-9 might represent their average cost. AB shows the demand in the sparsely populated area after competition has reduced markets to their minimum size. The price would be OP, and the rate of production would be OQ. In the densely populated area without competition the same price would lead to much greater quantities demanded than OQ. If the plant in the sparsely populated area had no competition, the quantity demanded at each price in the denser area would still be greater. Nevertheless, there could exist some amount of competition that would reduce the quantity demanded in the densely populated area to OQ at price OP. Even so, an increase in price in the denser area would result in less reduction of quantities demanded than in the sparser area because an increase in price will not reduce the market area of the arbitrarily shrunk denser area as soon as the area of the sparser area. An increase in price would reduce the number of consumers and their quantities demanded in the sparser area, while in the denser area, only the quantity demanded of each consumer would be

---

[18] The competitive boundary between two markets when pricing is f.o.b. can be described by the following equation:

$$p_1 + t_1 k_1 = p_2 + t_2 k_2$$

where
p_1 and p_2 = prices at the two plants
t_1 and t_2 = transport cost per unit per mile from the respective plant
k_1 and k_2 = respective distances from each plant

Then

$$t_1 k_1 - t_2 k_2 = p_2 - p_1$$

assume
$$t_1 = t_2$$
Then

$$t_1(k_1 - k_2) = p_2 - p_1$$
$$k_1 - k_2 = \frac{p_2 - p_1}{t_1}$$

Since the term on the right is a constant, the equation is that of a hyperbola. See Walter Isard, *Location and Space-Economy* (Cambridge, Mass.: The M.I.T. Press, 1956), footnote on p. 157.

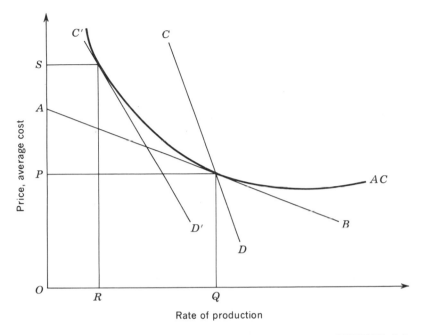

FIGURE 3-9

reduced. Thus, CD could represent the demand curve facing the firm in the dense area when its competition results in the demand OQ at price OP. Furthermore, there is room for more reduction in the trading areas by competition. This would be true until CD had shifted to $C'D'$ so that it was also tangent to AC. Therefore, price would be higher, the quantities sold by each firm less, and the extent of the market less in the dense area than in the sparsely populated area.[19]

Political boundaries and topographical features may distort market area sizes and shapes in similar ways. In international trade, tariffs and quotas are barriers to trade between countries. As a commodity crosses the border, if it is not completely excluded, the delivered price abruptly rises. In Figure 3-10 delivered price from plant A is shown by the line $BCDE$. The jump CD at the border is the tariff. Although there is not supposed to be interference with interstate commerce in the United States, there is. Labeling requirements on out-of-state products, inspection requirements, discriminatory taxes, and "buy at home" campaigns, especially by state institutions, may represent barriers to trade between states.[20]

[19] Lösch, *op. cit.*, pp. 180–181.
[20] Hoover, *op. cit.*, pp. 215–225; Lösch, *op. cit.*, pp. 196–214, 445–451.

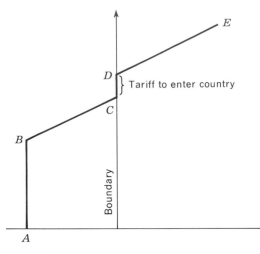

FIGURE 3-10

In international trade the increased cost of doing business in another country may not come from tariffs, but may arise from the problems of selling in an area with another language, with different tastes, and with different systems of weights and measures. All these factors require increased costs to be overcome. Advertising and correspondence must be translated, and products may need to be redesigned.

Border crossings may be few, just as river crossings and mountain passes are few, and thus extension of markets across the political or topographic boundary may be restricted. For example, in Figure 3-11 assume that a plant is established at A. If there are no trade barriers, the whole circle is the plant's market area. If there is a tariff at the boundary BC, the market can extend only to EFG on the other side of the barrier before demand vanishes. The delivered price to buyers along EFG would be the same as along BXC. The tariff has abruptly increased the delivered price at the border BC. If the boundary were a river with a bridge at H, a mountain range with a pass at H, or a political boundary with the only customs point at H, the market on the other side of the boundary would be reduced to JFI.[21]

Thus, there is a tendency for commodities with large market areas to shun the border area, and to locate nearer the center of population of the political entity. A large part of the market for such commodities would be cut off near the borders. Goods and services with small market areas,

[21] Hoover, loc. cit.

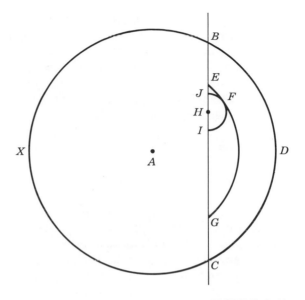

FIGURE 3-11

such as retail stores, would be unaffected by the boundary unless a tariff involved protection of their market. If one country had a tariff on a commodity but the other did not, the protected industry would tend to locate near the border. For example, there is the homely case of gas stations located on the outskirts of a city where they do not have to charge a city gasoline tax. Just inside the border of the city, service stations are few. They locate away from the boundary.

SYSTEMS OF SYSTEMS OF CITIES

As pointed out in previous sections of this chapter the size distribution and spacing of cities do not conform exactly to the simple model generated by assuming uniform population and resource endowments on a plain in which transportation costs are identical in every direction. A small part of the reason for the difficulty in checking the theory is the statistical one of defining the urbanized area. More important, however, are the divergencies of the assumptions of the model from reality. In the last section the impact of pricing policies, population density, differences in managerial talent, topography, and political boundaries on market sizes and shapes were described. Although changes in the sizes and shapes of trading areas were indicated, the hierarchical structure of these places was left undisturbed. With price discrimination or greater population density the market sizes would be smaller and places closer together, but the system is otherwise undisturbed.

There are, however, several other reasons for the difference between the theory and reality. There is no guarantee that every activity with the same size trading area will find it profitable to locate in the same place. Retailers selling convenience goods or groups of retailers selling shopping goods may locate together because these goods may be purchased by the buyer on the same shopping trip. Manufacturers, however, with the same minimum size market areas may not find any advantage to locating with other activities with the same size trading areas. To show that activities with the same range do not locate in the same place we need look at only a few cases. For most activities New York is the center of a trading area including the whole set of cities in the United States. International banking services, publishing, national advertising, and corporate finance are activities centering in New York City. The national political administration, however, is in Washington, D.C.; Detroit has in the past served a national market for automobiles; Chicago has provided the nation with meats and televisions; and Los Angeles has provided the nation with motion picture entertainment.

The reasons why these activities with the same market size may not be located in the same center are that resources are not uniformly distributed, that labor productivity is not uniformly distributed, and that some activities will be drawn to the same center even though they do not have the same market size. Furthermore, some locations are historical accidents. They are accidents in the sense that factors other than the economic created them. A good example would be the site of the nation's capital, Washington. From the point of view of minimizing transportation costs to the national population, some point in the Midwest near Chicago would be a better site.[22] The site, of course, was selected before the size of the eventual region was known, and indeed, may have been fairly central to the thirteen colonies.

Resources may draw plants from the center of their markets because lower input prices will cause the average cost curve of the firm to shift downward. It will be profitable for the plant to be located nearer materials if this reduction in the cost schedule is greater than the possible downward shift of the demand curve facing the firm, as its site is farther from the market center. In particular the total revenue will shift downward if population density is irregular rather than uniform. Thus, some places

---

[22] Chauncy D. Harris, "The Market as a Factor in the Localization of Industry in the United States," *Annals of the Association of American Geographers*, vol. 44, pp. 315–348.

that would be low-order places because of their trading area position become higher-order places as activities with much larger trading areas are
drawn to them because resources are near or labor productivity is
greater.

Another reason why activities with the same market size may not be
located in the same place is agglomeration economies. In particular it may
be profitable to locate a plant adjacent to other plants in the same industry
because they have common inputs, or it may be profitable to locate
adjacent to plants in supplying or buying industries. The reasons why
firms can profit by locating adjacent to each other and why it is profitable
to make one plant very large are agglomeration economies. These will be
discussed in the next chapter.

The surrounding area of a central place is a supply area and a market
area. The city is a production center buying inputs locally and from a wide
area, and the city is a trading center selling its products to the city and a
wide area. The supply area depends upon the commodities and services
produced in the city. A large center may require a very large supply area.
The commodities and services provided by the center are determined by
the resources available in the hinterland. Activities will locate in centers
which enable them to maximize profits.

Therefore, a group of cities, such as the group in the United States, is
really several systems rather than one. Wholesaling, retailing, banking,
professional services, and other services to households that are relatively
free of input constraints and are tied to markets fit into a hierarchical
system such as the simple model. This simple system, however, is overlaid
by the more complex development of places dependent exclusively or
partially upon manufacturing industries. The supply and trading areas of
these manufacturing places will depend upon the scale of production that
is profitable in the central place. The supply area may be a region and the
trading area may be the entire nation, as in the case of cottonseed oil
processing in Memphis and canning in New Orleans and San Diego. On
the other hand, the trading area may be only a region and the supply area
the world. Many combinations are possible.

When the problem of an urban hierarchy is thought of in this way, classification is difficult. Nevertheless, Duncan in his study, *Metropolis and Region,*
attempted an approach to classification.[23] Relying basically, although not
exclusively, on per capita wholesale sales as a measure of trading activity
and on per capita value added by manufacture as a measure of manufacturing activity, a dual structure of city hierarchies was established for

[23] Otis Dudley Duncan et al., *Metropolis and Region,* published for Resources for the
Future, Inc. (Baltimore: The Johns Hopkins Press, 1960), chap. 11.

the SMSAs of 300,000 or more inhabitants in 1950. The scheme is shown in Table 3-4. The classification scheme is not meant to be exact, but is suggestive. There are several marginal cases that might have been placed in different categories.

The five largest metropolitan areas with more than 3 million people were considered national metropolises because of their sheer size and complexity. Nevertheless, they do not serve the same functions. New York and Chicago are similar in being high in both manufacturing and trading functions. Los Angeles and Philadelphia show profiles more characteristic of a diversified manufacturing center than a trading center, and Detroit tends to show characteristics of a specialized manufacturing center.

The Regional Metropolises were places with high per capita wholesale sales and low per capita value added by manufactures. The same sort of reasoning was used to determine the Regional Capitals. Cities were divided between the two classifications depending upon their size and sphere of influence. Of all the categories listed these two are the only ones of much hierarchical significance.

The group of places with relatively high per capita value added by manufacture and low per capita wholesale values were put into the manufacturing cities. The classification, however, is not exact. This group of cities may be divided into those with metropolitan functions and those without. The cities range from those with no wholesaling function to those with as much wholesaling per capita as some of the regional metropolises. Manufacturing activity varied from those places at which only one industry concentrated to those places at which many different industries located. The latter are diversified manufacturing centers. The cities could be classified into three groups: Diversified Manufacturing with Metropolitan Functions, Diversified Manufacturing with Few Metropolitan Functions, and Specialized Manufacturing. There is no implication in the ordering of the groups that one group is subordinate to the other, although some regional capitals may be subordinate to cities in the Diversified Manufacturing Cities with Metropolitan Functions group.

The cases in Specialized Manufacturing are truly special. None of these cities appears to warrant its size in population, because per capita wholesale sales and value added in manufacture are so low. Our national capital is a special case. San Diego, San Antonio, and Norfolk-Portsmouth are homes of military bases, and without the bases they might not have reached their current sizes. The tourist trade has put Miami in its current position. Wilkes-Barre-Hazleton is based on coal mining, an unusual function for a city of its size. Tampa, Knoxville, and Phoenix also seem to be based on extractive industries. These are no coal centers, but centers of employ-

TABLE 3-4   CLASSIFICATION OF SMAs OF 300,000 OR MORE INHABITANTS ACCORDING TO METROPOLITAN FUNCTIONS AND REGIONAL RELATIONSHIPS

National metropolis

New York
Chicago
Los Angeles
Philadelphia
Detroit

Diversified manufacturing with metropolitan functions

Boston
Pittsburgh
St. Louis
Cleveland
Buffalo
Cincinnati

Regional metropolis

San Francisco
Minneapolis-St. Paul
Kansas City
Seattle
Portland
Atlanta
Dallas
Denver

Diversified manufacturing with few metropolitan functions

Baltimore
Milwaukee
Albany-Schenectady-Troy
Toledo
Hartford
Syracuse

Specialized manufacturing

Providence
Youngstown
Rochester
Dayton
Allentown-Bethlehem-Easton
Akron
Springfield-Holyoke
Wheeling-Steubenville
Charleston, W. Va.

Regional capital

Houston
New Orleans
Louisville
Birmingham
Indianapolis
Columbus
Memphis
Omaha
Fort Worth
Richmond
Oklahoma City
Nashville
Jacksonville

Special cases

Washington   Norfolk-Portsmouth
San Diego   Wilkes-Barre-Hazleton
San Antonio   Tampa-St. Petersburg
Miami   Knoxville
               Phoenix

SOURCE: By permission from Otis Dudley Duncan et al., *Metropolis and Region*, published for Resources for the Future, Inc. (Baltimore: The Johns Hopkins Press, 1960), p. 271.

ment in the industry defined as agriculture-forestry-fisheries. They also have concentrations of employment in construction, resulting from their recent fast growth rates. Their position may appear anomolous because they are emerging regional capitals.

SUMMARY

The size and location of cities are dependent upon their functions. Trading centers in which economic activities relatively free of input constraints locate tend to form a hierarchical system of cities. From this underlying trade framework differences occur because human and natural resources are not uniformly distributed; some plants therefore locate in centers that have smaller or larger trading function market areas but are near resources. Agglomeration economies may also cause some differences, as may historical accident. Thus, a group of cities and central places in a region is in fact a system of systems of cities.

CHAPTER 4

The simplest model of a system of cities, described in the previous chapter, was based on the assumption that population and resources were evenly distributed throughout the land. Furthermore, transport costs were assumed to be the same in all directions, since topography was also assumed to be homogeneous. The hierarchical scheme of places in this system was dependent on the number of activities locating at a particular place and the threshold size of those activities. Population in these centers had to increase over that of the hinterland and vary with production in the central place. In the simple model the population was assumed to be some proportion of the population served, where the population served included that of the central place itself. Thus, from a plain in which population was uniformly distributed, central places or cities arose with different populations. These places, however, were still treated as points. They did not have a geographic dimension.

In the first chapter it was stated that the location of production would be stressed rather than the location of people, because people tend to live near their jobs. In the last chapter employment in the agricultural sector was assumed to be evenly distributed because land was assumed to be equally fertile. People concentrated in places because of the nonagricultural employment opportunities in those places. These places were located in the center of the particular market area served. All activities with the same threshold market size were assumed to be located in the center of each market area of that size.

The assumptions of the model seem best fitted to trading activities such as wholesaling, retailing, and banking. If the geographic distribution of manufacturing industry could also be explained by the model, it would be expected that industrial production in each industry would tend to be distributed in the same way as markets. Of course, some industries sell more to other industries than to final consumer markets. But if industries selling to consumers were uniformly distributed with respect to markets, those industries which sold chiefly to industrial markets would also be distributed in the same way as the final consumer market, because their industrial markets would be so distributed.

In order to analyze the distribution patterns of manufacturing industries, this chapter will begin with a measure of the geographic dispersion of manufacturing industries with respect to the distribution of consumer markets in the United States. This will show the degree to which many manufacturing industries tend to be distributed in the same way as market areas, and the degree to which some are pulled away from such geographic dispersion. The rest of the chapter will discuss the reasons why such industrial concentrations arise away from market centers. These reasons are included in agglomeration economies and the geographic variation in input prices.

For any one industry the comparison of the geographic distribution of its production with that of its markets can lead to an understanding of the reasons for its particular pattern of location. Nevertheless, markets are also dependent on the location of industry. As employment centers arise away from the centers that would have occurred in the simple model of a system of cities, population is attracted to these places, and the consumer market takes on a new configuration. Thus, the distribution of consumer markets, which is the basis for comparing the geographic distribution of production of a particular industry, already includes the impact of both the central place hierarchy and manufacturing employment centers. Manufacturing employment centers, of course, do attract central place activities precisely because they represent markets. Thus, if the geographic distribution of *all* manufacturing production is compared with the geographic distribution of consumer markets, it would be appropriate to question which was indeed the dependent variable. They both are. For a single industry, however, it is appropriate to begin by comparing the geographic distribution of its production with that of its markets.

THE GEOGRAPHIC DISPERSION OF MANUFACTURING

If manufacturers' markets were equal to or smaller than the nine census regions listed at the top of Table 4-1, production in each manufacturing industry would be distributed among the regions in the same proportion as markets. The difficulty is how to measure markets. One measure of the size of markets in different regions is personal income (for a full explanation of personal income by regions, see Chapter 6), the total sum of money available to persons to spend. This measure reflects both the size of the population and the income received in each region. Thus, if the percentage distribution of production among regions was equal to that of personal income, the implication would be that manufacturing production centers were near their markets and that they tended to have the same distribution as trading activities. Furthermore, manufacturing would not distort the hierarchy of central places as much as many studies have suggested.[1]

[1] August Lösch, *The Economics of Location* (New Haven, Conn.: Yale University Press, 1954), pp. 365–374.

TABLE 4-1 COEFFICIENT OF LOCALIZATION, SELECTED GROUPINGS OF MANUFACTURING INDUSTRIES, UNITED STATES, 1962

Industry	United States ($1,000,000)	Region* (percentage distribution)									Coefficient of localization
		New England	Middle Atlantic	East North Central	West North Central	South Atlantic	East South Central	West South Central	Mountain	Pacific	
Personal income	$439,661	6.5	21.8	21.1	8.0	12.4	4.5	7.6	3.7	14.4	.11
All manufacturing (value added)	179,256	7.5	23.3	29.2	6.2	10.7	4.5	5.4	1.8	11.4	.11
Food and kindred products	20,856	3.9	20.0	24.8	12.3	10.0	4.9	7.1	3.0	14.4	.08
Tobacco products	1,645	—	7.5	—	—	71.6	17.2	—	—	—	.72
Textile mill products	6,098	14.0	19.4	—	—	53.6	7.4	1.0	—	1.6	.52
Apparel and related products	7,151	6.4	51.4	9.2	3.6	11.6	7.6	3.5	—	6.5	.33
Lumber and wood products	3,606	4.7	6.9	10.6	4.1	13.3	8.1	7.7	5.0	38.2	.30
Furniture and fixtures	2,838	5.0	18.6	25.9	3.6	22.4	6.0	5.0	—	11.2	.16
Paper and allied products	7,044	10.9	19.9	24.6	5.3	15.0	6.2	5.0	.7	11.3	.12
Printing and publishing	9,996	6.6	35.1	24.4	7.3	7.8	2.6	6.0	1.8	9.6	.17
Chemicals and allied products	16,062	3.0	26.3	20.8	5.3	17.2	8.2	4.0	1.0	6.0	.17
Petroleum and coal products	3,439	3.0	13.4	19.1	5.4	3.6	1.7	37.0	3.6	14.7	.30
Rubber and plastics	4,316	15.4	18.6	37.6	4.7	5.5	5.4	3.3	—	—	.26
Leather and leather products	2,102	29.4	25.8	17.6	10.2	4.1	6.0	—	1.0	—	.31
Stone, clay, and glass products	6,605	4.8	21.5	26.5	7.9	12.4	5.2	7.2	2.5	11.2	.06
Primary metal industries	13,744	4.4	26.4	42.2	2.4	7.2	5.1	3.6	3.0	6.3	.26
Fabricated metal products	11,119	8.8	22.3	38.2	5.4	5.8	3.8	4.0	.9	10.5	.20
Machinery, except electrical	16,068	10.6	20.5	44.3	7.0	3.8	2.2	4.0	1.0	7.8	.27
Electrical machinery	15,594	10.6	27.7	32.4	4.5	5.6	3.6	2.3	—	12.3	.21
Transport equipment	20,946	5.4	11.8	43.7	7.6	5.8	—	3.2	—	18.3	.26
Instruments and related products	4,303	12.7	45.2	19.3	6.2	—	—	1.6	—	—	.30

* For definitions of these regions, see Fig. 6-3.

SOURCE: Calculated from data in U.S. Bureau of the Census, *Annual Survey of Manufactures* (1962); and U.S. Bureau of the Census, "Personal Incomes by States," *Statistical Abstract of the United States* (1965), p. 334.

One measure of the geographic distribution of production relative to markets is the coefficient of localization. The first step in calculating the coefficient is to compute the percentage of total United States personal income received in each region. The next step is to compute the percentage of value added (value of shipments less purchases of materials from other industries) in each industry that is produced in each region. If value-added data are not available, employment may be substituted on the assumption that production is proportional to employment. Subtract the percentage of personal income in each region from that of value added by each industry in each region. For each industry sum either the positive or negative differences over all regions and divide by 100. This number is the *coefficient of localization*. If production in the industry were distributed exactly as personal income, the coefficient would be 0. If all the production in the industry were in one region in which there was little or no personal income, the coefficient would be 1. An implication of the coefficient is that it indicates the approximate percentage of production shipped between regions.[2]

Table 4-1 shows the distribution of personal income among the nine census regions of the United States in 1962, the distribution of value added for each of nineteen manufacturing industries among the nine United States census regions in 1962, and the coefficient of localization for each industry. The manufacturing of tobacco products is the most concentrated industry, with a coefficient of .72. The geographic distribution of production of stone, clay, and glass products and food and kindred products is closer to that of personal income than to that of any of the other industries. Their coefficients are .06 and .08, respectively.

There are several interrelated reasons why the geographic distribution of manufacturing production may be concentrated. In the first place the possible scale of production may be greater in size than one region. One plant may serve a firm's national market. So long as inputs are not a constraint, these plants or activities may be located at the center of the market so that transport costs to the national market may be minimized. This would mean concentration in the East North Central Region.[3] To test this presumption, one would need data on each firm's share of market and plant sizes. Nevertheless, a relative concentration of manufacturing in the East North Central Region does appear. Whereas only 21 percent of income was received in the East North Central Region, 29 percent of all manufacturing value added was produced in the East North Central Region.

[2] The calculation of the coefficient is a modification of the one developed by P. Sargent Florence, W. G. Fritz, and R. C. Gilles in "Measures of Industrial Distribution," in U.S. National Resources Planning Board, *Industrial Location and National Resources* (1943), chap. 5.
[3] Chauncy D. Harris, "The Market as a Factor in the Localization of Industry in the United States," *Annals of the Association of American Geographers*, vol. 44, pp. 328–331.

Moreover, a greater percentage of value added than of personal income was generated in this region in each of eleven industries.

Another possibility is that firms cluster in belts in an area endowed with resources required by the industry. Each plant has part of the resource area as a supply area, while its market is the whole nation. While this location would reduce material prices, it must not cause much reduction in the revenue schedules or it would not be a profitable situation. The concentration of tobacco production, textile mills, and furniture production in the South Atlantic States may be partly explained by resource endowments.

A more elusive possibility is that firms shift plant sites to areas where labor is more productive per wage dollar. The concept itself is hard to pin down. Nevertheless, the concentration of textile mills in the South Atlantic Region has often been cited as an example of this factor.[4]

Concentration of production in excess of market size may be caused by agglomeration economies. Perhaps the cost curves of each plant in an industry shift downward because of the expansion of the industry in one place. An example of this may be the concentration of the apparel industry in the Middle Atlantic Region. Agglomeration economies usually refer to concentration in a central place rather than in a region. Apparel production is not only concentrated in the Middle Atlantic Region, but in New York City in particular.[5]

Before the coefficient of localization is accepted as a measure of the dispersion of the industry, several qualifications should be made clear. The industrial groupings include the production of many different products, just as the grouping of all manufacturing in one lump includes a diversity of production, and thus the coefficient for each industry is an average for the diverse production included in each group. The coefficient of localization for all manufacturing (.11) indicates that manufacturing production tends to be distributed almost as personal income, and yet the coefficients of the industrial groupings range from .06 to .72. In the same way electrical machinery production includes such products as transformers, vacuum cleaners, radios, television sets, and electronic components. The coefficient of localization for electrical machinery is .21, but if the group were divided into subgroups, the coefficient for many of the subgroups would be much higher. Almost 50 percent of telephone and telegraph apparatus production takes place in Illinois. Petroleum and coal products is another example. The geographic locations of coal and petroleum may complement one another so that the coefficient of localization for coal and petroleum

[4] Harvey S. Perloff et al., *Regions, Resources, and Economic Growth* (Baltimore: The Johns Hopkins Press, 1960), pp. 419–420.
[5] Perloff et al., *op. cit.*, pp. 420–424.

products is only .30 for the two together. If separated, they would probably both be much higher.

Many industries, in fact most, do not sell directly to consumers, but they sell to other industries. This is another reason why the coefficient of localization will change as the large industrial groupings are broken up into smaller ones. To the extent that the geographic distribution of production of industries selling directly to consumers is not the same as consumer markets, other producers whose markets are these consumer industries will not be correlated with the distribution of consumer markets, but with the distribution of the consumer industries. The measure of the geographic distribution of markets for industries selling to other industries rather than consumers should be the geographic distribution of production in the industries to which they sell. If this were done, many of the coefficients of localization might be lower. But as suggested previously, to the extent that the consumer industries are distributed as their markets, industries selling to them would also be distributed as the consumer markets.

Another problem is how to divide the country into regions. This question will be discussed in great detail later. At this point, however, it should be noted that the level of the coefficient of localization for an industry may vary with the size of the regions used. If the United States had been divided into neighborhoods, only grocery stores, drugstores, and filling stations might have shown up as geographically distributed in the same way as markets, and none of the manufacturing industries listed above would have shown themselves as associated with markets. The neighborhood is not a large enough market for the establishment of a bakery or bottling plant and yet one or several of each are in almost every county in the nation. We have reduced the problem by including much larger areas in our regions. Still, the Mountain Region receives only 3.7 percent of total personal income, and is of insufficient size to cause the location of significant amounts of transportation equipment production. The Mountain Region is supplied by other regions. Yet, if the market demand of the area were greater, transport production would take place in the region. The lack of production of an item in a region does not necessarily indicate that the industry is not centrally located with respect to its markets. As we have pointed out, scale may be so large that one plant of the largest firms may serve the nation. That plant may be centrally located with respect to the entire market.

GEOGRAPHIC VARIATIONS IN INPUT PRICES

The first step in understanding the impact of variations in input prices on the location of industry is to define clearly what is meant by input price.

It could be the price per ton of material, the price per acre of land, the price per hour of labor, or the price per hour for using equipment or buildings. But each of these inputs may vary in quality from one place to another. By quality is meant productivity. A particular combination of tons of material and man-hours in one place may produce 100 units of a given product. In another place the same combination might produce 300 units of product. Strictly speaking, the production function would be different between places. Isoquants of a given rate of production in areas with more productive inputs would be reached with fewer units of inputs. The quality or productivity referred to is intrinsic quality, not productivity changes resulting from different combinations of inputs being put together. A fixed acreage of land used with varying numbers of workers would vary in productivity, but at the same time different soils have varying productivity even when the same number of workers is used on each plot. This is the quality difference referred to in this paragraph. Such quality differences may arise because of climate, nutrition, the factors causing one mineral deposit to be more concentrated in pure ore than another, the education and talents of a particular work force, etc.

For simplicity in the following analysis these differences in quality will be treated as differences in the price of a given input. Each input will be of a given quality everywhere. Differences in quality, such as a poorer quality of ore, will be priced at the cost necessary to cause the material to be equivalent in productivity. If three tons of poor ore is equivalent to one of pure ore, the price per ton of ore would be the price for three tons of poor ore or for one ton of pure ore. If three people in one place are equivalent to one person in another, the wage paid would be for three hours in the less productive location or for one hour in the place with more productive workers. In this way the production function would be the same in every place, and isoquants would not shift about from one place to another. Only prices of inputs would vary.

In addition to quality there are other reasons for these input prices to vary from one place to another. There are special problems with each class of inputs: land, labor, buildings, equipment, materials, and loanable funds.

Materials include raw materials as well as products purchased from other manufacturers. These material prices will increase with distance from the place of extraction, or the place of production, by the transport cost per unit per mile, just as the delivered price of any other product increases with distance from a production place. The way in which transport cost per unit per mile is related to distance of shipment will depend on the mode of transport. For example, trucking rates tend to be proportional to distance, railroad rates tend to increase at a decreasing rate with respect to dis-

FIGURE 4-1

tance, and water shipping rates also tend to increase at a decreasing rate with respect to distance. For short hauls trucks tend to be most economical, for medium-distance hauls rails tend to be most economical, and for long-distance hauls shipping by water tends to be most economical. These relationships might be shown as in Figure 4-1. The exact distance at which one mode of travel becomes more economical than another will depend on the particular routes, the type of commodity, the direction of haul, and the size and volume of shipment.[6]

It is obvious that part of the relation between transport cost and distance will depend on the circuity of routes for different modes of travel between the shipper and the destination. Differences in rates for the same distance and mode will vary with the volume or size of shipment. Less than carload, or truckload, shipments require more handling and terminal costs. Thus, the rates per ton increase if shipments are smaller than carload or truckload lots. Rates per ton will increase as the size of the product increases relative to its weight. A product light in weight but taking up a lot of space would require a greater transport rate than one of the same weight that was more compact. Some products require special equipment, such as tankers and refrigerator equipment, and their transport rates vary accordingly. Rates per ton also may vary with direction of travel. If more shipments move in one direction on a given line, the shipments in the opposite direction can be handled at lower costs. The barges, trucks, or freight cars must be returned over the route to the point of heavy ship-

[6] Edgar M. Hoover, *The Location of Economic Activity* (New York: McGraw-Hill Book Company, 1948), pp. 15–26.

ments whether empty or not. Therefore, loads going in the opposite direction to the main flow of traffic may be quoted a low rate, called a back-haul or "ballast" rate, because little or no cost is incurred by the transfer agency.

These variations in rates are more obvious than variations in the rate per ton that occur for different kinds of goods. Perishable or fragile goods, such as fruit, household appliances, and furniture, of course, are likely to cost more per ton to ship a given distance because the likelihood of loss is greater and increases the insurance rate. A less obvious factor causing increased transportation costs for different commodities is the higher value of some commodities per pound. Transport industries, except for trucking, tend to have high overhead expenses, and it has been difficult to allocate these expenses to the proper shippers. The practice has been to discriminate against goods with high value per pound because they are supposed to be able to bear higher transportation costs. The argument is a technical one, similar to that on geographic price discrimination. The demand for transportation services is derived from the demand for the products shipped. Thus, the demand for transport services will be more inelastic, *ceteris paribus,* if the particular transport service, such as railroads, is essential and there are no good substitutes, such as trucking, and if the total expense on transportation is a small part of the total production cost. In such a case the transport service can discriminate by charging different prices for high-value- and low-value-per-pound goods because the markets can be separated without much cost and the price elasticities of demand in the separate markets are different. If the transporter offered the same price for the two markets he would find that marginal revenue would be less in the more inelastic high-value-goods market than in the more elastic low-value-goods market. Revenues would be increased by increasing the price to high-value goods and lowering the price to low-value goods, thus shifting the business from high-value to low-value goods.[7]

Thus, material prices may differ in a variety of ways as distance between buyer and seller increases because of the variations in transportation costs caused by the mode of travel, the direction of travel, the kind of commodity, and the size and volume of shipment. It is perfectly true, of course, that these same comments apply to the delivered prices of final products.

Wage rates may differ for firms in different locations for reasons other than quality differences in the work force. Even if all labor were perfectly

[7] While competition from trucking has curtailed this kind of price discrimination in railroad rates, it still exists as is shown by the continued inroads of trucking into precisely this part of the railroad market in which railroads have tended to load overhead costs. See John R. Meyer et al., *Competition in the Transportation Industries* (Cambridge, Mass.: Harvard University Press, 1960), pp. 174–175.

mobile and equally skilled, differences in wages per hour would exist in different places at the same time. These differences in wages will be called "equalizing differences." They include the differences in wages required to compensate for the severe climate and absence of the comforts and pleasures of civilization that exist in some places, and the differences in wages allowed because people prefer some areas and climates and will accept lower wages because they consider the nonpecuniary benefits of the area to be part of their income.[8]

Some places can support only a small agricultural population, much less a large nonagricultural population, because of the barren terrain and unfertile soil. In these places food prices are high. If the higher costs required to bring food from distant places were not compensated for by lower house rents, clothing costs, and other living expenses, wages in the area would have to be higher by the increase in living costs. Within any particular city-region, living costs will be greater in the city than in the hinterland. Food must be shipped to the city, and the larger the population, the greater is the supply area needed to serve the city and the longer are the distances required to ship food for the city. Prices will have to be raised in the city to attract the supply from other places and compensate for the transportation costs. House rents will be higher because of the congestion of the city.

To the producer, however, sites in some areas of the city or region will enable him to pay lower wages than in other areas. Wages in the city are higher than in the hinterland to compensate for the higher living costs. At the same time, however, there is a large work force available in the city that may not be available in the hinterland. The producer can draw on a wide cross section of people with diverse skills without having to attract workers from more distant places, as he would if he located in a small town in which most of the people were already employed. If the producer would locate this enterprise near the center of the city, he could draw equally from workers all over the area. He would be conveniently accessible to the largest labor force. If he should locate on the fringe of the city, however, and he required a very large labor force, he would find that he would have to raise his wages above those of competitors near the center of the city because the commuter costs of the more distant workers would be greater. To attract workers from the opposite side of the city, the firm would have to raise wages high enough to compensate for the longer commuter trip, or the workers would work downtown to increase their real income.

---

[8] For the causes of differences in wage rates between places, see Bertil Ohlin, *Interregional and International Trade* (Cambridge, Mass.: Harvard University Press, 1957), pp. 212–229; Hoover, *op. cit.*, pp. 103–115; and Lösch, *op. cit.*, pp. 240–243, 455–461, 490–495.

If the market mechanism worked perfectly, then, wages would not be equal in different regions or in different areas of the same city-region. In addition, however, the market does not work smoothly, so that differences in wages will exist between different areas above the equalizing differences. Although we will discuss the imperfections of the labor market in more detail in Chapter 8, it is enough at this point to see that workers may not have knowledge of their alternatives, that they may not have sufficient funds to make a move, or that the wage difference may be insufficient to justify the cost of migration.

Mobility of the input is a key to understanding how input prices may vary from one place to another. Material prices varied with the transportation cost of shipping them from their point of origin. Wages vary with skills, cost of living, amenities, and the mobility of workers. Land is perfectly immobile as are buildings and other real property fixed to the land. We would expect the rent of land, then, to vary tremendously from one site to another, and it does. In this case, however, the rents vary between sites within city-regions, while the average rent may not be so different between regions. Thus, land rent is important for determining the specific site for a plant within a region, but not so important for determining the most profitable region or city. Land rents will be the topic of the next chapter.

Funds for investment have often been thought to be costless to transfer from one place to another, so that a common assumption in economic analysis is that the cost of borrowing, the interest rate, is equal everywhere. The assumption is incorrect. Interest rates often vary from one to two percentage points from the East Coast to the West Coast in the United States. In this case the reason why funds are not shifted to places where they can earn more interest, and thus force equality in interest rates everywhere, is that investments in a distant place are riskier to the investor than are local investments because he has less information on the distant place. Furthermore, any information required to check on a buyer will cost more with distance. There will be more middlemen through whom business will have to be transacted.[9]

Although taxes indirectly reflect the price of government services available in a particular place, there is not a direct correspondence. Thus, taxes cannot be considered input prices. Nevertheless, they are expenses; they do vary from place to place; and they may be low in some places because inadequate government services are provided. Therefore, lower taxes may influence a firm to move to one site or another. The variations, however, are somewhat like land rents in that there may be more variation within

[9] Lösch, *op. cit.*, pp. 462–477.

regions than between regions. These variations, then, are more important in determining the profitability of sites within a region than the profitability of a particular city-region.[10]

ORIENTATION

We are now in a position to show how these geographic variations in input prices may cause producers to find their most profitable sites far from the center of their market. In Chapter 2 the general conditions for an optimum location were explained. These general conditions, however, do not reveal likely location patterns for particular industries. Specific revenue and cost figures for alternative sites are needed to determine plant sites. Nevertheless, if some special assumptions are made about the production function, total cost curve, total revenue curve, and markets, a few general statements can be made about the geographic distribution of production.[11]

Assume that there is no substitution between inputs in the production process of firms in a particular industry. The isoquants do not look like those in Chapter 2. Addition of just one of the inputs will not increase the rate of production. Therefore, the isoquants would look like Q_1 and Q_2 in Figure 4-2. Combinations of inputs represented by points A and B are the least-cost combinations whatever input prices are. Assume that inputs are required in the same proportion whatever the rate of production. To achieve double the rate of production it is necessary to double the amount of each of the inputs. Thus, given input prices, total cost will increase proportionately with the rate of production.

Furthermore, assume that only one rate of production can be sold in the market. There may be more than one market, but the market or markets are all considered as geographic points, not spatial markets, and a specified amount of the final product is sold in each. The delivered price of the product in each market is also specified in advance. In addition the firm pays the transportation cost of the product to market. Thus, the net price at plant is the delivered price less transportation cost to the market or markets.

Since the price per unit received for the product and the cost per unit of production do not vary with the rate of production, the most profitable site

[10] John F. Due, "Studies of State-Local Tax Influences on Location of Industry," *National Tax Journal* (June, 1961), pp. 163–173.
[11] These assumptions are from the traditional least-cost approach to location theory found in the following works: Alfred Weber, *Theory of the Location of Industry*, translated by C. Friedrich (Chicago: The University of Chicago Press, 1929); Hoover, *op. cit.*, pp. 27–46; Walter Isard, *Location and Space Economy* (Cambridge, Mass.: The M.I.T. Press, 1956), pp. 77–142; Walter Isard, *Methods of Regional Analysis: An Introduction to Regional Science* (Cambridge, Mass.: The M.I.T. Press, 1960), pp. 233–249.

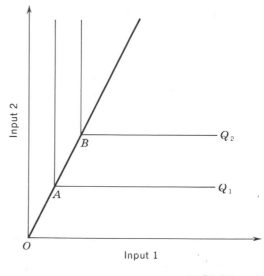

Input 2

Q_2

B

Q_1

A

O

Input 1

FIGURE 4-2

can be determined by comparing the net price at plant with the unit cost at plant at each site. The site with the greatest profit per unit would be the optimum site. The profitable site, however, can be found a different way under these conditions. The difference in profit from site to site only depends upon the transport cost per unit of product from plant to market, the transport cost of the material per unit of final product, or the differences between sites in other input costs per unit of final product.

The simplest case is the firm faced with one market and one material source. The market is a point market at A; the material source is at B. The wage costs per unit of final product are the same at both sites. In this case the only variables changing with the changing location would be the transportation costs of material and final product. The most profitable site will be where transportation costs are a minimum. This can be found by comparing the transportation cost per unit of final product from B to A with the transportation cost of material per unit of final product from B to A. The most profitable plant site will be the market A if the transport cost on the final product is greater than the cost of shipping the material. The most profitable site will be at the material source B if the transport cost of shipping the material is greater than the cost of shipping the final product.

The transportation cost of materials is most likely to be greater, and the plant site is most likely to be attracted to the material source, when there is a considerable weight loss in the production process. For example, ore smelting, sugar refining, and operations requiring a great deal of fuel tend to locate near the source of materials. Production processes using fuels that are burned up in the process, or causing waste that is discarded in the process and does not become a part of the final product to be shipped, tend to be attracted to material sources. Production processes using material that is perishable, as in the case of canning and freezing, tend to be attracted to the material source. The transportation cost of the material includes the probability of losses.

Transport costs per unit of product will tend to be greater than the transport cost of the materials necessary to make one unit of final product for firms in intermediate and late stages in the production process. Weights of material and product will not be very different. Thus, it is likely that later stages of processing will be market-oriented. There are several reasons why transport cost on the final product will be greater than on transport costs of materials. In the early stages of processing, bulky raw materials are refined. In later stages, such as metal fabricating, there is not so much reduction of cheap raw material as machining and forming of the material. The final product becomes more valuable per ton or per pound. It is more likely to be difficult to package and transport. It may be fragile, as in the case of watches, and it is distributed in smaller quantities to widely dispersed customers. Delivery to customers needs to be quick to obtain and expand business. Some prepared foods are more perishable than the materials used to make them. All these reasons make the final product more costly to handle and ship, causing the transport costs of the final product to be greater than those of the materials. Some production processes are weight-gaining rather than weight-losing and thus tend to cause the transport cost on the final product to be higher too. For example, a soda-bottling plant combines a soft-drink syrup with water, bottles the product, and distributes it. In this process, water, a ubiquitous material, adds weight to the final product to be shipped. Water has relatively the same price in most locations. Thus the transport cost on the final product can be avoided by locating at the market. Ink and beer production also add ubiquitous materials and tend to be located near the market.

So far we have been considering whether the plant should be located at either the market or the material site; we have neglected the possibility of any intermediate location. To compare these possibilities we need to compare the total transport cost per unit of output for each alternative site. Consider the most economical transport route between B, the material site, and A, the market site. If transport costs are proportional to

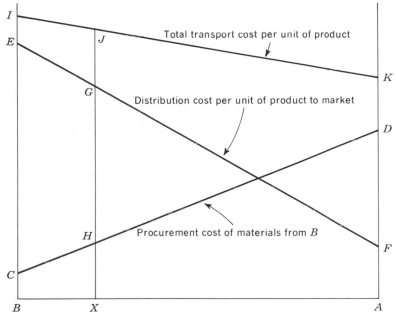

FIGURE 4-3

distance, then CD in Fig. 4-3 traces the transport cost from the material site to intermediate locations and to market for tons of material necessary to produce one unit of final product. The transport cost of shipping materials to the production site is the procurement cost. For example at location X, HX is the procurement cost. The distribution cost is the transport cost of shipping a unit of final product to market from the material site or other alternative sites between the material source and the market. BE is the distribution cost at the material site. At location X the distribution cost is GX. The total transportation cost per unit of output is the sum of the distribution and procurement costs at each site. IK traces the total transport cost per unit of output at each site from the material source to the market. In this case the market site is the minimum transportation cost location. The material source and all other intermediate locations require greater transportation costs.

If the distribution cost were exactly equal to the procurement cost, any location would be equally desirable. If transport costs were proportional to distance and the transportation cost per unit of output per mile were just equal to the transport cost per mile per tons of material necessary to produce one unit of product, the total transport cost line IK in Figure 4-3

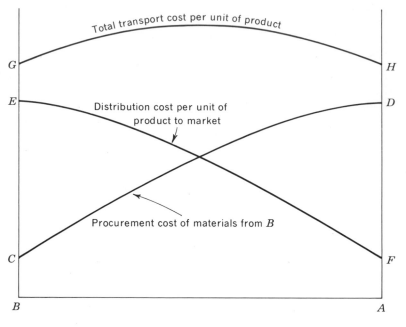

FIGURE 4-4

would be parallel to the base AB. If transport costs were not proportional to distance but increased at a decreasing rate as CD and EF in Figure 4-4, no intermediate sites would be considered, even if the transport cost on the final product were equal to the transport cost on material. The reason is that as sites are considered that are away from the material site and toward the market, the distribution cost decreases more slowly than the procurement cost increases. Total transport cost increases until the midpoint is reached. At that point movement toward the market results in the distribution cost's falling faster than the procurement cost increases. Since the rates are the same, we would be indifferent between locating the plant at the market or the material site. Thus, intermediate sites under these assumptions are unlikely to be selected.

Although intermediate locations have been shown to be unlikely locations for industry, there are cases in which such locations are feasible, and others in which the intermediate location is the minimum-transport-cost location.

Suppose that there is a transshipment point between the material source and the market. For example, point X in Figure 4-5 is a transshipment point at which goods passing through must be transferred from boats to railroads. It could also represent a transfer from trucking to railroads, or any

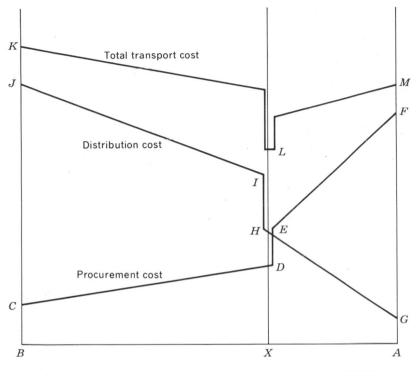

FIGURE 4-5

other kind of break in transit. An additional shipping cost is incurred when goods are transferred from one mode of transport to another. Thus, the distribution cost of shipping the product from material source B to market A in Figure 4-5 would be BJ. This includes a transshipping cost of IH at location X. The procurement cost of material would be AF, if the plant is located at the market. This cost includes transshipping cost DE at location X. If the plant should be located at X, the transshipment point, the cost of unloading, transferring, and loading the cargo to another mode of transport would be avoided. In some cases, as in Figure 4-5, transportation costs would then be a minimum. It would cost DX to procure material for one unit of product and HX to transport a unit of product to market. The extra transshipment cost would be avoided.

Transshipment points may be the minimum-transport-cost locations for plants or establishments when the transport costs on material and product are nearly equal and transshipment costs are high, as in the case of bulky commodities. In addition, wholesaling activities would have the further advantage that the transshipment point is located at a place from which it is less costly to distribute to many smaller markets.

Some plants, particularly flour milling, may locate at intermediate points and be allowed "in-transit" privileges by the railroads. When producers are granted this privilege the transport rate is the same on the material and the finished product. There is no particular advantage to the intermediate site when this is done, although it eliminates the site's disadvantages; rather, these privileges are a result of negotiation to prevent flour milling and other processing plants from moving off to more profitable sites as changing conditions make their current locations less advantageous than others.

This analysis, a traditional one in location theory, is easily adapted to situations with more than one market and one material source. Each point, whether a market, a material source, or a cheap input site, is treated as if it were the source of a mechanical force. The force at each point is the transportation cost for final product, the transportation cost of material per unit of final product, or the savings in labor or other input costs per unit of final product that would be saved if the plant were located at the point. The most savings will occur at the site (not necessarily either a market or an input source) at which the many forces are in equilibrium. This equilibrium site occurs where no movement in any direction will allow more savings. For example, consider two markets and three different input sources where one or another input price would be a minimum, as pictured in Figure 4-6. These points are A through G. P might be the best plant site.

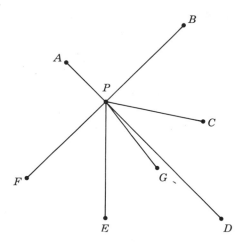

FIGURE 4-6

If it were not the best site a shift of the plant toward one of the points, say a market site, would reduce transportation costs per unit of final product more than the other costs per unit of product would increase because of increased distance from the other points. The plant site would be shifted in the direction of the cost savings until no further savings could be achieved by shifting the plant to another site. This last equilibrium point would be the best or most profitable site for the plant.

Given that the production process is the same for all firms in a given industry, the analysis so far would suggest that every firm in a particular industry would have the same orientation and would use the same inputs and use them in the same ratio. This conclusion is too simple. Firms or plants in the same industry may be market-oriented in one place and material-oriented in another. Moreover, the production process, the combinations of inputs used, will change to take advantage of cheaper inputs in particular places. The theory can be extended to include these points by utilizing the more traditional economic theory of the firm described in Chapter 2, rather than this specialized location theory. Three main assumptions can be relaxed: markets are assumed to be spatial rather than punctiform; demand in the market varies with the delivered price rather than being fixed; and the isoquants are the more typical kind shown in Chapter 2, allowing substitution of inputs in the production process to achieve the same rate of production. The following analysis will outline the change in the analysis of the location of the firm and then will be extended to an industrial analysis to show how particular patterns of the geographical distribution of production may arise.

Consider two alternative sites. One, site A, is at the center of a firm's market; the other, site B, is at a place where one of the input prices is a minimum. The production process of the plant to be located requires two inputs, input 1 and input 2. The price of input 1 is the same everywhere. The price of input 2 is lowest at site B and relatively higher at site A.

The lower price of input 2 at site B causes the isocost lines, such as AB in Figure 4-7, to shift to AC. More of the inputs can be purchased with the same outlay at site B than at site A. Furthermore, this means that a greater rate of production, Q_2, can be produced at B with the same outlay as at A. Another way to say this is that each rate of production, such as Q_1, can be produced for less at site B than at site A. Thus, the total cost curve for the plant would shift down as the plant site was located nearer B. Taking all factors into account, however, this may not be the most profitable site. Since population density is not uniformly distributed and A is the center of density of the market, the total revenue curve will also shift downward, perhaps to TR' as in Figure 4-8. The actual shift in the total cost schedule

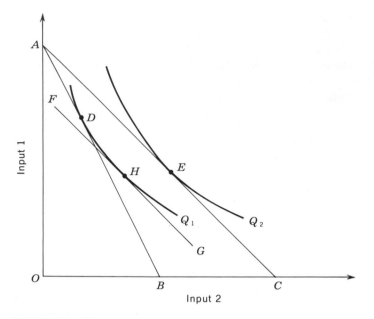

FIGURE 4-7

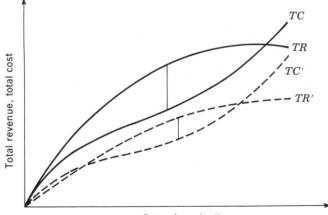

FIGURE 4-8

takes into account the possible substitution of the cheaper input for the relatively more expensive input 1 at site B. For example, the combination of inputs represented by H in Figure 4-7 represents a greater ratio of input 2 to input 1 at site B than would be used at site A, as represented by the input combinations determined at point D. The slope of FG represents the input prices at B. The actual shift in the total cost schedule also takes into account any possible changes in economies of scale that might occur by shifting location.

The test, then, of whether the shifting of the plant from the market center to an input source is an optimum solution depends on which is the most profitable. The profitability at the input source depends on the downward shifts in the total revenue and total cost curves. Comparison of the maximum difference between revenues and cost at site A and site B will determine which would be the more profitable site.

Now consider the problem of the geographic distribution of all firms in a particular industry rather than the selection of a site by one firm. Each firm will try to maximize profits. In our previous illustration the first firm to choose a site would select the market site, since it would yield the greatest profits. There are still many market areas left to serve in the entire region. Under the given conditions about market density and prices of input 2, the question to be answered is what is the geographic distribution of all the firms in the industry. Thus the problem is the same as that tackled in Chapter 3 in which trading areas on a plain were analyzed. In this case the impact of variations in demand and resource endowment on patterns of trading areas is discussed in more detail.

Assume that there is no collusion, and that prices are established f.o.b. (free on board) at plant. Disregard the total revenue and total cost schedules suggested as possibilities in Figure 4-8 in order to consider a wider range of alternatives. Three cases will be accounted for: (1) All plants will locate at the inexpensive input site, (2) plants will locate at both the inexpensive input site and the center of the market, or (3) all plants will locate at the center of density of the market.

If the price of the final product at B turned out so low, even with a single seller setting a monopoly price, that the delivered price at A was less than the average cost of producing the product at A at any rate of production, production would occur only at B. If the total market area was sufficiently large for several sellers to survive, they would all locate at B and sell at the same f.o.b. price. This analysis in effect says that the marginal cost of production at the least-cost rate of production rises from B and does so at a greater rate than the delivered price of the product, in spite of the possibility of some substitution in production. The more traditional approach to location of industry explained why transport cost on material per unit of output might be greater or less than that of the final product. With substitution the marginal cost of production does not necessarily rise as fast as the transport cost of the material.

A second case occurs when marginal cost of production at each rate of production rises by less than the delivered price of the product from B, taking account of the substitution possibilities. In this case the center of density of the market would also become possible as a production site because the marginal cost of production would be less than the delivered price from B. Will it become a production center? This depends upon the size of demand. Under the above circumstances firms at A and B could both survive as spatial monopolists, if the monopoly prices established at A and at B would carve out circular markets that did not intersect. Note that the price at plant at B is probably less than at A and that its market is somewhat greater in geographic area.

A more complicated situation arises, however, when the market areas of the producers at A and B intersect. One possibility is that both plants and many more may survive, but with excess profits eliminated by the restriction of market size to each producer. Another is the possibility of a continuously unstable situation with few sellers. The end solution depends on the barriers to entry in the industry, including the minimum sales necessary to achieve a competitive price—the threshold size. The difficulty is that when the markets intersect, each firm must take into account what his competitor will do when a price change is made. At this point the solution would appear to be the one suggested in the previous chapter, that market sizes will be reduced until the firm's aggregate demand schedule is tangent to the average-cost curve. In this case, however, each firm's average cost is different. Therefore, the price at plant for each firm will be different. This implies that market sizes will be different, but that the delivered price at the boundary between two firms must be equal. It is not clear that this is necessarily an equilibrium situation. Some excess profits because of position may appear, and price discrimination may appear, so that firms can encroach on other firms' markets.[12]

A third case may arise in which marginal cost of production again rises slower than the delivered price of the final product as distances increase from B. In this case however, the places A and B are so close that B is included in the monopoly market of a plant producing at A. Although production at B could be at a lower plant price than at A, no plant can

[12] For further analysis of these possibilities, see Melvin Greenhut, *Plant Location in Theory and in Practice* (Chapel Hill, N.C.: The University of North Carolina Press, 1956), pp. 57–83.

survive at B because the market area that could be carved out of A's market area would not be sufficiently large to enable the producer at B to achieve a threshold size. This result would occur because of the disparity in the density of consumers in the two areas. Of course, if input prices were also lower at the center of density of the market, firms would concentrate at the center of the market so long as the marginal cost of production increased from A at a faster rate than the delivered price of the product.

Introducing the variations in market demand and the possibility of input substitution has made the analysis less definite. Nevertheless, it has been shown that as long as delivered price of the final product rises less rapidly than marginal cost of production from the least-cost site, firms will tend to concentrate where the input price is least. On the other hand, if the delivered price of the product from this least-cost site should rise more rapidly than the marginal cost of production, plants might exist at the market center, the material source, or both sites. It is important to see that plants in the same industry may be in the center of density of their market *and* at sites with input price advantages with a less dense market area. A strategic transportation node may also be occupied by a firm in the same industry. The point is that markets are not points. Markets are areas.

The interdependence of firms on each others' actions has just been mentioned with respect to pricing when markets intersect. In the next section the interdependence of other firms' locations on the cost curve of firms will be discussed. These effects are agglomeration economies or diseconomies, and show another reason why firms are not always located at the center of their market.

AGGLOMERATION ECONOMIES[13]

The name "agglomeration" comes from the agglomeration of people attracted to one place because many firms are in that place or because one large plant is in that place. Thus, the reasons why firms can profit by locating adjacent to each other and why it is profitable to make one plant very large are agglomeration economies. Agglomeration economies may be divided into four classifications: transfer economies, internal economies of scale to the firm, external economies of scale to the firm that are internal to the industry, and external economies of scale to an industry.

Before describing these economies in detail a few qualifications are re-

[13] This section relies heavily on Hoover, *op. cit.*, pp. 116–128; and J. A. Guthrie, "Economies of Scale and Regional Development," *Regional Science Association Papers and Proceedings*, vol. I (1955), pp. J1–J10. Other sources will also be mentioned as they arise.

quired. First, external economies of scale may be mobile or immobile. Only immobile external economies would cause firms to be located adjacent to each other. Mobile external economies would occur as an industry expanded, whether all the firms were in one place or in several. Immobile economies, however, would not occur unless firms in the industry or group of industries were located at one place.[14] Second, in analyzing external economies of scale, we usually think of these economies as being generated by the size of the output of the industry or industries. Some economies, however, may be a result of increases in population rather than output. Third, economies of scale may vary with the organization of industry in the community.

Transfer economies are the savings in transportation cost to each firm from locating adjacent to others. Plant locations are usually restricted to the existing transportation network. The reason is that transportation costs would increase at locations away from the network because of the difficulty of moving goods. Highways, canals, and railroads, however, are built from one place to another so that there is choice in where they should go. They may connect existing places in a built-up area, they may create new places in an underdeveloped area, or they may connect existing places with new places and create new town sites in developed areas. The number of potential industrial locations is sometimes limited to junctions and nodes. As already indicated, firms with many dispersed markets and material sources will find junctions advantageous in order to minimize transfer costs. Nodes are junctions strategic to an entire transport network, and are thus important points for many businesses.

Industrial linkages may cause industries to locate together in order to obtain transfer economies. Transfer economies between successive stages of production may be obtained by adjacent location. This is unusual, as earlier stages are generally located near material sources and later stages of production are generally near markets.

Further transportation economies occur when groups of stores locate together. Businesses selling goods and services that consumers in the same trade area are likely to purchase on the same shopping trip will locate near each other. A drugstore, grocery store, dry cleaner, and barbershop may locate together for this reason. Sales of each store will increase because consumers save travel time and expense by shopping in the shopping center. This may be one reason for assuming that firms of different industries with the same trading area locate in the same place. Furthermore, firms selling the same type of shopping goods, such as furniture,

---

[14] E. A. G. Robinson, *The Structure of Competitive Industry* (Chicago: The University of Chicago Press, 1958), pp. 124–126.

may find that sales increase when they are located adjacent to other firms selling the same goods, because shoppers like to compare styles and quality before buying. Furniture stores, new and used car dealers, and shoe stores often locate together for this reason. This kind of agglomeration creates different shopping center arrangements rather than the previous hierarchical arrangement of central places.

Internal economies of scale are so large for some plants that employment in the plant might create a town. Places formed by the employment size of one enterprise will, of course, be situated where the enterprise will make the greatest profit. If the enterprise is a mine or refinery, the town will be situated near the resource deposit. This, however, does not mean that every resource deposit will have a city, as will be shown in Chapter 5. If the enterprise is a university, military base, or government administration center, the town will be situated by political pressure, by the necessities of defense, or by centralness to the administered population.

Nevertheless, the influence of internal economies of scale on location can be complicated. Internal economies of scale are the lower average cost of production that results from an increased rate of production. The total operation of the firm, however, can be separated into four functions: technical production, management, marketing, and finance. Minimum average cost for each function may occur at rates of production different from each other. A large firm may be able to reduce average costs by the way in which it combines the scale of operation of each function. In the marketing function a very large size may bring savings in distribution costs per unit of output, as it would if the product needed to be differentiated through national brand advertising. If minimum average cost for technical production should be for a smaller scale of production, several plants within the firm would be operated. Depending on the product, the plants might be located together near a raw material source or dispersed near markets. Branch plants in cigarette production are near materials; branch plants in beer production are near markets. Thus, internal economies may not result in concentration at one place.

Economies may result from large-scale operation of a multiproduct plant because the plant can shift products with the vagaries of consumer demand and price. In this case optimum size may be much larger than in the single product case.

Immobile external economies of scale to the firm but internal to the industry are reductions of cost per unit of output to the firm, as the industry expands in a particular place. These cost reductions refer to a downward shift in the cost curves of a firm with the expansion of the industry. Cost reductions that we have previously mentioned—transfer economies and internal economies—refer to a shift in the curves by moving from one place to another to avoid transport cost or to moving along the same cost curve with expansion of output within the firm. If many enterprises in the same industry locate in the same place because of the advantages of external economies of scale to each firm, the city formed in this way will be situated where the industry could most profitably locate.

One of the most common reasons given for external economies to the firm is a large and skilled labor pool available to each firm in an area in which the industry is concentrated. Other examples include the possibility of firms existing to process waste materials that may not be possible without a large industry, the facilitation of research, and the development of markets for raw materials with resultant savings in cost. Moreover, as an industry expands in one place, firms may specialize and make one or two parts for the industry. Figure 4-9 is useful in seeing how this is possible. In this figure the solid line TAC is the total average cost of the firm. AC is the average cost of making specialized machinery, or, perhaps, of some other function such as repair of specialized machinery for rates of production of the final product. There are economies of scale available within this one function. As the industry expands, it is possible for this function to be performed by separate plants and firms because of the demand from

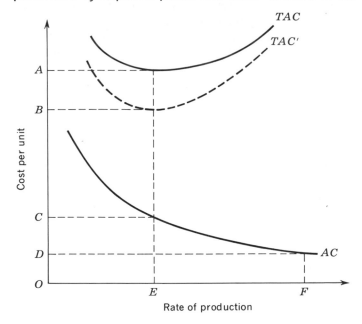

FIGURE 4-9

many plants and firms rather than from just one. Thus, the specialized plant obtains the economies of scale that each production firm could not have achieved on its own. For example, the total average cost for a single plant with a rate of production OE might be OA. The average cost of a particular function might be OC. If the industry expanded and this function was performed by a specialized firm, such as a carburetor manufacturer for several automobile manufacturers, the average cost of the specialized function would be OD because the specialized firm could sell to all producers whose total rate of production is OF. The average cost of the specialized function to the original firm falls to OD and his total average cost falls to OB. The new total average cost of each firm shifts to the dotted curve TAC'.[15]

External diseconomies of scale are upward shifts of the average-cost curves of each firm as the whole industry expands in one place. External diseconomies may occur because raw material costs are pushed up by transport costs on more distance sources or by increased production costs of intensive development of local sources. External diseconomies may occur because land values rise from the scarcity of good building sites caused by the general concentration of production and population. External diseconomies may also occur because wages are pushed up by labor organizations in a specialized production center.

External economies of scale to firms in many industries are the downward shifts in average-cost curves of each firm as many industries grow in one place. These have been called urbanization economies. Urbanization economies include the availability of improved transportation services, such as terminal facilities; a larger and more flexible labor market; commercial and financial services, such as banks and utilities; and public services, such as fire and police protection. All these may cause the average costs of a firm to fall for the same rate of production if it locates in a larger rather than a smaller community, or in any community rather than outside a community altogether.

With more firms and industries the specialization of functions can be finer. Previously, it was shown how each firm in an industry locating in one place could take advantage of the industry's joint demand for specialized machinery or specialized repair needs. In the same way each firm in many industries locating in the same place can reduce average cost through the formation of specialized functions. A firm can rent rather than own its equipment and space so that it will be more flexible in adjusting to unstable demand. An apparel firm can rely on many specialized shops each making

[15] George J. Stigler, "The Division of Labor is Limited by the Extent of the Market," *Journal of Political Economy*, vol. 59, no. 3 (June, 1951), pp. 185–193.

one part of a garment, such as buttonholes or buttons. For the head-quarters of firms, metropolitan places are advantageous because of the specialists a firm can reach immediately when problems arise. These specialists include lawyers, accountants, engineers, other business consultants, advertising firms, and investment houses. It is often important that these contacts be made quickly, so that the city is advantageous for quick face-to-face contact.

Smaller inventories are necessary in the city with wholesalers close by. There are transfer savings from large-scale transfer facilities and terminal handling. One might also want to include the amenities of city living. Locational decisions by executives may be influenced by the cultural activities available only in cities: opera, nightclubs, libraries and bookstores, society life, exotic restaurants, foreign movies, theaters, and varied athletic events.

Walter Isard tries to define more rigorously the agglomeration function of urbanization economies.[16] He constructs a net economies curve for each utility and service provided in cities. For example, assume that each city size can be identified with a particular output of electric power, that prices of power per Btu are not different by geographic location, and that there is no excess capacity beyond that required for peak loads. The net economies curve, as drawn in Figure 4-10, shows the savings per year in power generation for each city size over costs in the number of cities of 1,000 population that would be necessary to add up to the city size. Such a curve could be applied to transportation and labor. Nevertheless, it is obvious that cities would have to be standardized for relative amounts of industrial activity and commercial land use patterns, and journey to work and commodity flow patterns. The curves would reach a peak and decline because of deglomeration factors—higher land values, congestion, higher cost of food, etc. Isard suggests that such a curve could be calculated for municipal functions: fire protection, police protection, education, gas facilities, water facilities, sanitation facilities and services, and recreation facilities and services. Although it would be tempting to sum these curves for a net urbanization economies curve, it cannot be done, as Isard points out. First, there are no standard cities. Second, each service should be weighted differently depending upon industrial composition, consumption patterns, etc. Third, economies with each service depend upon those of the other services. For example, power economies influence transportation and education. Labor economies influence transportation.

Benjamin Chinitz has developed the concept of agglomeration economies

---

[16] Walter Isard, *Location and Space Economy* (Cambridge, Mass.: The M.I.T. Press, 1956), pp. 182–188.

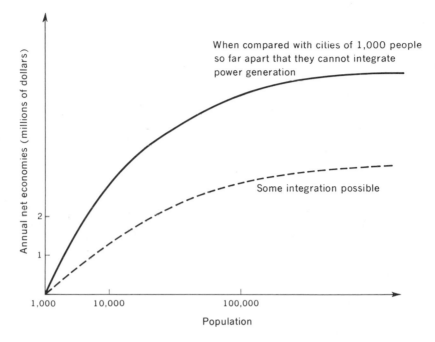

When compared with cities of 1,000 people so far apart that they cannot integrate power generation

Some integration possible

FIGURE 4-10

SOURCE: Reprinted from *Location and Space Economy* by Walter Isard by permission of The M. I. T. Press, Cambridge, Massachusetts (copyright 1956 by The Massachusetts Institute of Technology).

further by pointing in detail to the way in which industrial organization may affect external economies of scale. He sets forth the following tentative hypotheses:

1. There are more entrepreneurs per dollar of output in competitive industries than in oligopolies.
2. The cost of "transfering confidence" is high so that a small firm has a better chance for loans at home. But if the traditional organization of industry in the community is oligopolistic, a small firm will find it difficult to obtain loans from banks. The reason is that the banks may not have learned to make money from many risky loans rather than a few, sure, large ones to large companies, such as U.S. Steel and Westinghouse.
3. The wage rate and wage structure of the dominant industry influences that of the rest of the community. The dominant industry, steel in Pittsburgh, may establish its plants over such a wide geographic area that the traditional advantage of a metropolitan labor force is absent. Furthermore, the work schedule has an impact. For example, in steel

the workers rotate on three shifts: 8 A.M. to 4 P.M., 4 P.M. to 12 midnight, and 12 to 8 A.M. A housewife is discouraged from working when her husband is on such a schedule.

4. The character and emergence of transport and other services to industry depend upon which industries cause development. Large firms incorporate these services internally; small firms need outside specialists. Thus, if services are not available a new firm must start big.[17]

SUMMARY

Industrial location patterns may change the size and spacing of cities that would occur under the simple conditions for a system of central places based on trading areas. The exceptions have probably been somewhat exaggerated. Nevertheless, there are several factors in the location of industry that may cause plants not to be located in places with the same trading areas as the plant. Geographic variations in input prices could cause the most profitable location for a plant to be attracted away from the center of its market. Furthermore, a plant so attracted to a material source could create a town because of its production. Agglomeration economies could also cause the most profitable location for a plant to be attracted away from the center of its market. These economies were reductions in costs or downward shifts in a firm's cost schedule if it located near other firms producing the same commodity or just near centers of economic activity.

The attraction of a plant to a particular site is often called its orientation. The central place analysis would depict most plants as market-oriented. A plant attracted to a material source would be material-oriented, and a plant attracted to a cheap labor site would be labor-oriented. An example of a material-oriented industry in Table 4-1 is the tobacco products industry. An industry in Table 4-1 that has often been claimed to be labor-oriented is the textile mill products industry. An example of an industry in Table 4-1 attracted to concentration in one place because of agglomeration economies is the apparel industry.

Traditionally the conditions for orientation to an input source have been based on a model of a plant with very restricted assumptions. Economies of scale, substitution of inputs, and variations in demand have been omitted from the analysis. Taking all these factors into account makes it difficult to set down simple rules about orientation.

[17] Benjamin Chinitz, "Contrasts in Agglomeration: New York and Pittsburgh," *American Economic Review*, vol. 51, no. 2 (May, 1961), pp. 279–289.

In the previous two chapters we investigated the factors determining the size and spacing of cities, the regional distribution of industry, and the impact of this distribution on the size and spacing of cities. So far, then, we have developed the economic rationale for the clustering of population into cities and the geographic distribution of these cities. In this chapter we shall investigate the determinants of the spatial arrangements of economic activity within the city and its hinterland. Supply areas of extractive goods for the city market will be discussed first. An explanation of a simple model of land rent and land use will follow with particular reference to agricultural production. The model will then be extended to commercial, industrial, and residential land use. All models are simplifications of reality, and this one is no exception. Therefore, we shall also try to show how more realistic assumptions might change the land use patterns determined by the model. Finally, empirical evidence on the spatial distribution of population density, the spatial distribution of manufacturing employment, and the spatial distribution of different types of residential structures will be shown to be consistent with the theory.

The theory is not only useful in understanding the factors underlying the distribution of land use. The theoretical framework also provides a way of determining the impact on land use of changes in the factors, that are thought to be important, such as changes in transport cost. In this chapter the structure of the theory will be developed. Its use in determining the impact of changes in important variables on land use structure will be developed in Chapter 9.

SUPPLY AREAS[1]

The simplest problem of land use is determining which coal mine, oil well, limestone deposit, or other natural resource that is not ubiquitously located will be used to supply any particular market. Mining operations are thought of as resource-oriented, but it is important to realize that not all resource locations are mined. All the other factors determining the maximum profit location of a plant discussed in Chapter 2 are relevant in determining which resource location will be used.

The market is considered to be a point in space and there are several sites in the area around the market for obtaining the raw material. The

---

[1] Edgar M. Hoover, *Location Theory and the Shoe and Leather Industries*, Harvard Economic Studies, vol. 55 (Cambridge, Mass.: Harvard University Press, 1937), chap. 2.

problem is to determine which sites will be utilized and to what extent. The industry is competitive so that no one plant produces enough of the commodity to affect the market price. Therefore, the price of the product is determined at the market. The supplier receives a price equal to the market price less transportation costs from his site to the market. Because the firm has no influence on price, the firm will receive the same price per unit no matter how many units it produces per time period. Thus, the net price is the marginal revenue to the firm, and the maximum profit rate of production will be that rate at which price (marginal revenue) is equal to marginal cost. Furthermore, the quantities that will be supplied by each plant with variations in price will be determined by the marginal cost curve of the plant. The market supply curve is the horizontal sum of the individual mines' supply curves, assuming no external economies of scale.

The solution of the problem can be more clearly understood with the aid of Figures 5-1 and 5-2. In Figure 5-1, M is the market site. To the right of M along the horizontal axis the quantity of product per time period is measured. The market demand curve is DD. To the left of M, the scale is miles from the market M. A and B are two mining sites MA miles and MB miles

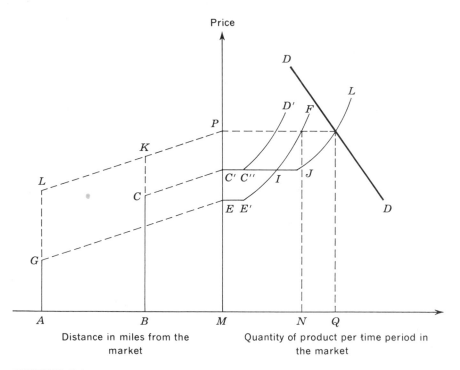

Distance in miles from the market   Quantity of product per time period in the market

FIGURE 5-1

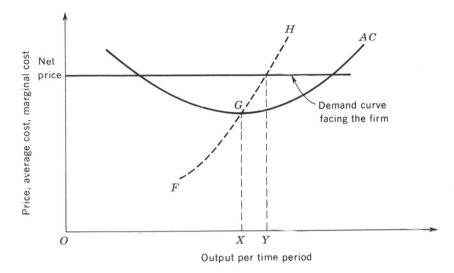

FIGURE 5-2

from the market. AG and BC measure the marginal cost at each site equal to total average cost in the long run. If price to the plant is less than long-run average cost, the mine will not be operated because it will not yield a sufficient return. GH in Figure 5-2 shows the portion of the marginal cost curve above long-run average cost that represents the supply curve of the mine. To maximize profits the producer will make that rate of production, OY, that causes net price at plant to be equal to marginal cost.

GE and CC' in Figure 5-1 are transport gradients. Their slope is the transport cost per mile to ship a unit of product. The price received at the plant is the market price less total transport cost (cost per mile times miles). If the quality of the ore in the two mines were different, the transportation costs would be different. The transport cost per ton-mile of the purer ore would be less than that of the less pure ore.

The price in the market must reach EM in Figure 5-1 before A will begin production. The price in the market must reach $C'M$ before B will begin production. $E'F$ and $C''D'$ represent the marginal cost curves of plants A and B respectively. For example, $E'F$ in Figure 5-1 is the same curve as GH in Figure 5-2 except that it is shifted upward by the cost of shipping a unit of output from A to M. $E'F$ and $C''D'$ are the marginal cost curves of each plant in terms of *delivered price* rather than *net price*. Added together horizontally the two curves form $E'IJL$, the market supply curve. The quantity demanded and the quantity supplied are equal at price PM. Plant A produces MN units of the ore; plant B produces NQ units of the ore.

With the aid of this diagram one can analyze the impact of changes in transportation costs, mining technology, and shifts in the demand curve on the supply area, and the quantity of ore supplied by each source. For example, in the above case the more distant site A can be mined more cheaply than the closer site B. If the demand curve shifted to the left because of a new, cheaper source of fuel (i.e., coal versus oil) so that it intersected the supply curve $E'IJL$ to the left of I, plant B would shut down. The supply would come from plant A.

Admittedly, one supplier could extract monopoly profits. The quantity supplied would be less and the price higher than shown by the competitive solution in the diagram. Nevertheless, the principles of the competitive situation are depicted by the diagram. The number of material sites was reduced to two for expositional purposes. In reality there would be many more potential sources of the material for any market.

SIMPLE MODEL OF AGRICULTURAL LAND RENT AND LAND USE[2]

To simplify the analysis assume that there is a market center at which agricultural products from the surrounding hinterland are sold. The surrounding land is uniformly fertile, and transportation is equally costly in any direction from the market. The prices of farmers' products are determined in the marketplace at that price that equates the quantity supplied and demanded. The price received by the farmer is the market price less transportation cost from the farm to the market. The farmer who can bid the most for a site is the one who will occupy it. His bid is dependent upon the market price of his product less transportation cost and less other production costs. Furthermore, in equilibrium farmers producing the same product would not have incentive to shift locations.

Let us first study one crop, corn, and then add another, such as soybeans or potatoes. We will start by determining the rent that the producer can pay at the market center for land, and will then analyze the rent that he would be willing to pay at some distance K from the market center. Assuming that corn requires only land and labor, the production function for corn is depicted in Figure 5-3. Q_1 traces those combinations of acres of land and man-hours of labor that would yield a rate of production of Q_1 bushels of corn per crop period. Q_2 depicts the combinations that would yield a higher rate of production, Q_2 bushels per crop period.

The producer is in a competitive market. Each individual producer supplies such a small part of the total supply that changes in his supply alone will

[2] William Alonso, *Location and Land Use* (Cambridge, Mass.: Harvard University Press, 1964), pp. 37–42; Richard F. Muth, "Economic Change and Rural-Urban Land Conversions," *Econometrica* (January, 1961), pp. 1–23.

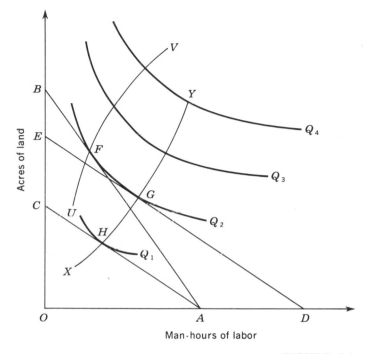

FIGURE 5-3

not affect price. Therefore, revenue will increase proportionately with rates of production. If the producer is located at the market, transport costs are not subtracted from price, since the producer requires no transportation to get his goods to market. The market price is the price received by the producer. TR_m in Figure 5-4 is the total revenue line of the producer at the market.

Profits are total revenues less total costs. Total costs are made up of the wage per man-hour times the number of man-hours plus the rent per acre times the number of acres. The wage rate is assumed to be the same throughout the hinterland of the market. Rent per acre is the only input price that varies. Given some level of total expenditures and dividing by the wage rate we would find that OA man-hours could be purchased if no land were rented (Figure 5-3). To find out the maximum rate of production for that level of expenditures we need to know the rent per acre. Suppose that rent per acre is such that if the whole of the expenditure were used to purchase land, OB acres of land could be purchased. The isocost line would then be AB. The maximum output that could be obtained would be Q_2. The least-cost combination of land and labor to produce the rate of produc-

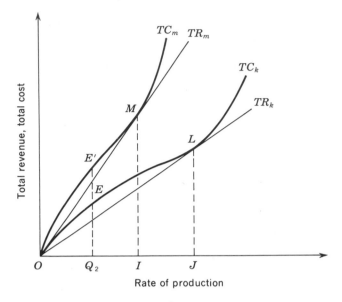

FIGURE 5-4

tion Q_2 with the given wages and rents is represented by the coordinates of the point F. Still holding the rent and wage level constant, UV traces the least-cost combinations for other rates of production. As discussed in Chapter 2, there is a total cost curve associated with the expansion path UV.

Suppose, however, that the rent per acre were higher than represented by the isocost line AB. Then if all the expenditure were used to buy labor we would still obtain OA man-hours of labor but could rent fewer acres of land, say OC acres. The least-cost combination of inputs would be represented by the coordinates of point H. The rate of production achieved, however, would be less than it was previously with the lower rent per acre. The rate of production for the given expenditure would now be Q_1. The expansion path given the higher rent schedule is traced by the curve XY in Figure 5-3. To get the same output, Q_2, with the higher rent level requires an increase in costs. This is shown by the shift of the isocost line AC upward to ED. The least-cost combination of the inputs is represented by the coordinates of the point G. At the rate of production Q_2 total cost is higher with the higher rent represented by the isocost line ED. Q_2E' in Figure 5-4 is the total expenditure necessary to obtain this rate of production at the higher rent levels. If rents are lower as represented by the isocost line AB, total costs are less, as shown by the height of the curve TC_k at Q_2, Q_2E.

If there are no differences in the economies of scale between the two expansion paths UV and XY in Figure 5-3, then the total cost for the higher rent per acre will always be more at each rate of production. Thus, TC_m traces out the total cost at each rate of production, given the high rent per acre, and TC_k traces out the total cost at each rate of production, given the low rent per acre.

Now, given the total revenues TR_m received by the producer at the market, how much would he be willing to bid for land at the market? He would certainly be willing to pay the low rent as it would yield large profits at the rate of production at which the maximum difference between TR_m and TC_k exists. The producer, however, would also be willing to pay the higher rent, but no more. At the higher rent level the total cost, TC_m, is everywhere higher than total revenues, except at point M where it is tangent to the total revenue curve. Total costs equal total revenues at M. Thus, the higher rent is the maximum rent per acre that the producer would be willing to pay for land at the market center for the production of corn.

Let us proceed in the same fashion to determine the maximum rent per acre that the producer of corn would be willing to pay at some distance from the market center. Total revenues to the producer are lower at each rate of production. He now receives the market price of corn per bushel less the transport cost per bushel to get the corn to market. TR_k in Figure 5-4 shows the lower total revenue schedule of the producer at location K. Wages are the same as at the market. The maximum rent per acre that the producer will be willing to pay is the rent per acre associated with the total cost curve that is tangent to the total revenue curve from above, such as TC_k at point L in Figure 5-4. The rent per acre offered will be lower than at the market because the total cost curve, to be tangent to the lower total revenue curve, *must* be lower than the total cost curve associated with the maximum rent per acre at the market.

In Figure 5-5 are shown the maximum or ceiling rents per acre that the producer would be willing to pay at different distances from the market. OA is the ceiling rent per acre at the market. KB is the ceiling rent per acre at a location K miles from the market in any direction. At OC miles from the market the producer would be unwilling to pay any rent. AC shows the ceiling rent at each distance and is called the rent bid curve. As the producer moves farther from the market, the price per bushel that he receives is less by the amount of the transportation cost, and the ceiling rent decreases.

Suppose that potatoes are also produced. To determine which area will be used for corn production and which for potato production, the rent bid

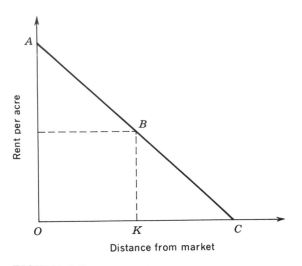

FIGURE 5-5

curve for potatoes must be calculated. The ceiling rent at each location would be calculated in the same way as for corn production. DF in Figure 5-6 represents the rent bid curve for potato production.

In the competitive market for land the highest bidder for any particular site obtains it. Thus, farmers in potato production outbid farmers in corn production for all land to OL miles from the market in Figure 5-6. For this area the segment of the rent bid curve for potato land, DG, is higher than the segment of the rent bid curve for corn land, AG. It is also important to see that all farmers, wherever located, have their choice between corn and potato production. Up to OL miles from the market they would choose potato production because they would be losing money if they did not. They could make more by renting the land to someone else to produce potatoes than by growing corn. From OL miles to OC miles from the market corn will be produced.

In the final equilibrium no producer must be able to profit by moving to another site in the potato production area. This will occur only when the rents paid are equal to the maximum bids at each location. The same equilibrium situation must hold in the corn production area. Thus, the curve $DGBC$ is the rent gradient or surface tracing the rents paid at each distance from the market. Rent surface expresses the three-dimensional character of the rents paid with respect to distance from the market. In Figure 5-6 the rent structure is shown for only one direction from the market. If the figure $ODGBC$ is revolved on the vertical axis, a cone similar to the

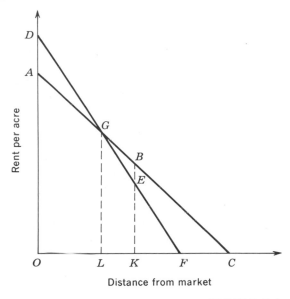

FIGURE 5-6

demand cone is generated that shows the way in which rents decline from the market in every direction from the market.

The analysis can also indicate which crop will be produced closer to the market. The production of those crops for which the rent bid curve is steeper will be closer to the market. Three factors would affect the slope of the rent bid curve. The ceiling rent per acre would decline faster with distance from the market center the greater the transportation cost per unit of product per mile, the greater the yield per acre, and the less possible it would be to substitute cheaper land for nonland inputs.

As sites away from the market center are considered, the net price received by the farm will decrease because of the increased transportation costs. The higher these transportation costs, the faster net price will fall with each additional mile the site is moved away from the market. Thus, the total revenue curve will also shift downward faster with each additional mile away from the market, if the transport cost is greater. The total cost curve will accordingly also have to shift downward faster. For this to occur the ceiling rent per acre will have to decline faster with respect to distance compared to the decline in rent per acre for production of some other crop for which transportation costs are not so great.

The rent bid curve for production of a crop that has a greater yield per acre will also be steeper. For each rate of production, the crop with the greater yield per acre will show more output and more revenue per acre. As the site is shifted away from the market center the transportation cost for the output of an acre of land will increase faster for the product with the greater yield just because there is a greater amount of product to be shipped for each acre. Thus, the absolute decline in rent per acre must also be larger in order for the more distant site to yield the same rate of return as the close-in site.[3]

As rent per acre decreases, the least-cost combination of inputs changes. For example, in Figure 5-3 the coordinates of point F represent the least-cost combination of inputs for a lower rent than the coordinates of point G. More land is used if rent per acre is lower; the substitution of land rises as rent per acre falls. Therefore the fall in the ceiling rent per acre will become correspondingly smaller because the same downward shift in the total cost curve would be accomplished by a greater fall in rent per acre if the acreage did not increase. The increase in acreage absorbs some of the decrease in rent per acre.

Because the slope of the rent bid curve may change with substitution of land for nonland inputs, it is possible that the same use could pay the highest ceiling rent in two different places. For example, in Figure 5-7 AB might be the rent bid curve for one crop, say corn, and CD might be the curved rent bid curve for another crop, wheat. Wheat would be produced in both the innermost ring and the outermost ring under these circumstances since from O to L and from M to D the wheat rent bid curve is higher. Production of wheat in these areas would allow a greater ceiling rent than production of corn.

---

[3] These two points can be easily made with the aid of a simple mathematical model. Consider that farm production requires fixed inputs for each rate of production achieved and that increases in production can only be achieved with proportional increases in all inputs. The price of the product is competitively determined in the market. The net price received by the farm is the market price less transportation costs from farm to market. The market is a point in a featureless plain in which transportation costs are the same in every direction and are proportional to distance. The amount available for rent per acre is equal to revenue per acre less other costs per acre less transport cost of the product to market, where the product is in terms of yield per acre. This can be expressed in the following equation:

$$R = E(p - a) - Efk$$

where
 R = rent per acre
 E = yield per acre
 p = market price per unit of commodity
 a = production cost per unit of commodity excluding rent and transportation cost to market
 f = transport rate per mile for each commodity
 k = distance in miles
The rent bid at market would be $E(p - a)$, since $k = 0$ at the market. The rent bid declines by an amount equal to Ef for each increase in distance from the market site. Thus, either a greater yield or transport cost could cause one crop to have a steeper rent bid curve than another. See Edgar S. Dunn, Jr., *The Location of Agricultural Production* (Gainesville, Fla.: University of Florida Press, 1954), pp. 6–7.

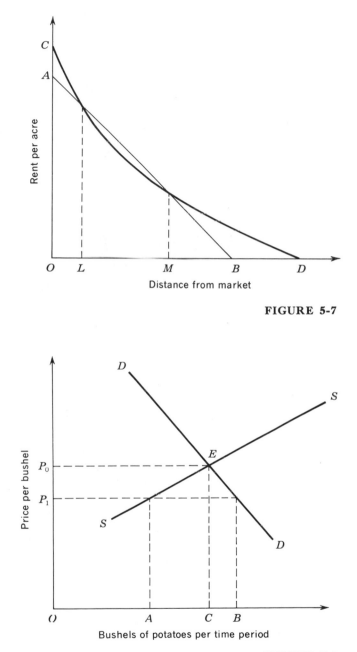

FIGURE 5-7

Distance from market

Price per bushel

Bushels of potatoes per time period

FIGURE 5-8

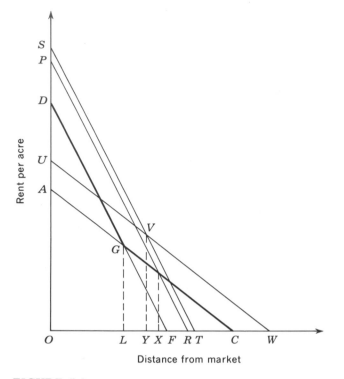

FIGURE 5-9

So far, it has been assumed that the amount of a crop supplied and the quantity demanded were equal at the market price. If, however, the acres of land in Figure 5-6 within OL miles of the market times the yield per acre was not sufficient to supply the quantity of potatoes demanded at the market price, the market price would have to increase so that the rent bid curve would shift upward, more land would be put into potatoes, and the quantity supplied would increase. In Figure 5-8 SS is the supply curve of potatoes given the price of corn, and DD is the market demand curve. At the current market price of P_1 per bushel the quantity supplied is only OA and the quantity demanded is OB. The market price will be forced up by the excess demand. As the price per bushel in the market rises, the rent bid function for potato land will shift upward. It shifts upward because the increased price causes the total revenue curve to rotate upward. Thus, higher maximum rent bids are feasible at each location. If it would take the area of land within OX miles of the market (see Figure 5-9) to supply OC bushels of potatoes to the market, the price would have to rise to P_o.

The rent bid curve for potatoes, DGF, would shift to PR and the highest bid for land within OX miles of the market would be for potato production.

Suppose, however, that the corn price had equated the quantity demanded and supplied at that price. The absorption of some corn land for potato production would have caused a shift to the left of the corn supply curve. An excess demand for corn would then exist at the current price. The price of corn per bushel would rise in order to increase the quantity of corn supplied. This would raise the rent bid function for corn land. The rent bid functions would continue to shift until the quantity supplied of corn and potatoes equaled the quantity demanded at the market price. The rent gradient or surface would be similar to DGC in Figure 5-9, except that the boundary at which land is shifted from potato production to corn production might be at a different distance from the market, and corn production would probably extend farther into the hinterland than OC. For example, the final rent gradient might be SVW. Potatoes would be produced from O to OY miles from the market; corn would be produced from OY to OW miles from the market.

COMMERCIAL AND INDUSTRIAL LAND USE

The idea of utilizing the simple model of agricultural production location for commercial and industrial urban location has been appealing to many location theorists. In agriculture the central importance of the market as a point in space with transportation costs from that market decreasing the price received by the producer allowed an analysis of location with respect to distance from the point center. The importance of a point market center is less easily recognized for commercial and industrial location. Several factors, however, can be shown to be important in affecting the profits of a store or plant as its location is varied with respect to the center of the market or metropolitan area. Retail stores, banks, advertising agencies, corporate headquarters, and government offices will maximize the volume of business that they transact if they are located near the center of the daytime population of a city.

For these kinds of economic activities accessibility is the key to a profitable location. Accessibility affects profits through the total volume of sales or transactions that the activity can make in different locations. If we assume a market center at which most transactions take place, such as the central business district of a city, establishments can maximize their sales in the central location rather than an outlying one. Although the price at which goods are sold may not differ by location, nor may the operating costs excluding land differ by location within the metropolitan area, the total number of transactions will differ. The reason is that if the establishment is located downtown more people will walk by it than if it were located five miles away. To make the same number of transactions five miles from the large concentrated daytime pedestrian traffic would require a much larger advertising campaign, larger parking facilities, and other selling costs. Total revenue net of these selling costs to attract the attention of many people decreases with distance from the central market. Total revenue net of these selling costs at the market might be depicted by the curve TR_m in Figure 5-10. Total revenue net of these selling costs at a location K miles from the market center would be lower, and might be depicted by the curve TR_k in Figure 5-10.

The only other cost item that would be influenced by location would be the rent per acre. In the same way as we did for the agricultural producer, we can imagine a production function which shows how acres, or in this case square feet of land, and man-hours of labor can be combined to achieve the same volume of transactions. In Figure 5-3, Q_1 could reflect number of transactions; OB could reflect the square feet of land, given the rent and the total outlay; and OA could reflect the number of man-hours that could be purchased with the same outlay. Using the same logic as in the case of agricultural production, we can show that if wages and other nonland costs are the same throughout the metropolitan area, there

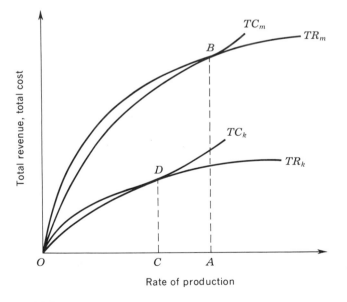

FIGURE 5-10

is some rent per square foot that will raise the total cost function until it is tangent to the total revenue function. For example, TC_m in Figure 5-10 is associated with the highest rent, or ceiling rent, that a firm in this business can pay for a central site. The establishment would transact a volume of business OA per time period, and total receipts and costs would be AB, including the "normal" return to stay in business. For each kind of business there would exist different production, revenue, and cost functions. But each establishment in the same line of business, we will assume, would have identical production, revenue, and cost functions.

The downtown revenue function represented by TR_m in Figure 5-10 could be for a ladies' shoe store. To see the rent per square foot that could be paid at some location K miles from the downtown area, we first take into account the downward rotation of the total revenue curve, such as TR_k in Figure 5-10. For an establishment to break even at location K, the total cost curve must be shifted downward to TC_k. This could be accomplished by paying a lower rent per square foot. The rent associated with the cost curve TC_k would be the ceiling rent at location K. The ceiling rent at location K would have to be less than that at the center of activity to shift down the cost curve. Thus, we can generate a rent bid function for each urban activity concerned with accessibility to the largest daytime population.

The next step is to investigate why the slopes of the rent bid functions of two kinds of urban activities dependent upon accessibility would be different. Three factors would affect the slope of the rent bid curve. The ceiling rent per acre would decline faster with distance from the market center the greater the increased selling costs to achieve the same volume of business, the greater the number of transactions per square foot of floor space, and the less possible it would be to substitute cheaper land for other inputs. There is no need to explain these factors since the principle is the same as for the decline in ceiling rent for agricultural production. In this case selling costs take the place of transportation costs, transactions per square foot of floor space take the place of yield per acre, and the substitution of land for nonland inputs is the same.

The factors causing the rent bid curve for manufacturing plants to decline with distance from the central market area are different from those we have mentioned for agricultural and urban activities dependent upon accessibility. The total revenues of a manufacturing plant are usually derived from sales not only to the local area, but to many metropolitan areas or city-regions. Total revenues will not noticeably shift as the plant is located at different distances from the city center, since we are initially assuming that transport costs are equal in every direction. Total costs, however, may change. They may change in two different ways. In the first place, wages per man-hour may increase with distance from the center of density of the population. To obtain a given work force a firm located on the fringe of the city would have to pay a higher wage to compensate for higher commuting costs of the workers, since (as explained later) the density of residences is less and a greater area would be required to obtain the same number of workers. In the second place, if rent per square foot fell, the plant would use more land and fewer nonland factors per unit of output. The plant would be spread out all on one floor rather than confined to a narrow space with three or four stories. A layout all on one floor would enable the plant to have a more efficient flow in the assembly process, and greater economies of scale could be achieved than in cramped quarters.

In Figure 5-12, isocost line AB represents low wages per man-hour and high rent per acre. The coordinates of point I would be the least-cost combination of labor and land for the rate of production Q_1. Isocost line CD represents the same level of expenditure for a lower rent and higher wage rate. The same rate of production, however, cannot be reached. In Figure 5-11, the total cost curve TC_m represents the total cost curve when rent per acre is high, wage per man-hour is low, and the plant layout is in

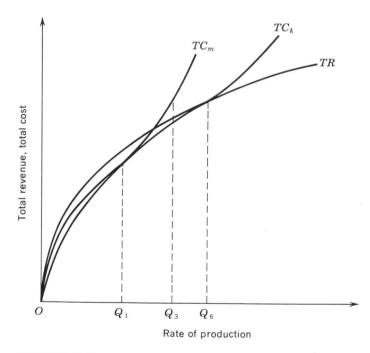

FIGURE 5-11

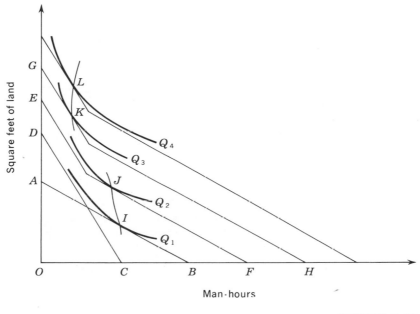

Man-hours

FIGURE 5-12

a three- or four-story building. TC_k represents the total cost curve when rent per acre is lower, wage per man-hour is higher, and the plant layout is in a sprawling one-story structure. For the rate of production Q_1 the high-rent site is the least costly. CD would have to be shifted upward to be tangent to Q_1 in Figure 5-12, and would thus represent a higher expenditure level than AB, since AB and CD originally represented the same expenditure level.

Some low rents per acre would cause the total cost curves to lie below the total revenue curve TR in Figure 5-11. TC_m and TC_k in Figure 5-11 represent two cost curves associated with a high and a low rent per acre that would be just tangent to the total revenue curve at locations M and K. The ceiling rent that the plant would be willing to pay must fall as the plant moves some distance K from the market. If it did not, labor costs would increase, the plant layout would not change, and therefore the total cost curve would rise above the total revenue curve, and the plant would not be able to locate profitably at K. For low rates of production the single-floor layout is inefficient, but for higher rates of production, beyond Q_3 in Figure 5-12, the single-floor layout will yield a greater output for the same level of expenditure. This is also seen in Figure 5-11. Total cost is lower at

Q_3 for the location K with low rents per acre, single-floor layout, and higher wage costs.

Thus, for manufacturing plants we can also determine a rent bid function that shows the declining ceiling rents per acre that a plant would be willing to pay as its location became more distant from the market center, or the center of daytime population. The slope of the function depends upon the increase in the wage rate, the decrease in rent per acre necessary to offset this wage increase, and the economies of scale made possible by the substitution of more land for nonland factors of production. Even if there were no economies of scale, increases in wage rates at locations K miles from the market would make K unprofitable unless rents per acre fell sufficiently to reduce the total cost curve until it was tangent to the total revenue curve. If wages per man-hour did not change with distance but if economies of scale caused the cost curve to rise for low outputs per day and to decrease for greater ones with lower rent per acre, the plant would be indifferent between the two locations. The slope of the rent bid curve, then, would be steeper the faster wages per man-hour rose with distance, and the less the substitution of land that is necessary for a more efficient layout.

RESIDENTIAL LAND USE[4]

In purchasing housing space, households will be willing to pay more for housing close to the market center, in order to reduce their transportation expenditures for the journey to work (assuming most employment is in the market center) and for shopping trips. To determine the rent bid function for residential land use we will first see why the price of housing decreases with distance from the market. Houses will be constructed and owned by builders, who rent them. The price per unit of housing that they receive decreases with distance from the market so that the ceiling rent per acre that they are willing to pay for land has to decrease.

To explain the way in which transportation costs reduce the amount that a consumer is willing to pay for the price of a house at different distances from the market center we shall have to introduce indifference curve analysis.[5] The analysis is parallel to that of the production function of the

[4] This section relies heavily on Richard F. Muth, "The Spatial Structure of the Housing Market," *Papers and Proceedings of the Regional Science Association*, vol. 7 (1961), pp. 207–220. A similar model is in Alonso, *op. cit.*, pp. 59–75.
[5] If this discussion of indifference curves is inadequate, see a good intermediate economic analysis text, such as Richard H. Leftwich, *The Price System and Resource Allocation*, 3d ed. (New York: Holt, Rinehart and Winston, Inc., 1966).

firm. The consumer household receives an income from various sources: employment, renting nonhuman resources, and profits. Given this income and the prices of goods and services, households must make their choice of the things they wish to buy. One of the most important purchases is housing. The price of housing from here on is the monthly, or annual, value of the services of a standard unit of housing.

Suppose the household has an income equal to OC in Figure 5-13. The household has a choice among food, clothing, many other items, and housing. At the market center of the city the price of a standard unit of housing is so high that if the household spent all its income on housing it could buy OD units. The budget line CD shows all the combinations of income spent on other things and amounts of housing that the household could purchase with the income OC. Which of the various combinations will the household select? The household will select the combination that yields the greatest satisfaction to its members. For example, the coordinates of point A may represent the "best" choice for a particular house-

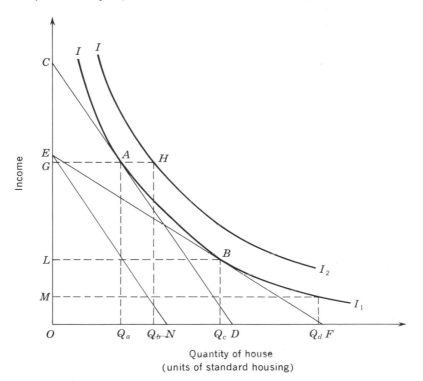

Quantity of house
(units of standard housing)

FIGURE 5-13

hold. OG of the household's income would be spent on all other goods and services, and OQ_a standard units of housing would be purchased.

The household, however, might feel equally well off with other combinations of housing and other goods. For example, the coordinates of point B might represent a combination that would make the household equally well off. With present prices and income, however, the household cannot reach B. The curve II_1 traces all the combinations of goods, services, and housing that would make the household as well off as would the combination A. II_1 is an indifference curve because the consumer is indifferent to which of the combinations traced out by the curve he should obtain. Combinations OG and OQ_b represent a choice that would make the household better off because it would have an increased amount of housing and the same amount of all other goods and services. Indifference curve II_2 shows all the combinations of housing and other goods between which the household would be indifferent at this higher level of well-being. We could fill in the entire graph with indifference curves. The ones closer to the origin would be combinations representing less satisfaction; the indifference curves farther from the origin would be combinations representing greater satisfaction.

Indifference curves have the following characteristics: they cannot intersect, they slope downward from left to right, and they are convex to the origin. By definition if each indifference curve represents combinations that are equivalent, two indifference curves representing different levels of satisfaction cannot intersect. If they did, the curves would not represent different levels of satisfaction. The curves slope downward from left to right because we assume that households will be logical in their choices. The choice represented by the coordinates of A in Figure 5-13 will be equivalent to other combinations of housing and other goods in which housing is purchased in larger quantities, only if the quantities of other goods are reduced. The consumer cannot be just as well off if he gets the same as A but in addition has more of one or the other commodities. To be equally well off with more housing the consumer must give up some of the other goods. The convexity assumption is that as more of one good, say housing, is obtained, additional increments are valued less. As the household increases the quantity of housing from OQ_a to OQ_c to OQ_d in equal increments, less reduction in the amount spent on other goods (LM is less than GL) will make the household equally well off.

The combinations of housing and other goods available to our household at the market that are within its budget are represented by the budget line CD. The household selects the choice yielding the greatest satisfaction. The choice is represented by the point on the budget line tangent to an indifference curve. This is the highest level of satisfaction that can be reached with the given budget. The household reaches this level of satisfaction with OQ_a of housing and OG of other goods and services.

The same household K miles from the center of shopping and employment, however, will have a lower real income. Given the same earnings and prices, the budget line will shift to EN. The reason is that the household has greater transportation costs to work and to shopping than at the market. His real income is less by the cost of transportation. With the given level of income the household would prefer to live at the market center. Nevertheless, there would be a reduced price per unit of standard housing that would make the household indifferent between the market and K miles from the market. With income (after transport costs) of OE the consumer could buy only ON units of standard housing K miles from downtown, while at the market he could have bought OD units, if the whole income were spent on housing. If the price per unit of standard housing should decline, the reduced income OE could buy more housing if it were all spent on housing. Suppose that the price at K was sufficiently lower so that OF units of standard housing could be purchased with all of income OE. The new budget line would be EF. There would exist some reduction in the price per unit of standard housing that would rotate the budget line upward from EN to EF so that it would be tangent to indifference curve II_1, and a combination of housing and other goods equivalent in satisfaction to that in the market could be purchased. In this case, it would be OL of other goods and services, and OQ_c of housing.

If all households had the same income and the same tastes (the same indifference curves), the price per unit of standard housing would have to decrease with distance from downtown for the household to be indifferent between any two locations different in distance from the market. More housing, however, is purchased as distance from the market increases. The builder is in a competitive market so that the price per unit of standard housing that he receives does not vary with the quantity that he sells. The total revenue curve for the builder is less at K miles from the market than at the market center for each rate of production because the household is only willing to pay less per unit of standard housing. The meaning of rate of production is slightly different than we have indicated for other producers. In this case, it must mean the standing stock of units of standard housing that the builder constructs and maintains at any location. In the long run, which we are analyzing, the builder's rate of production is the standing stock of housing that he maintains. As one unit depreciates to nothing, another is rebuilt. Or each house is maintained to its new condition by annual expenditures.

The total costs of the builder include expenditures for many nonland inputs such as labor and materials. The prices of these inputs per unit will be considered the same throughout the city-region. Land rent per acre will be the only price allowed to vary. Just as in each of our previous analyses, there is some rent at which the total cost curve of the firm is tangent to the total revenue curve from above. There is some rent per acre at which the firm will just make "normal" profits and no more. Since the prices of other inputs are equal throughout the hinterland, the builder at a location K miles from the market could not make a profit unless the rent per acre decreased and total costs decreased. The rent per acre associated with each of these total cost curves is the ceiling rent of the builder. We could also draw a rent bid curve tracing the ceiling rent that the builder would be willing to pay at the market and each location around it. Once again the ceiling rent per acre would decline with distance from the market.

The slope of the rent bid curve depends upon the decreased price per unit of housing as distance from market increases, the amount of house per unit of land, and on the substitution of land for nonland inputs as rent decreases. In the case of housing, high-rise apartments using little land relative to other inputs will be built near the market. As the distance increases and rent declines, the builder will shift to duplexes, to single-family houses, and finally to single-family houses on large acreage.

SPATIAL EQUILIBRIUM

Let us now superimpose all the rent bid curves on the same graph. For each agricultural activity, urban activity dependent upon accessibility, manufacturing activity, and housing, there could be constructed a rent bid function depicting the ceiling rent per acre that would be paid by firms and plants engaged in these activities at different distances from the market center, or as we might alternatively call it, the center of density of the daytime population. In Figure 5-14, the rent bid functions for each activity in these groups are considered the same. We do not distinguish between the rent bid function for potato production and corn production, or among offices, banks, and stores, or between manufacturers of different commodities. The core or market center would be occupied by offices, banks, stores, etc., from the center to OK_1 miles distant; manufacturing plants and warehouses might be located from OK_1 to OK_2 miles distant; housing might occupy the land from OK_2 to OK_3 miles distant, manufacturing plants using a single floor might be located from OK_3 to OK_4 miles distant; and agricultural uses would occupy the land OK_4 and more miles distant. The activity able to pay the highest ceiling rent for a particular location

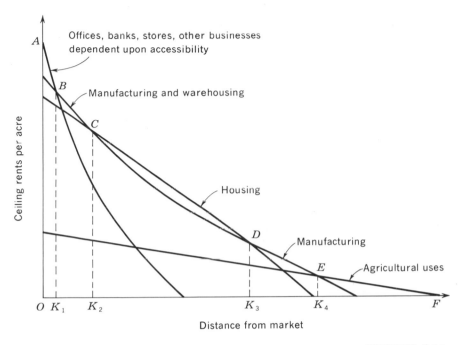

FIGURE 5-14

would occupy it. The curve $ABCDEF$ would be the rent gradient for this particular city region.

By rotating the rent gradient around the vertical axis OA, a rent surface would be generated. The land use picture that would emerge would be that of Figure 5-15. Economic activities would occupy rings around the core. At one time it was suggested that this was in fact the way the distribution of land uses around the city might look from the air, and it was called the concentric theory of land use.[6] The analysis we have used to arrive at the concentric zones, however, was absent.

We are, however, not finished with analyzing the land use and rent structure. For there to be complete equilibrium such that no use or firm has any incentive to move, several conditions must hold, as was briefly shown in the discussion of the simple agricultural model. First, each plant maximizes profits by utilizing the least-cost combination of resources and scale of operations that yields the greatest profit. Second, plants producing

---

[6] Chauncy D. Harris and Edward L. Ullman, "The Nature of Cities," in Paul K. Hatt and Albert J. Reiss, Jr. (eds.), *Cities and Society: The Revised Reader in Urban Sociology* (New York: The Free Press of Glencoe, 1957), pp. 237–247.

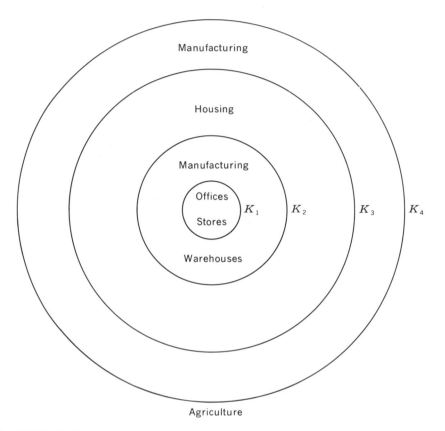

FIGURE 5-15

the same commodity or providing the same service must be indifferent between locations in which that use occupies the land. In the land market for that use the only difference between rent per acre in two locations is the difference necessary to eliminate all but normal profits between the two sites. Third, the land market is in equilibrium because each site is occupied by the use that can pay the highest ceiling rent at that location. Fourth, prices of products equate the quantity supplied and demanded at that price. The price of the product is one of the factors determining the height of the rent bid function of each curve. The rent bid function of each activity shifts up or down with upward or downward price changes until the land that can be occupied for the production of the particular commodity will provide a sufficient supply to meet the quantity demanded at that price. The position of a particular land use depends upon the slope of the rent bid curve. Those with steeper rent bid curves are closer to the market or do not occupy any site. The slope of the rent bid curve, you will remember, depends on the output per acre, the transportation or selling costs, and the possibility of substitution between land and nonland resources.

TOWARD MORE REALISM

Anybody who has thought about land use knows that the land use of our cities does not conform to a concentric land use pattern. Part of the difference between the idealized model and reality is the limiting assumptions of the model. It is surprising how few assumptions we have to modify for the model to take on the form of land use patterns exhibited in cities of the United States. We need modify only four assumptions: uniform fertility of the soil, uniform topography, equal transportation costs in every direction from the market center, and the single market center.

The city that arises around a port cannot possibly be concentric. Chicago is a half circle; St. Louis is a circle with a river through the middle; New York is three-quarters of a circle. Mountains may restrict development of the city in particular directions, as in Los Angeles.

Since not all soil is equally fertile for every crop, the productivity of land in particular places will affect the profitability of its use for a particular crop. Nevertheless, this does not change the impact of the previous analysis. Distance from the market will still determine the ceiling rent that can be paid. The rent bid curve for a particular product, however, will decline continuously only over land of the same fertility. As fertility changes, the rent bid curve may shift up or down.

A more dramatic change occurs when we modify the assumption that transportation costs are the same in every direction from the market center. For example, we can assume that there are four main expressways through the market center, as in Figure 5-16. The rent bid functions for each use will have different slopes depending upon the direction from the center being considered. For each activity, the faster and easier travel along the main highways will reduce the cost of transportation, and therefore it will reduce the slope of the rent bid function.

The total revenue curve for agricultural products will fall less rapidly with distance from the center along the highways because transport cost per bushel per mile will be less. For urban activities that are dependent upon accessibility, selling costs of reaching the same volume of transactions would increase less rapidly along the highways than between them because of the greater volume of traffic on the highways. Therefore, the total revenue curve and ceiling rent for these activities would fall less rapidly along the

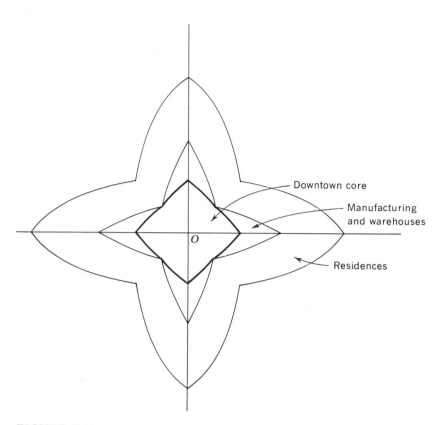

Downtown core

Manufacturing
and warehouses

Residences

O

FIGURE 5-16

highways. The rent bid function for residential land would fall more slowly along the highway because the commuter cost to the core would be less per mile, causing the price per unit of standard housing to fall slowly and the revenue curve of the builder to shift downward more slowly.

Manufacturers sell to other cities and procure inputs from other areas. Therefore, a new element must be considered for urban manufacturing locations when transportation costs are unequal in different directions. The total revenue curve will shift downward for locations away from the intercity highways because of the increased transportation costs to markets. Furthermore, material costs will also increase for locations away from the intercity highways because of increased transport costs. As the manufacturer considers locations at different distances from the market center, the rent bid function for land will fall sharply for directions between the highways because in addition to wage considerations the total revenue curve will be falling faster, and the cost curve will be rising faster.

If we would now introduce a railroad network, or even just one rail line through the city-region, can you predict the changing pattern of land use by analyzing the rent bid functions? If the railroads are used for intercity traffic and not for commuting, the only land use whose rent bid function will be changed is that for manufacturing plants. If railroads are also used for commuting, however, their impact on the rent surface and land use would be the same as highways. If the railroad goes through the market center, manufacturers will dominate along the tracks, and ceiling rents for manufacturing will decline with distance from the center. If, however, the railroad does not pass through the center, the ceiling rent for manufacturers will at first decline with distance from the market, but will increase as distance is less to the railroad.

So far, we have maintained the assumption of a single market center. In Chapter 3, we have seen how systems of cities develop around regional centers. Cities of different sizes provide services to different-sized trading areas, and within cities shopping areas show a similar hierarchical arrangement. Thus, there is not just one market center, or one concentration of daytime population. These subsidiary market centers will cause peaks in the rent surface. The heights of the peaks, however, will not be as high as that of the central business district.

Rent per acre is bid up at the points accessible to a large trading area that is conveniently reached by car or bus. To occupy the land in the midst of residential use, the shopping area uses must be able to pay a ceiling rent higher than that paid for residential use. At locations that are easily accessible to large populations, selling costs are less and ceiling rents can be higher than at poor locations.

The rent gradient in one direction from a regional center might appear as in Figure 5-17. Three subsidiary market areas are shown. Between K_3 and K_4 miles a neighborhood shopping center might rise in the midst of a residential area. The neighborhood centers would include convenience goods and perhaps a bank. Farther out one might find a regional shopping center, as at K_6 to K_7 miles from the center in Figure 5-17. It, too, will be in the midst of a residential area, but it will also be farther from the competing shopping goods center in the central business district. Regional centers would include a large department store, and some specialty shops. The third subsidiary center is much farther from the central business district. The satellite city K_{10} to K_{11} miles from the center in Figure 5-17 is meant to show how the rent gradient might be affected around a town of lower order in a system of cities. The ceiling rents in the center of the

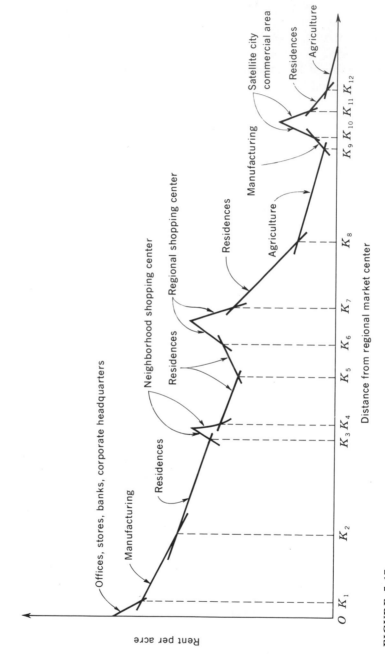

FIGURE 5-17

satellite do not rise as high as those in the center of the higher-order city because prices of products do not need to be forced so high to cause sufficient quantities of production to move to the smaller places.

SOME EMPIRICAL EVIDENCE ON THE THEORY

Several statistical regularities that have been observed are consistent with the analysis just outlined.[7] A few will be mentioned here to show the nature of these observations.

Manufacturing production would tend to be small scale toward the center of the city and large scale toward the fringe because rents would be high in the center and low at the fringe. Production at the fringe could substitute land for nonland inputs and take advantage of assembly-line technology. Table 5-1 shows the percentage distribution of manufacturing jobs in zones of the New York Metropolitan Region. Indeed there is some indication that small firms tend to be located in the core, while large ones are located farther out.

In the same way residential buildings should shift from multifamily structures to single-family structures as distance from the core is increased,

[7] For a survey, see Peter Haggett, *Locational Analysis in Human Geography* (New York: St. Martin's Press, Inc., 1966), pp. 153–182.

TABLE 5-1   DISTRIBUTION OF MANUFACTURING JOBS IN ZONES OF NEW YORK METROPOLITAN REGION BY SIZE OF PLANTS, 1956

	Number of employees (thousands)	Percentage shares of region's employment (NYMR = 100)		
		Core	Inner ring	Outer ring
All industries covered by table	1,310.4	49.6	32.0	18.4
Industries with average establishments of:				
60 or fewer employees	734.6	61.2	24.7	14.1
61 to 240 employees	435.3	43.3	37.2	19.5
More than 240 employees	140.5	7.7	54.1	38.2

SOURCE: Reprinted by permission from Edgar M. Hoover and Raymond Vernon, *Anatomy of a Metropolis* (Cambridge, Mass.: Harvard University Press, 1959), p. 50. Copyright 1959 by Regional Plan Association, Inc.

TABLE 5-2 TYPES OF HOUSING IN NEW YORK
METROPOLITAN REGION, 1950

| | Percentage of dwelling units in: | | | |
Area	All types of structures	Single-family structures	Two-family structures	Multi-family structures
Region	100	32.2	15.0	52.8
Core	100	14.6	13.1	72.2
Manhattan	100	1.8	0.8	97.4
Rest of core	100	18.9	17.2	63.9
Inner ring	100	51.7	19.2	29.0
Outer ring	100	69.8	15.2	14.7

SOURCE: Reprinted by permission from Edgar M. Hoover and Raymond Vernon, *Anatomy of a Metropolis* (Cambridge, Mass.: Harvard University Press, 1959), p. 138. Copyright 1959 by Regional Plan Association, Inc.

because the lower rents allow substitution of land for nonland inputs. This in turn should be reflected in lower densities of dwelling units per acre as distance from the core increases. Even single-family structures should have more land on the lots as distance from the core increases. Table 5-2 shows that 97 percent of the residential structures in Manhattan are multi-family structures and 70 percent of the residential structures in the outer ring are single-family structures. In Table 5-3, dwelling units per acre in the New York Metropolitan Region are shown to decline with distance from Manhattan.

A corollary would be that population density should decline with distance from the core. In Table 5-4, population density in the New York Metropolitan Region is shown to decline with distance from the core. Richard F. Muth has shown that the analysis of residential land use and rent is consistent with a gross population density that varies negatively and exponentially with distance from the core.[8] He found that the negative-exponential function was probably the best simple approximation to urban residential density patterns in 1950 in the forty-six United States cities that he studied.

Patterns in the spatial distribution of agricultural production have also been found to be consistent with the theory. Chisholm, for example, has found that the type of agricultural production in Sicily changes with dis-

[8] Muth, *loc. cit.*

TABLE 5-3   NET RESIDENTIAL DENSITY OF MUNICIPALITIES IN LAND USE SURVEY AREA, IN RELATION TO TRAVEL TIME TO MANHATTAN, 1954–1955

Municipalities classified by access zones (zone 1 is closest to Manhattan)	Dwelling units per acre of residentially developed land
1	25.7
2	7.1
3	5.4
4	3.7
5	3.2
All municipalities in land use survey	6.4

SOURCE: Reprinted by permission from Edgar M. Hoover and Raymond Vernon, *Anatomy of a Metropolis* (Cambridge, Mass.: Harvard University Press, 1959), p. 137. Copyright 1959 by Regional Plan Association, Inc.

TABLE 5-4   POPULATION PER SQUARE MILE OF INTENSIVELY DEVELOPED LAND IN COUNTIES OF NEW YORK METROPOLITAN REGION, 1953–1956

Area	Thousands per square mile
Entire region	13.9
Core counties	44.7
Inner ring counties	9.9
Outer ring counties	5.2

SOURCE: Reprinted by permission from Edgar M. Hoover and Raymond Vernon, *Anatomy of a Metropolis* (Cambridge, Mass.: Harvard University Press, 1959), p. 136. Copyright 1959 by Regional Plan Association, Inc.

tance from settlements and is related to the ratio of nonland inputs. Consistent with land use theory the agricultural products requiring greater man-hours per acre were closer to the settlement, as would be expected if rents were higher toward the settlements.[9]

[9] M. D. I. Chisholm, *Rural Settlement and Land Use: An Essay in Location* (London: Hutchinson University Press, 1962), p. 63.

SUMMARY

Briefly, the center of market activity of the metropolitan area is the place most accessible to the whole population of the area. Urban activities dependent upon accessibility for total revenue will occupy the valuable central core. These activities include banking, corporate headquarters, department stores, specialty shops, furniture stores, and investment and insurance agencies. The rent gradient will decline in all directions from this center, except that peaks will occur along railways and waterways that provide intercity transportation, and around subsidiary market centers providing services to smaller groups of the population than the entire metropolitan area. Peaks in the rent gradient will also occur around satellite cities.

Manufacturing plants will most profitably locate along the major routes in and out of the metropolitan area. Plants closer to the core will be smaller operations using very little land, while those farther from the city will spread out their operations on one floor and pay lower rents per acre.

Residential areas will fill in between and around the urban commercial activities and manufacturing plants. Higher rents per acre will be paid closer to the center, and thus we will find high-rise apartments close in. These will grade off into duplexes and finally single-family residences at greater distances from the market. Therefore, we would expect housing units per acre and population per acre to decline with distance from the market center. Two points need to be brought out here. First, the rent bid function for residential use was based on commuter and shopping transport costs. Therefore, the rent should be higher around the subsidiary shopping centers and employment complexes. Second, neighborhood amenities have not been taken into account in evaluating the rent bid function for residential use. In spite of higher commuter costs households will be willing to pay more per unit of standard housing if the house is located away from the dirt and grime of industry and close to a large park or lake, or if it is located high on a prominance to the windward of industry. Thus, these sites, too, will have high ceiling rents per acre for residential use.

The size of the urban area, the land occupied by urban rather than agricultural uses, is determined by the amount of land necessary to supply the quantity demanded of urban goods and services. The rent bid functions adjust so as to bring about equilibrium in the goods and services markets. At some distance in each direction agricultural uses will outbid urban activities for the use of land. In general the agricultural uses will not necessarily be those yielding the greatest production per acre. Productivity helps, but ceiling rent is also dependent upon the market price of the product, the transport cost to market, and other costs. What can be pointed out is that market price and transportation cost are not necessarily oriented to the nearest city. Ceiling rent for crops depends upon market price and distance from the main market center for that crop. For example, the rent bid function for agricultural uses beyond K_{12} miles from the regional center in Figure 5-17 depends upon distance from the regional center and not upon distance from the satellite city between K_{10} and K_{11} miles from the regional center. This same principle holds in determining which mineral deposits will be operated.

PART TWO

MEASUREMENT
AND CHANGE
IN REGIONAL
ECONOMIC ACTIVITY

CHAPTER 6

MEASUREMENT
OF REGIONAL
ECONOMIC ACTIVITY

The last three chapters have developed the rationale for the spatial order-ing of economic activity. We have analyzed the formation and location of cities, the hierarchical ordering of cities, the geographic dispersion of industry, and the utilization of land in city-regions. It is difficult for us to keep in mind all the prices, quantities, locations, transportation costs, etc., for any one city-region, much less the economic variables relevant to under-standing many city-regions. Furthermore, when we come to analyzing the growth of an area, or its response to business cycles, we will need some aggregate measure of income and employment. Thus, we need to find a way to aggregate the information that we have been discussing for any particular region that we might be interested in studying. The measures selected have not been chosen at random, but with a view to the measures needed for an analysis of stability and growth covered in subsequent chapters.

DEFINING THE REGION[1]

The discussion in Part 1 on the structure of regions brought out the con-tinuous nature of the spatial order of the economy. The whole system of cities is interrelated, and the hinterland of each city is related to the city and through it to other cities in the same economy and to other systems of cities. If there is such a concept as a natural region, it is a city and its hinterland. As we have seen, however, there may be several hinterlands of different sizes depending upon the number and variety of functions per-formed by an individual city. Therefore, any delimitation of economic areas will be arbitrary and will not depict a true natural economic region.

Nevertheless, there are at least two reasons for exploring the problem of delimiting regions. First, is the statistical problem of presenting detail on a massive amount of data. For example, data on population for the entire United States and for each county are tabulated. The characteristics of age, family size, sex, income, education, etc., can be tabulated for each county and presented, and it is done. But there would be a considerable savings in tabulating and cross-tabulating expense if this information were

---

[1] Rutledge Vining, "Delimitation of Economic Areas: Statistical Concepts in the Study of Spatial Structure of an Economic System," *Journal of the American Statistical Association* (March, 1953), pp. 44–64.

presented for 501 State Economic Areas instead of for each of over 3,000 counties. Such an aggregation would yield better areal information than data enumerated by states, or by nine regional groups of states. The second reason for studying the problem of delimiting regions is that studies of small areas must be bounded in order to collect data for evaluation. Thus, in these cases some way must be found to bound part of the economic landscape.

Basically, two approaches have been taken to organizing the economic landscape of the United States into reasonable regions for meaningful presentation of greater statistical detail. The first approach is based on the *functional integration principle.*[2] This is a long name for the simple notion that areas tied to the same central node should be called a region. The Standard Metropolitan Statistical Area used by the Bureau of the Census is a standard definition for metropolitan areas used by governments and many other private and public agencies, and is defined by the functional integration principle. Essentially the SMSA is defined (except in New England) as a county or group of contiguous counties that contain at least one city of 50,000 inhabitants or more, or "twin cities" with a combined population of at least 50,000. See Figure 6-1 for SMSA boundaries in 1967. In New England, SMSAs consist of towns and cities, rather than counties. In addition to the county, or counties, containing such a city or cities, contiguous counties are included in an SMSA if (1) 15 percent of the workers living in the county work in the central county of the area, (2) 25 percent of those working in the county live in the central county of the area, or (3) other measures such as telephone calls from the county to the central county and newspaper circulation indicate their integration with the central county.[3]

In theory the functional integration principle could define the whole United States as the hinterland for some metropolitan areas. Lower-order cities would have regions carved out of the hinterland of higher-order cities. In practice, however, the SMSAs include only areas in which a high proportion of the workers is employed in the central city. We shall find that this is a good criterion for income and product accounts, since it avoids the difference between income of residents and income earned in an area. The larger hinterland is excluded. Nevertheless, any criterion used to break off part of the hinterland would be arbitrary.

The second approach used to define reasonable regions for meaningful presentation of greater statistical detail is based upon the *homogeneity*

[2] Morris B. Ullman and Robert C. Klove, "The Geographic Area in Regional Economic Research," in *Regional Income*, vol. 21, Conference on Research in Income and Wealth, National Bureau of Economic Research (Princeton, N.J.: Princeton University Press, 1957), pp. 92–94.
[3] U.S. Bureau of the Budget, *Standard Metropolitan Statistical Areas* (1964), pp. 1–2.

principle. As one would expect from the name, this approach to defining a region tries to form regions that are as much alike as possible throughout, and different from other nearby areas. State Economic Areas (SEAs) of the Bureau of the Census grouping counties together for substate regions and the regional geographic divisions grouping states into eight regions used by the Regional Economics Division of the Department of Commerce are based upon the homogeneity principle. For a map of these latter eight regions see Figure 6-2.

SMSAs make up some of the 501 SEAs aggregated from two or more counties. The rest of the areas are defined on the basis of eighty-eight statistical indices, such as population density, income, race, births and deaths, and percentage of employment by main industry. Contiguous counties are grouped so that variations in the indices are greater between SEAs than within SEAs.

The regional groupings of states were based on a visual comparison of income payments; industrial distribution of employment; population size, distribution, and growth; racial and ethnic composition; level of living; transportation and communication; health; and history. Nine series of statistics, including per capita income in 1951, telephones per 1,000 population in 1950, infant deaths per 1,000 live births in 1949, and net migration from 1940 to 1950 as a percentage of 1950 population, were selected to test the homogeneity of the groupings of states into regions. For each statistic the variance between regions and between states within regional groupings was calculated. The smaller the variance between states in the same region and the larger the variance of the statistic between regions, the better would be the regional groupings by the homogeneity standard. The new regional groupings were compared with the several other groupings currently in use.[4] In these comparisons the Southeast Region was divided into an Upper South and a Lower South. One of the alternative definitions with which this nine-region breakdown was compared was the U.S. Census nine-region breakdown. (See Figure 6-3.) The new regional breakdown was found to be better on all but a few measures. Nevertheless, the only branch to adopt the new regions was the Regional Economics Division of the Department of Commerce.

In analyzing small areas it is necessary to define the boundaries of the area. For example, to analyze a river basin project a cost-benefit analysis must be undertaken. The benefits of the project will not accrue to the entire United States, nor does the demand for power and water services come from the entire United States for any particular irrigation project

---

[4] Ullman and Klove, *op. cit.*, pp. 87–109.

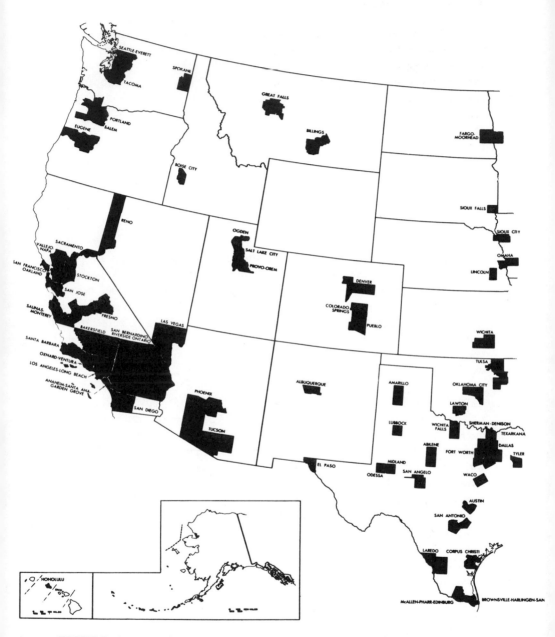

FIGURE 6-1 STANDARD METROPOLITAN STATISTICAL AREAS (areas

SOURCE: U. S. Bureau of the Budget, *Standard Metropolitan Statistical Areas*, 1967.

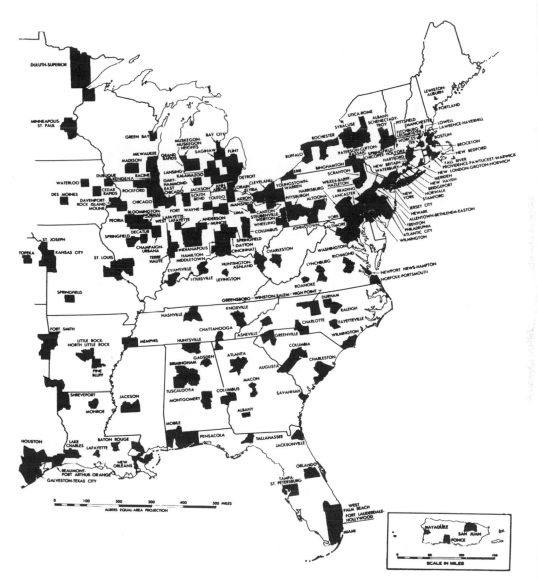

defined by U. S. Bureau of the Budget to March, 1967)

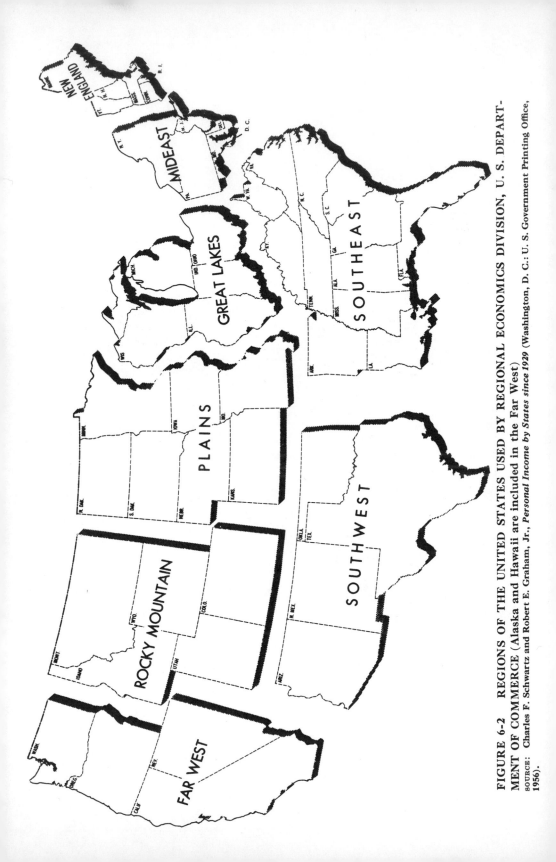

FIGURE 6-2 REGIONS OF THE UNITED STATES USED BY REGIONAL ECONOMICS DIVISION, U. S. DEPART-
MENT OF COMMERCE (Alaska and Hawaii are included in the Far West)

SOURCE: Charles F. Schwartz and Robert E. Graham, Jr., *Personal Income by States since 1929* (Washington, D. C.: U. S. Government Printing Office, 1956).

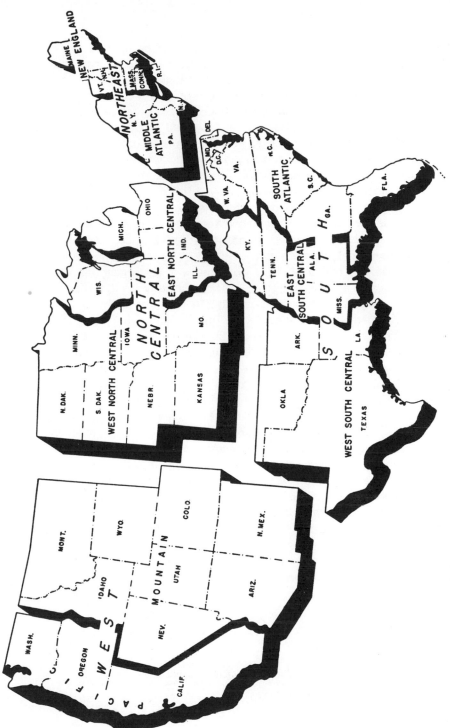

FIGURE 6-3   MAP OF THE UNITED STATES SHOWING CENSUS REGIONS AND DIVISIONS (Alaska and Hawaii are included in the Pacific)

SOURCE: U. S. Bureau of the Census, *Statistical Abstract of the United States, 1957*, 78th ed., 1957.

or hydroelectric project. For these studies a region must be defined so as to include the major areas impacted by the project. In this case the definition of the area will depend upon the interrelationship of the immediately adjacent area with other more distant areas. Not only must the drainage area of the project be considered, but adjacent areas dependent on the study region for local services and employment must be included.

To study the future development of the New York Metropolitan Area the New York Metropolitan Region Study defined a twenty-two-county area for study. All the counties were connected with the urban core of Manhattan through employment. In fact in studying this central node of the United States there were many instances in which the study group had to reach out to study the interrelations between New York and Chicago, New York and Boston, New York and Philadelphia, and New York and Los Angeles.[5]

To study the municipal finances of a central city of one of our large metropolitan areas, the region of study would have to be larger than the political boundaries of the central city itself. At the very least the area including the residences of employees working in the central city should be included. Revenues and costs incurred by the city will depend upon the fortunes of business in the region, and upon where employment and residences will be located within that region, all of which require a study of the core and its hinterland. In spite of the data difficulties, one author has suggested that boundaries of urban regions be redefined on the basis of the labor market of the area instead of along county lines. These geographic units of analysis would be called Functional Economic Areas and would be more useful than the current SMSAs and SEAs for the analysis of the impact on the area of business cycles, the removal of a plant, the loss of a government base, or the loss of a government contract to an important local business. Indeed Karl Fox has shown how county boundaries in Iowa might be redrawn on the basis of the concept of a labor market area in order that data might be collected for such units to facilitate economic analysis.[6]

DESCRIPTIVE INPUT-OUTPUT MODEL OF A REGION

Once we have defined a region for study we could relate the region to other regions and the hinterland by analyzing the functions performed by higher-order regions, and by the functions performed by the region of study for

[5] Raymond Vernon, *Metropolis 1985* (Cambridge, Mass.: Harvard University Press, 1959).
[6] Karl A. Fox and T. Krishna Kumar, "The Functional Economic Area: Delineation and Implications for Economic Analysis and Policy," *Papers and Proceedings of the Regional Science Association*, vol. 15 (1965), pp. 57–85.

lower-order regions within it. There is, however, another way of summarizing the economic activity of a region and its connections with other areas. An input-output matrix is a useful framework for describing these interrelationships.

For any place, the input-output flow matrix sums the flows from each industry and household to every other household and industry. Each row shows the distribution of the production of an industry to other industries and demand sectors or the distribution of the resources of households to industries and demand sectors of the economy. Each column shows the flows of inputs into a particular industry from industries and households. The descriptive framework just described is not an analytical model, but a framework for collecting and integrating the transactions between households and businesses in an economy. Under particular assumptions about the production function of each industry the matrix can become an analytical tool.[7] In this study we shall refer only to the descriptive usefulness of the technique. As an analytical tool the input-output matrix has been limited in regional analysis because of the cost of collecting data. As a descriptive framework it is the best way to see how aggregation leads to regional income accounts.

To explain the statistical framework of the input-output matrix let us begin with the production function of an individual plant. The production function relates the rate of output of the plant to the use of resources and other inputs. Instead of showing all the possible rates of output with their associated quantities of resources, we shall take a snapshot for one time period. For one year we shall record the total output of the plant and the total consumption of man-hours, materials, and purchases from other firms necessary to produce the indicated rate of production. In a column such as the one in Table 6-1, we can record the quantities of inputs used for the given level of output.

[7] See Hollis B. Chenery and Paul G. Clark, *Interindustry Economics* (New York: John Wiley & Sons, Inc., 1962), for an excellent text that discusses the input-output matrix as an analytical tool in handling national and regional economic problems. For a good simple introduction, see William Miernyk, *The Elements of Input-Output Analysis* (New York: Random House, Inc., 1965).

TABLE 6-1   WIDGET INPUTS

Resources:	
Iron and steel	500 tons
Labor	400 man-hours
Total production	1,000 widgets

TABLE 6-2 DISTRIBUTION OF WIDGET OUTPUT

Industry	Purchased by these sectors				
	Iron and steel	Consumers	Govern- ment	Exports	Total distribution
Widgets	20	800	100	80	1,000

The next step is to trace the distribution of the widgets. We want to know whether the product was sold to consumers, government, other businesses, or was exported from the region. In a row such as the one in Table 6-2, we can record the quantities of widgets distributed to industries and demand sectors of the economy.

Within the same framework we can sum the use of inputs and the distribution of widgets produced by all widget plants within the region under study. Thus, the summation put together in the same table might look like Table 6-3.

Although it is conceptually possible to construct tables showing the use of inputs and the distribution of total product for each product produced in a region, it is more practical to try to estimate these tables for groups of industries because of the cost of collecting the necessary data. The grouping of the industries will depend upon the regions under study. In the United States an eighty-industry grouping was used in constructing the 1958 input-output matrix.[8] For one county within the United States,

[8] Morris R. Goldman, Martin L. Marimont, and Beatrice N. Vaccara, "The Interindustry Structure of the United States," *Survey of Current Business* (November, 1964), pp. 10–29.

TABLE 6-3 SUMMARY OF WIDGET INPUTS AND OUTPUTS

Purchased from these sectors	Purchased by these sectors				
	Widgets	Iron and steel	House- holds	Govern- ment	Exports
Widgets		200	8,000	1,000	800
Iron and steel	5,000 tons				
Labor	4,000 man-hours				

or for a small underdeveloped country, only twelve industries might be necessary to usefully analyze the regional economy. Not every industry is represented in every region. Many small and unimportant industries may be grouped together. In an agricultural county with little manufacturing the industry groupings might be corn, soybeans, other agriculture, mining, food processing, electronics, other manufacturing, services, households, and government.

Table 6-4 is a hypothetical set of input-output accounts for a region. It is an accounting system summarizing all the transactions of a region. The table is simplified in order to bring out the major relationships to be under-

TABLE 6-4 HYPOTHETICAL INPUT-OUTPUT ACCOUNTS
(In millions of dollars)

Producing sectors	Interindustry demand						Final demand					
	Agriculture and mining	Construction	Food and kindred products	Electrical machinery	Other manufacturing industry	Real estate and finance	Household consumption	Investment	Government	Exports	Total final demand	Row totals
	(1)	(2)	(3)	(4)	(5)	(6)	(7)	(8)	(9)	(10)	(11)	(12)
(1) Agriculture and mining	25	1	33	—	11	—	1	—	—	29	30	100
(2) Construction	—	—	—	—	—	—	—	38	—	2	40	40
(3) Food and kindred products	10	—	17	—	5	—	31	—	1	36	68	100
(4) Electrical machinery	—	2	—	4	11	—	—	15	—	68	83	100
(5) Other manufacturing industry	2	6	2	3	17	11	6	5	1	47	59	100
(6) Real estate and finance	4	1	1	1	6	1	22	8	1	5	36	50
(7) Households	50	14	26	45	40	36	1	—	10	—	11	222
(8) Imports	9	16	21	47	10	2	30	—	—	—	30	135
(9) Column totals	100	40	100	100	100	50	91	66	13	187	357	

stood. Rows 1 through 6 detail the distribution of production in each of the six industrial sectors of the region. Columns 1 through 6 of each row detail the interindustry demand, that is, the distribution of production to other industries that will be used in the production process again. For example, $33 million worth of production in agriculture and mining is sold to the food and kindred products group. This would include grain to be made into flour and then into cakes and bread. Columns 7 through 10 of each row detail the distribution of products to their final use. The products sold for final use will be consumed and not used for further production. Final use includes production sold within the region directly to households for consumption; to business for investment to build new plants and to increase their equipment; to government for all local government operations; and to industry, households, and government outside the region.

Although purchases for business investment are used to produce other goods and are depreciated in the process, they are not part of the final product of these other goods. Investment goods purchased by industry have reached their final use, and are thus considered part of final demand. By convention all government purchases are considered purchased for final use, as are purchases by households. Such a case can be thought up as some little old lady's buying jars and paraffin to use for selling homemade jelly, which is really an interindustry transaction. The total of these cases is probably small in dollar volume and not worth the very large cost of accounting separately for them. Exports include all sales to industry, government, or households outside the region, whether for intermediate use or for final use. As far as the region under study is concerned, all goods sold outside the region will not have an intermediate use within the selling region. Therefore, exports are for final use.

Instead of going across the rows of Table 6-4 column by column we shall now discuss the columns row by row. Each of the first six columns summarizes the purchase of inputs for production in each of the industrial sectors. For example, column 1 shows that during the year $25 million worth of product was purchased by the agriculture and mining industry from itself for intermediate use. This would include the production of feed for livestock. Another $10 million was spent to purchase goods from the food-processing industry, $2 million for the production of other manufacturing industries, and $4 million for the real estate and finance services of the region. These are only the interindustry purchases. These inputs were combined with labor and capital owned by households. Households, row 7, received $50 million in wages, interest, and profits for their contribution to the production of goods in agriculture and mining. Row 8, however, shows that not all the inputs needed for production could be found within the study region. Imports of $9 million were made to produce goods in the agriculture and mining sector.

There are entries of household services sold directly for final use to households and to government. There is also an entry showing imports sold directly to consumers for final use. Domestic servants would be an example of labor services bought directly by households for final use. The government hires employees. Their wages, $10 million, are purchases by government for final rather than intermediate use. It is easy to see that consumer households would purchase goods directly from other regions. In this hypothetical table $30 million was spent on consumer imports.

The first six row items in column 12 show the total market value of output in each industry. The value of output is exactly equal to the value of goods and services used in their production including the profits to entrepreneurs. If all the production were not sold in the same year, the value of unsold production would appear as an increase in inventories, and thus an investment. For example, part of the $15 million (row 4, column 8) spent on investment by the electrical machinery industry might have been an increase in inventories in that industry.

The total for each of columns 7 through 10 shows the total spent for local consumption, investment, government, and exports from the region. The sum of consumption, investment, government, and exports is $357 million, which is the total for column 11. But the $357 million final demand does not represent production in our hypothetical region because the $357 million spent on final demand includes some expenditures for imports. Subtracting total imports (row 8, column 12), $135 million, from $357 million yields $222 million. This $222 million measures the value of output from this region purchased during the year for final use, and is the region's production.

Interindustry or intermediate purchases were excluded from the region's production. If they were included, the value of the interindustry transactions would be included twice. The reason is easy to see. Purchases by one industry from another become a part of the value of the new product. For example, the $33 million of production from agriculture and mining sold to the food-processing industry is part of the cost of processing food for final use. The value of the sales of the food processing industry for final use includes this cost.

Another way to look at this problem is to study row 7, the value of household services. The value added by each industry is the value of services bought from households and excludes the purchase of inputs from other industries. The payments for the goods and services of households—the wages, interest, rents, and profits earned by households for selling the services they own—represent the value added in each industry from resources of the region. The term value added is used to describe this contribution to the value of the product in each industry. The sum of value added in the region (row 7, column 12), $222 million, is equal to the value of the regional product for the year.

The net product of a region is the reproducible annual output of the region. An adjustment may need to be made to the $222 million to arrive at the reproducible or net regional product. Part of the investment expenditures may have been for building new plants and equipment and for expanding production capacity, but part of it may have gone for replacing worn-out plants and equipment. If total output were consumed and none were used to replace the equipment and plants, the potential level of output in subsequent years would be less because of the reduction in capital equipment. Economists define the expenditures necessary for replacement of used-up capital as the capital consumption allowance. The net output of the region is the total regional product, defined above, less a capital consumption allowance. The latter account does not appear in Table 6-4.

In Table 6-3, which summarized the production and distribution of one product, rows could be summed, but columns could not be summed. The rows could be summed because they were measured in the same physical units. The columns, however, could not be summed, since column 1 was tons of iron and steel, and man-hours of labor. The sum of man-hours and tons would be meaningless. If Table 6-4 had been estimated using physical units, as in Table 6-3, it would not have been possible to calculate the total value of inputs, the total value of consumption, total exports, or total regional product, since some items would be in tons, others in man-hours, and others in bushels, crates, or boxes. Therefore, prices were used to measure the value of transactions.

To the extent that the economic organization of a region is competitive, prices measure the value of goods and services to the economy. Using money prices, however, is not without its problems. In the first place the purchasing power of a dollar varies over time and space. In the second place those goods and services that we provide ourselves outside the marketplace are not valued and added into the output.

The first problem can be partially overcome by using index numbers. For example, the Consumer Price Index is calculated by first finding the average budget for a typical family in a base year that is arbitrarily selected. Each year the same items in the budget are priced and added up.[9] We then

---

[9] As prices change, the family will change the pattern of its expenditures, buying less of the more expensive items and more of the cheaper items. But the change in the pattern is ignored, and thus, the new budget is higher than it might be.

take the ratio of the new cost to the old cost and have a price index for two years. The index can be used to deflate to constant dollars the dollar estimates of the net regional product in two different years. For example, if the regional product were $15,180 million in 1950 and $25,904 million in 1963, the difference between them is an overestimate of the increase in output because prices have also increased during this time. The Consumer Price Index was 83.8 in 1950 with a base year as the average of 1957–59. In 1963 the Index was 106.7. The constant dollar estimates of product are found by dividing the current dollar figures by the appropriate index.

$$\frac{\$15,180}{83.8} = \$18,114 \qquad \frac{\$25,904}{106.7} = \$24,277$$

The difference between the new estimates is closer to the actual change in total product from 1950 to 1963.

The second problem, that nonmarket transactions are excluded, can also be partially overcome. Some nonmarket outputs are the work of housewives, the rental value of owner-occupied houses, food grown and consumed on farms, and wages paid in room and board rather than money. We can impute value to these goods and services by using prices for comparable goods and services that are sold in the market. In practice the income and product accounts for the United States have included imputed values for all the above nonmarket transactions, except the work of housewives. To the extent that their production is shifted from the home to the market the accounts show an increase in production where none exists. Over a decade or a few years such changes are probably so small that they can be ignored.

PERSONAL INCOME BY REGIONS

The complete information necessary to construct the accounting system illustrated by Table 6-4 for the nation or for subnational regions would be exceedingly expensive to obtain. Nevertheless, an input-output set of accounts is available for the United States for the years 1947 and 1958.[10] A few tables have been estimated for regions.[11] Net National Product, however, has been estimated for each year since 1929 by the Department of Commerce. Without going through the input-output matrix described

---

[10] Goldman, Marimont, and Vaccara, *loc. cit.;* and W. Duane Evans and Martin Hoffenberg, "The Interindustry Relations Study for 1947," *Review of Economics and Statistics* (May, 1952), pp. 97–142.

[11] Two of these studies are Werner Z. Hirsch, "Interindustry Relations of a Metropolitan Area," *Review of Economics and Statistics* (August, 1959), pp. 360–369; and Roland G. Artle, *The Structure of the Stockholm Economy* (Ithaca, N.Y.: Cornell University Press, 1965).

above, the value of goods and services sold for final use and the value added by industries can be estimated. These two approaches yield two estimates of Net National Product.[12] To construct similar income accounts for regions within the United States, difficult data problems would have to be overcome.

Census data are available for national accounts that may not be available for a small area because of disclosure rules. The Bureau of the Census will not disclose information on firms that might lead to the identification of firms with particular information on sales, employment, wages and salaries, etc. Moreover, if data are developed from national surveys, they are inadequate for a local area. To achieve the same statistical accuracy a much greater sample would be needed for each local area. Large corporations and the Federal government, and for smaller regions the state governments, are institutions whose operations span many regions. These institutions may find no need to keep records that would be helpful in allocating their operations to the correct region. The large corporation with many branches may show all its dividends paid in the county of its headquarters. Total sales are usually shown as being from the main plant or headquarters instead of from the plant from which the goods were shipped. So far, the benefits of developing a detailed set of accounts for many regions have not been considered worth the cost of estimation.[13]

The Department of Commerce, however, has estimated one component of Net National Product by states and regions. Estimates of personal income are available by state and region from 1929 to the present. Personal income is defined in the following way:

> State personal income is the current income received by residents of the States from all sources. It is measured before deduction of income and other direct personal taxes, but after deduction of individuals' contributions to social security, government retirement, and other social insurance programs. While cash income makes up the overwhelming bulk of the total—more than 95 percent on a national basis—personal income also includes several types of nonmonetary income, or income in kind, in order to improve the scope of the estimates and thereby make the basis of comparison by States more meaningful.[14]

[12] For a discussion of the two approaches and their reconciliation, see the *National Income Supplement to the Survey of Current Business* for 1958.
[13] For a more detailed discussion on these points, see Werner Hochwald, "Conceptual Issues of Regional Income Estimation," in *Regional Income*, vol. 21, Conference on Research on Income and Wealth, National Bureau of Economic Research (Princeton, N.J.: Princeton University Press, 1957), pp. 9–34.
[14] Charles F. Schwartz and Robert E. Graham, Jr., *Personal Income by States since 1929* (Washington, D.C.: Government Printing Office, 1956), p. 49. Current estimates are published twice a year in the *Survey of Current Business*, once in April and once in July or August.

Personal income is related to net product in the following way. First, indirect business taxes and other items between the market value of production and payment to factors of production must be subtracted. Second, undistributed corporate profits, corporate tax liability, and business contribution to social security must be subtracted from net product because they are not payments to individuals. On the other hand, transfer payments such as gifts and welfare payments must be added. Although they are not transactions increasing national product, these shifts of wealth from government and business are income receipts to individuals and households.

These personal income estimates by state and region are the best available measures of overall economic activity.[15] We shall now use these estimates to trace the short- and long-run trends in income for eight regions of the United States. The long-run trends are to represent the differential growth trends between regions. Over the long run there will be changes in population, plant and equipment, and geographic position relative to resources and markets as new transportation techniques come into use. In the long run a large increase in income might not really increase the welfare of the population, since population might grow at a faster rate or at the same rate as income. Thus, a better measure of long-run trends in growth is per capita income. In the short run, population growth will be small relative to the swings in personal income. The description of the relative impact of swings in the business cycle may be shown best with the amplitude of the fluctuations in total personal income.

Using estimates of personal income by regions for 1840, 1880, and 1900 by Richard Easterlin, for 1920 by Maurice Leven, and for 1930, 1940, 1950, and 1960 by the Department of Commerce, long-run trends in relative personal income per capita are shown in Table 6-5. The second row in Table 6-5 shows the personal income per capita for the whole United States in constant dollars. The original income per capita was divided by a consumer price index with a base 1957–1959 = 100. The rows for each region are not in dollars; they are the ratios of the region's per capita income to the United States per capita income for the corresponding year. For example, in 1960 personal income per capita in the United States was $2,150, while it was 111 percent of $2,150 in New England, 94 percent of $2,150 in the Plains region, and 72 percent of $2,150 in the Southeast.

In 1840, before the Civil War, New England and the Mideast had the highest

[15] It would be better for some purposes to have regional product accounts. Estimates on these, however, are not readily available. See George H. Borts, "The Estimation of Produced Income by State and Region," in *The Behavior of Income Shares*, Studies in Income and Wealth, vol. 27 (New York: National Bureau of Economic Research, 1963), pp. 317–364; and J. Thomas Romans, *Capital Exports and Growth among U.S. Regions* (Middletown, Conn.: Wesleyan University Press, 1965).

TABLE 6-5   UNITED STATES PERSONAL INCOME PER CAPITA AND
RATIO OF PER CAPITA PERSONAL INCOME IN EACH REGION TO
UNITED STATES LEVEL, 1840–1960

Region*	1840	1880†	1900	1920	1930	1940	1950	1960‡
United States	$ 65	$ 95	$113	$680	$ 624	$ 595	$1,491	$2,217
Value in 1957–59								
dollars§	337	386	483	974	1,072	1,219	1,779	2,150
New England	128	137	130	116	129	127	109	111
Mideast	118	122	123	123	143	133	118	116
Great Lakes	71	107	106	111	110	112	111	107
Plains	78	95	106	99	82	81	95	94
Southeast	89	58	56	53	50	58	68	72
Southwest		67	78	88	64	70	86	86
Rocky Mountain		183	163	109	86	89	96	94
Far West		199	157	149	131	132	120	118

* For definitions of these regions, see Fig. 6-2.
† Southwest excludes Oklahoma.
‡ Includes Hawaii and Alaska in Far West.
§ The index used to deflate per capita income to constant dollars was the Consumer Price
Index (1957–1959 = 100) listed below. The source is the Consumer Price Index of the
Bureau of Labor Statistics for 1920–1960, and the Burgess index from 1840 to 1900 in the
U.S. Bureau of the Census, *Historical Statistics of the United States, Colonial Times to 1957*
(1960), table E158, p. 127.

Consumer Price Index (1957–1959 = 100)

1840	19.3
1880	24.6
1900	23.4
1920	69.8
1930	58.2
1940	48.8
1950	83.8
1960	103.1

SOURCE: 1840, 1880, 1900—Richard A. Easterlin, "Interregional Differences in Per
Capita Income, Population, and Total Income, 1840–1950," tables A-1, A-2, A-3, pp. 97–104,
in *Trends in the American Economy in the Nineteenth Century*, Studies in Income and
Wealth, vol. 24 (New York: National Bureau of Economic Research, 1960).
1920—Maurice Leven, *Income in the Various States* (New York: National Bureau of
Economic Research), pp. 249, 253–256.
1930, 1940, 1950—Charles F. Schwartz and Robert E. Graham, Jr., *Personal Income by
States since 1929* (Washington, D.C.: Government Printing Office, 1956), pp. 142–143.
1960—*Survey of Current Business* (August, 1964), table 2, p. 16.

per capita income, while the Great Lakes and Plains, which were just
beginning to be developed, had the lowest per capita income. The Southeast fell in between, close to the national per capita income; and the
Southwest, Rocky Mountain, and Far West were yet to come into the
Union. By 1880 all the states were settled with the exception of Oklahoma
in the Southwest. In 1880 the highest per capita incomes were in the

Rocky Mountain and Far West regions, although New England and the Mideast still held favorable positions above the national level of per capita income. Only the Southeast, Southwest, and Plains areas were below the national average. The Southeast, however, fell from 89 percent to 58 percent of the national per capita income. Thus, the impact of the Civil War was still seen 15 years later.

From 1880 to 1900 the relative positions of the regions remain about the same. After 1900 the relative position of the Rocky Mountain region falls from second to fifth. Per capita income falls to 86 percent of the national average in 1930. Another significant change after 1900 is the switch in the relative per capita incomes of New England and the Mideast. Both regions have per capita income above the national average for the whole period, but the Mideast rises above that of New England in 1920 and stays there.

From 1880 to 1960 there has been a tendency for the relative personal income per capita of each region to converge toward that of the nation. As personal income per capita for the nation has risen, per capita income in each region has come nearer to the national average in percentages. In 1880 per capita income ranged from 199 percent of the national average in the Far West to 58 percent of the national average in the Southeast. In 1960 per capita income ranged from 118 percent of the national average in the Far West to 72 percent of the national average in the Southeast. Nevertheless, the absolute dollar differences between per capita income in each region and the national average have not converged. The absolute difference of per capita income in the Southeast from the national average in 1880 was $162, while that of the Far West was $382. The absolute difference of per capita income in the Southeast from the national average in 1960 was $602, while that of the Far West was $387.

Short-run fluctuations of personal income in the separate regions of the United States can be studied only for the period since 1929 because annual data are not available for previous periods. Since 1929 there has been only one significant business cycle, that of the great depression. From a peak in 1929, national product and income declined to a low in 1933, and rose to another peak in 1937 before declining again. Another decline took place in 1938, but lasted for only a year. In the postwar period cyclical fluctuations in income have been so slight that they have been called recessions rather than depressions. These recessions are observed in quarterly and monthly data on income and product for the nation. State and regional data, however, are not available, except on an annual basis.[16] The postwar recessions

[16] A new series of quarterly estimates of state personal income is being developed by the Regional Economics Division of the Department of Commerce. See Edith T. Burton, "Quarterly Estimates of State Personal Income: A New Series," *Survey of Current Business* (December, 1966), pp. 13–15.

of 1949, 1954, 1958, and 1961 appear in the annual personal income figures either as a slight decline in one year for the nation and some regions, or as merely a decline in the rate of increase in income for one or two years. Nevertheless, there was substantial unemployment in the late 1950s and early 1960s.

Therefore, to illustrate the way in which different regions may react to short-run fluctuations in national income the depression of 1933 has been selected. Total personal income for the peak year 1929 is shown in Table 6-6 for the United States and each of eight regions. Instead of showing the actual income in the succeeding years to the next peak in 1937, only the ratios of the incomes in each year to that of 1929 in the respective regions are shown. The ratios facilitate comparison of the amplitude and duration of the cycles between the regions.

The first row of Table 6-6 shows that personal income in the United States declined each year from 1929 to 1933. In 1933 personal income was 55 percent of its 1929 high. By the time of the next peak in 1937, personal income had reached 86 percent of its previous high in 1929. The peak years for each region were the same as for the nation. The trough of the depression was in 1933 for each of the regions except in the Southwest. By 1932 personal income in the Southwest reached a low of 54 percent of its 1929 high and then remained at that level through 1933 before beginning to rise again. Thus, any differences in the timing of the cyclical fluctuations during this period are insignificant. Differences in timing might appear in monthly or quarterly data.

TABLE 6-6   1929 PERSONAL INCOME AND RATIO OF 1930–1937 INCOME TO 1929 INCOME, BY REGIONS (In millions of dollars)

Region*	1929	1930	1931	1932	1933	1934	1935	1936	1937
United States	$85,611	90	77	58	55	62	70	80	86
New England	7,125	92	82	66	62	68	72	81	84
Mideast	27,465	93	81	63	58	64	69	79	83
Great Lakes	20,235	86	71	52	48	57	66	76	85
Plains	7,584	90	74	56	50	55	72	74	85
Southeast	9,990	86	75	57	58	68	76	87	95
Southwest	4,254	86	72	54	54	60	70	79	90
Rocky Mountain	1,614	92	73	58	55	64	77	90	91
Far West	7,394	92	78	60	57	65	72	87	92

* For definitions of these regions, see Fig. 6-2.

SOURCE: Charles F. Schwartz and Robert E. Graham, Jr., *Personal Income by States since 1929* (Washington, D.C.: Government Printing Office, 1956), pp. 140–141.

The amplitude of the depression, however, varied with the regions. Personal income in New England, Mideast, Southeast, and Far West in 1933 did not fall as far below the 1929 high as that of the United States as a whole. Personal income in New England declined the least, while that of the Great Lakes declined the most. The decline of income in the Southwest and Plains regions may have been more a result of the "Dust Bowl" than a reaction to fluctuations in income elsewhere in the United States. Personal income in none of the regions surpassed their 1929 level, but income in the Southeast, Southwest, and Far West surpassed 1930 levels, which happened in none of the other regions.

We have now described some of the short- and long-run trends in large regions in the United States. In the next few chapters explanations for differences in short-run and long-run trends between regions will be discussed. In Chapter 7 the theory of short-run fluctuations in income will be discussed, along with reasons for the different amplitude of these cyclical fluctuations between regions. In Chapter 8 the short-run theory will be extended to incorporate the long-run forces causing change in income and per capita income.

INTERREGIONAL TRADE

So far we have shown the long- and short-run changes in total and per capita incomes in individual regions. We have not shown how the income accounts of one region are linked to other regions. In Table 6-4, we have already noted that part of the production of the region is purchased by other regions. The value of these exports was part of the value of production of the region under study. We also noted that production in each industry required inputs that were purchased from other regions. The value of these imports was not a part of the value of the region's production and had to be deducted from the value of total sales in the region of study. In order to concentrate on the interregional links in the accounting system the following model summarizes all final demand sectors into domestic final demand and exports.

Table 6-7 is a simple input-output matrix showing the interregional links in the accounting framework for three regions. The columns show the purchases made by a region, or the uses of income earned from production in the region. The rows show the distribution of a region's production.[17] In the more detailed accounting system net regional product was equal to the sum of consumption, net investment, government expenditures, and

[17] Lloyd Metzler, "A Multiple-region Theory of Income and Trade," *Econometrica* (October, 1950), pp. 329–336.

TABLE 6-7 SIMPLIFIED INTERREGIONAL INPUT-OUTPUT MATRIX*

	Purchases by region 1	Purchases by region 2	Purchases by region 3	Net regional product
Production in region 1	$C_1 - M_1$	M_{12}	M_{13}	Y_1
Production in region 2	M_{21}	$C_2 - M_2$	M_{23}	Y_2
Production in region 3	M_{31}	M_{32}	$C_3 - M_3$	Y_3
Total purchases by each region	C_1	C_2	C_3	

* C_i = net domestic final demand in region i and is equal to the sum of consumption, investment, and government expenditures less the capital consumption allowance. Consumption expenditures include purchases of local as well as imported goods and services.
M_i = total imports into region i.
M_{ji} = exports from region j to region i.
Y_i = net regional product for region i.
where i and j stand for regions 1, 2, and 3 where appropriate.

exports, less imports. In the abbreviated framework of Table 6-7, net regional product is equal to the sum of net domestic final demand and exports less imports. For example, the sum of the first three items in the first row in Table 6-7 is net regional product for region 1. This is the sum of net domestic final demand less imports plus exports to region 2 and region 3. The first column shows the regions from which goods and services were purchased by people in region 1. The purchases include those goods and services produced locally, which is net domestic final demand less imports; and imports from regions 2 and 3.

Since trade between states and regions in the United States is relatively free without customs at the border of each state, it is difficult to find statistics showing the exports and imports of regions within the United States.[18] Thus, there are no general accounts at the present time showing the above relationships between regions in the United States. Nevertheless, a few attempts have been made to detail exports and imports for particular regions within the United States. These have been done for regions in which exports and imports are more easily traced, such as Puerto Rico and Hawaii.[19] Many community studies have made estimates of the economic base of the community. These community studies have attempted to estimate the exports of a town or city.

[18] Trade barriers do exist, although border checks are not required as in international trade. See Edgar M. Hoover, *Location of Economic Activity* (New York: McGraw-Hill Book Company, 1948), pp. 216–222, and the literature cited there.
[19] For example, James C. Ingram, *Regional Payments Mechanisms: The Case of Puerto Rico* (Chapel Hill, N.C.: The University of North Carolina Press, 1962).

Since data are not directly available on exports and it is often too costly to make a direct survey, indirect methods have been used to estimate exports.[20] Among several indirect approaches the location quotient has been the most widely used. Furthermore, since product accounts are not available for regions (only the personal income estimate is available) employment data are used instead.[21] Employment data are available by community in fairly good industry detail. The first step is to calculate the national employment in each industry and divide it by total employment in the United States. This ratio yields the percentage of national employment devoted to each industry. Now, we assume that if every state were self-sufficient and had the same economic structure as the nation, it would have the same percentage of employment in each industry as the nation. Therefore, for each region the ratio of the employment in each industry is divided by the total regional employment. If the regional ratio for each industry is divided by the national ratio for each industry, the new ratios are location quotients, which indicate exports and imports for each region. Quotients greater than 1 indicate industries exporting from a region, because the percentage of employment in the industry is greater in the region than in the nation. Quotients less than 1 indicate industries importing into a region, because the percentage of employment in the industry is less in the region than in the nation.

A further refinement of the technique is to calculate the total number of employees that would be expected in an industry in a particular region if that region had the same percentage of employment in that industry as the nation. The estimated employment is subtracted from the actual employment. If the actual employment is greater than the expected employment, the extra workers are considered to be producers of exports. Summing all this export employment in all industries yields total export employment. The percentage that export employment is of total employment is assumed to be equal to the percentage that exports are of total production.

Estimating exports on the basis of employment is crude at best. Employment figures do not take into account differences in productivity between regions, nor do they take into account differences in value added per worker in different industries in the same community or region. An alternative that partially corrects for these errors is to substitute value added by

[20] A good elementary discussion of these techniques is in Charles M. Tiebout, *The Community Economic Base Study*, Supplementary Paper no. 16 (Committee for Economic Development, December, 1962).
[21] With the availability of the estimates of state personal income, substate regional income estimates have been easier to make. For details, see Walter Isard, *Methods of Regional Analysis* (Cambridge, Mass.: The M.I.T. Press, 1960), Chap. 4.

each industry in each region for employment in each industry in each region and to substitute personal income in each region for total employment in the region. Value added takes into account the differences in productivity between industries, and personal income takes into account the different impact of earning power on markets between regions.

The first step in estimating this alternative measure of the location quotient is to calculate the ratio of value added for each industry in the nation to total personal income for the nation. The second step is to calculate the ratio of value added for each industry in each region to the total personal income for that region. Dividing the second ratio by the first ratio for each industry and region gives the estimate of the location quotient for each industry in each region. A ratio above 1, as before, indicates an export; a ratio below 1 indicates an import; and a ratio equal to 1 indicates that production is equal to consumption.

Table 6-8 shows the location quotients in the nine census regions of the United States for each of several manufacturing industry groups in 1962. By reading down a column, say the first column listing the location quotient for each of the industries in New England, the exports and imports of the region may be tentatively identified. According to the location quotients, New England exports textile mill products, paper and allied products, rubber and plastic products, leather and leather products, fabricated metal products, machinery, and instruments. Another way to read the table is across the rows. For example, food and kindred products are produced in every region, and the location quotients are nearly 1 in every region. Nevertheless, the West North Central Region and the East North Central Region would appear to be exporting regions, while the New England, South Atlantic, and Mountain Regions would appear to be importers. Tobacco production shows a clearer trading pattern. The South Atlantic and East South Central Regions export tobacco products to the other regions of the United States.

The location quotient method, however, is still unsatisfactory.[22] The first main criticism is that the technique assumes that households in every region have the same tastes and expenditure patterns. This is simply not true. People in California do not buy as many hats as people in New England. People in the north consume far more coal and fuel than people in the south. Similarly, people in the north buy houses with more insulation and central furnaces than people in southern areas. Thus, the location quotient of 0.29 for petroleum and coal products in the South Atlantic Region may indicate more importing of these products than actually takes

[22] The discussion in Chap. 4 of the implication of interindustry sales relating to the coefficient of localization is also applicable to the location quotient.

TABLE 6-8   LOCATION QUOTIENTS FOR SELECTED MANUFAC-
TURING INDUSTRIES IN UNITED STATES REGIONS, 1962

Industry	New England	Middle Atlantic	East North Central	West North Central	South Atlantic	East South Central	West South Central	Mountain	Pacific
All manufacturing	1.15	1.07	1.38	0.78	0.86	1.00	0.71	0.49	0.79
Food and kindred products	0.60	0.92	1.18	1.54	0.81	1.09	0.93	0.81	1.00
Tobacco products	—	0.34	—	—	5.77	3.82	—	—	—
Textile mill products	2.15	0.89	—	—	4.32	1.64	0.13	—	0.11
Apparel and related products	0.98	2.36	0.44	0.45	0.94	1.69	0.46	—	0.45
Lumber and wood products	0.72	0.32	0.50	0.51	1.07	1.80	1.01	1.35	2.65
Furniture and fixtures	0.77	0.85	1.23	0.45	1.81	1.33	0.66	—	0.78
Paper and allied products	1.68	0.91	1.17	0.66	1.21	1.38	0.79	0.19	0.78
Printing and publishing products	1.02	1.61	1.16	0.91	0.63	0.58	0.53	0.49	0.67
Chemicals and allied products	0.46	1.21	0.99	0.66	1.39	1.82	1.58	0.27	0.42
Petroleum and coal	—	0.61	0.90	0.68	0.29	0.38	4.87	0.97	1.02
Rubber and plastics	2.37	0.85	1.78	0.59	0.44	1.20	0.43	—	—
Leather and leather products	4.52	1.18	0.83	1.28	0.33	1.33	—	0.27	—
Stone, clay, and glass products	0.74	0.99	1.26	0.99	1.00	1.16	0.95	0.33	0.78
Primary metal industries	0.68	1.21	2.00	0.30	0.58	1.13	0.47	0.39	0.44
Fabricated metal products	1.35	1.02	1.81	0.68	0.47	0.84	0.53	0.24	0.73
Machinery, except electrical	1.63	0.94	2.10	0.88	0.31	0.49	0.53	0.27	0.54
Electrical machinery	1.63	1.27	1.54	0.56	0.45	0.80	0.30	—	0.85
Transport equipment	0.83	0.54	2.07	0.95	0.47	—	0.42	—	1.27
Instruments and related products	1.95	2.07	0.91	0.78	—	—	0.21	—	—

* For definitions of these regions, see Fig. 6-3.

SOURCE: Calculated from data in U.S. Bureau of the Census, *Annual Survey of Manu-facturers* (1962); and U.S. Bureau of the Census, "Personal Income by States," *Statistical Abstract of the United States* (1965), p. 334.

place. If the quotient had been 1, it could easily have indicated exports because of the lower fuel consumption per dollar of income in the South Atlantic.

The second main criticism is that the aggregation into industry groupings of plants producing many different items hides products that are totally exported. For example, the location quotient for food and beverages in the Pacific Region is 1.00. Food and beverage products include meat packing, grain products, dairy products, soda bottling, canning, preserving, freezing, bakeries, breweries, and wineries. The quotient of 1 would indicate no exports from this region of food and beverage products, and yet the Pacific Region is a major exporter of wine and canned fish, fruit, and vegetables.

SUMMARY

To measure economic activity it is necessary to bound a region. Any definition of a region is arbitrary and depends upon the purpose of a particular study. Once the region is defined, a regional accounting framework can be shown to provide the necessary data for short- and long-run economic analysis. The framework itself is dependent on the type of economic analysis proposed. Thus, the measures of economic activity suggested in this chapter are a reflection of the subsequent analysis in the next two chapters.

The many problems and costs encountered in attempting to fill the empty cells in the accounting framework described in this chapter have prevented the full development of aggregative economic measurement at the regional level. Another major problem has been forecasting income and employment by regions. Although the conceptual framework of the accounts leads into interregional income and employment theory of the next chapter, only qualitative statements with respect to the cyclical fluctuations of income will be possible to empirically implement the analysis based on the accounting framework of this chapter. Nevertheless, the concepts and the analysis which follow do contribute to our understanding of the economic stability of regions.

CHAPTER 7

INTERREGIONAL
THEORY
OF INCOME
AND TRADE

The meanings of the short run and the long run are different for different aspects of economic analysis. In the chapter on the location of the individual producer the long run was a planning horizon during which the firm was free to change the scale of its plant or even decide whether to shut down completely. The short run in the same context is the period during which the firm already has a plant and will not be able to change its scale. The problem then is not an investment problem nor a location problem, but a problem of how to price the product and what output to produce so that profits will be greatest, or losses least, given the previous investment. In this chapter the short run will mean the time period over which changes in the location of economic activity, changes in investment, or changes in export demand will result in changes in total income and employment rather than changes in wages and prices. During a short period of time wages will be sluggish. Rather than take a wage cut workers will prefer to be unemployed for a brief period. The following short-run analysis assumes that there are no changes in technology, wages, prices, the distribution of income, and resources in the economy.

SHORT-RUN MODEL OF AN OPEN ECONOMY[1]

In the last chapter we showed that the net product or income of a region was the sum of consumption expenditures, investment, government expenditures, and the value of exports of the region, less the value of imported raw materials, intermediate goods, and goods for final use. In the short run the level of imports, consumption, and investment will depend upon the income of the region. Imports, of course, will also depend upon exports, since imports may be used to produce goods for export.

The demand for the resources and products of any region is the sum of all the individual demands on their resources and products. The quantity of goods demanded depends upon price, income, and tastes. In the short run we shall assume that prices and tastes are given. Therefore, total

[1] Lloyd Metzler, "A Multiple-region Theory of Income and Trade," *Econometrica* (October, 1950), pp. 329–354. Those who have difficulty with the basic economic concepts should consult a good economics text such as Paul A. Samuelson, *Economics*, 6th ed. (New York: McGraw-Hill Book Company, 1964), pp. 179–267, 635–660. A recent advanced article on this topic is Joseph Airov, "The Construction of Interregional Business Cycle Models," *Journal of Regional Science* (Summer, 1963), pp. 1–20.

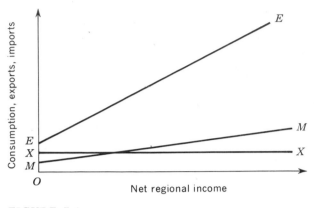

FIGURE 7-1

consumption, investment, and import expenditures depend upon the total level of income in the region. Income varies with the use of resources, including labor, owned by households. The exports of a region will depend upon the income of the regions to which the exports are shipped. All but import purchases are demands upon the local region.

Thus, we might show the relation between total expenditures on consumption, investment, and government and total income by the line EE in Figure 7-1. The line MM shows the way imports vary with income. Exports depend on income in other regions, not on incomes in the exporting region, and so the line XX showing exports varying with domestic income is a constant. The aggregate demand for the region's production is the sum of the expenditures (EE) and exports (XX) less imports (MM). Let $E'E'$ in Figure 7-2 represent the result of this summation. This line $E'E'$ then shows the aggregate demand for the region's products as its net income changes in the short run.

The line OY in Figure 7-2 shows a supply curve. Since prices and wages are constant, the horizontal axis measures not only income, but use of resources. The higher the income, the more resources are being used. If income falls, it is because workers are unemployed, or some capital is unemployed and its owner is not receiving his interest or profits. The line OY can be said to depict the level of factor income generated by the level of employment of resources measured on the horizontal axis in dollars.

Thus, $E'E'$ shows the level of desired expenditures or purchases against the region's resources and OY shows the level of income generated in the region from production. For levels of income or use of resources less than

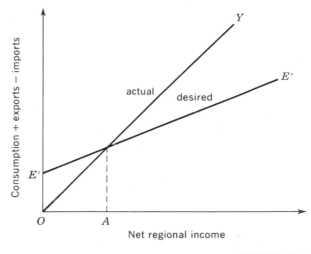

FIGURE 7-2

OA, desired expenditures are greater than incomes. Firms would find that their inventories were falling below desired levels and they would increase production. For levels of income above OA, firms would find that inventories were building above desired levels and they would reduce production. Employment and income would then fall in the short run. Therefore, there would be a tendency for employment and income to approach the level OA. Under our present assumptions there is nothing that assures us that this level should be one at which all the region's resources are fully employed.

Observed levels of income, however, will always fall on the line OY, whether the region is near equilibrium or not. If the economy should find itself below OA, the *desired* level of expenditures is greater than *actual* income. The businessmen intended to invest more in inventories, but they found after the fact that they could not maintain their intended targets because consumers purchased them. If the economy finds itself above OA, the *desired* level of expenditures is less than the *actual* income. Businessmen intended to invest less in inventories, but they found after the fact that they could not sell as much as they thought so that inventories built up greater than intended. Only at OA is *intended* purchases equal to *actual* purchases and income.

Now suppose that demand for the region's exports should rise. There are a number of reasons why this might happen. There may have been a change in taste for the products of this region. Technological change may

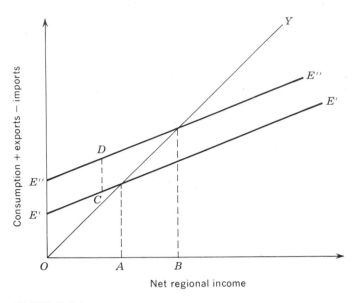

FIGURE 7-3

have made the region a more accessible source for the product to a larger market. For some reason exports increase. The line XX in Figure 7-1 shifts upward by the amount of the increase. Exports do not vary with the income of the region, so that XX remains parallel to the horizontal axis in Figure 7-1. The upward parallel shift in exports causes exactly the same upward shift in the demand for the region's products, the curve $E'E'$ in Figure 7-2. Thus, the new demand for the region's products is $E''E''$ in Figure 7-3, which has the same slope as $E'E'$ but is vertically higher by the increase in exports. CD in Figure 7-3 is the increase in exports. After this change, income will tend toward OB rather than OA, since OB will then be the level of income at which desired expenditures will equal actual expenditures.

Not only can we demonstrate that an increase in exports will cause an increase in income and employment, but we can also indicate how much the increase in income will tend to be so long as exports are maintained at the new higher level. An increase in income resulting from the increase in exports will initially be equal to the increase in exports. This increase in income, however, is earned by local households from wages, interest, and profits earned from producing the exported products. With the increase in income the households will increase their spending by some proportion. In the aggregate this is equal to the additional expenditures divided by the additional income. This is the same as the slope of EE in Figure 7-1. Part of these expenditures end up in imports. Therefore, to find the income generated by the expenditures of households producing exports, we must subtract the incremental increases in imports resulting from the increase in income. The resulting proportion showing the increase in expenditures generating local income from an increase in income is the slope of the $E'E'$ schedule. The slope of the $E'E'$ schedule is the marginal propensity to spend locally. It is the marginal propensity to consume (slope of EE) less the marginal propensity to import (slope of MM).

These local purchases by the families whose incomes increased from exporting cause a second-round increase in income. These increases will cause a second-round increase in expenditures. For example, suppose that the marginal propensity to consume out of increases in income is 50 percent and the marginal propensity to import is 30 percent; the marginal propensity to spend locally would be 20 percent. Thus, an initial increase of $100 in exports would cause a direct increase of $100 in incomes in the export sector plus $20 (.20 × $100) in other sectors providing goods to households in the export sector plus $4 (0.20 × 0.20 × $100) created by the expenditures of the second-round earners. These rounds of increased expenditures take place quickly and the total increase in income rapidly approaches $125.

Algebraically it is the sum of an infinite geometric series such as the following:

$$dX + sdX + s^2dX + s^3dX + s^4dX + \cdots$$

where dX is the change in exports and s is the marginal propensity to consume less the marginal propensity to import. The sum of such a series can be shown to be equal to the following:

$$\frac{1}{1-s}dX$$

The term $1/(1-s)$ is called the multiplier. In the above case the multiplier was $1/[1-(.50-.30)] = 1.25$. With the given assumptions an increase in exports would cause the equilibrium level of income to rise 1.25 times the initial increase in exports.

Once resources are fully employed, however, there can be no further increases in real income to the region. The only ways that increased product and income could come about would be by increases in population via natural growth or migration, by increases in capital equipment, and by new finds in natural resources. It is true that in the short run a region might expect increases in prices as the demand for the region's resources and product exceeded the potential supply.

Three other comments are appropriate. First, the multiplier may work in either direction. An increase in exports will cause a multiple increase in income, but a decrease in exports will cause income to decrease by the same multiple. Second, other changes can have the same impact on the equilibrium level of income. For example, a change in taste or in business expectations may cause an upward shift in desired spending at each level of income. The line EE in Figure 7-1 may shift up or down. The amount of the shift will have the same impact on the level of income as a shift in exports. Shifts in the import function can also cause the same impact. In this case, however, an upward shift in imports would cause a downward change in income, while a downward shift in imports would cause an upward shift in income. Third, the multiplier is an *underestimate* of the likely increase in regional income. The reason is that as income increases the amount of imports from other regions will increase. This will cause incomes in other regions to increase because their exports have increased. As incomes in other regions increase, the other regions will buy more exports from the region in question with the original increase in exports and income, so that exports will shift upward again. This will cause further increases in the equilibrium level of income in the region with the initial increase in exports and income.[2]

---

[2] The simple model presented in this section can be described mathematically as follows: The accounting equation is

$$(1) \quad Y = E + X - M$$

where

Y = net regional product
E = expenditures on net investment, consumption, and government
X = exports
M = imports

The expenditure relations are as follows:

$$(2) \quad E = a + bY$$
$$(3) \quad M = c + eY$$
$$(4) \quad X = \bar{x}$$

where

a = level of expenditures when Y is zero
b = marginal propensity to spend
c = level of imports when Y is zero
e = marginal propensity to import
$\bar{x}$ = given level of exports

Substituting (2), (3), and (4) into (1), we obtain the following solution for the equilibrium level of income:

$$Y = a + bY + \bar{x} - c - eY$$
$$(5) \quad Y = \frac{a - c + \bar{x}}{1 - (b - e)}$$

The change in the equilibrium level of income with respect to a change in $\bar{x}$, a, or c is equal

ECONOMIC BASE STUDIES[3]

As noted in Chapter 6, data on income by small areas are not available in sufficient detail to work out the above model and calculate the multiplier for a particular region. In its place economic base studies have been developed. Because of the availability of employment data by small areas, these studies usually use employment as a proxy for production and income in a region. Then, on the basis of the location quotient, some modification of the quotient, or a survey, total employment for the region is split into the number of employees producing goods for export (basic employment) and the number producing goods solely for local consumption (nonbasic employment).

If we assume that employment is proportional to income, the proportion of income spent locally may be calculated. In our previous model this would be total expenditures less imports divided by total income. In this employment model the proportion of income spent locally is total employment generated by local consumption (nonbasic employment) divided by total employment. Imports are indirectly taken into account because only income spent locally generates local employment. Moreover, if we can assume that the average propensity to spend is equal to the marginal propensity to spend, the multiplier can be calculated. This is an uneasy assumption. It means that the aggregate spending curve $E'E'$ in Figure 7-2, after subtracting exports, goes through the origin and is a straight line. The assumption presumes that the marginal propensity to spend locally will not change with different levels of total regional income.

Under these assumptions the multiplier is as follows:

$$dY = \frac{1}{1 - s} dX$$

where dY is the change in total employment as a proxy for income, dX is the change in basic employment as a proxy for exports, and s is the proportion of nonbasic employment to total employment as a proxy for the mar-

---

to the multiplier:

$$\frac{dY}{d\bar{x}} = \frac{1}{1 - (b - e)}$$

A change in $\bar{x}$ is a change in exports. A change in a is an upward or downward shift in the EE curve described by equation (2). A change in c is a similar shift in the MM curve, described by equation (3). b and e in the multiplier are the marginal propensities. $(b - e)$ is the marginal propensity to spend locally.

[3] The basic references for this section are Charles M. Tiebout, "The Urban Economic Base Reconsidered," *Land Economics* (February, 1956), pp. 95–99; Charles M. Tiebout, *The Community Economic Base Study*, Supplementary Paper no. 16 (Committee for Economic Development, December, 1962); Walter Isard, *Methods of Regional Analysis* (Cambridge, Mass.: The M.I.T. Press, 1960), pp. 189–205; and Ralph Pfouts (ed.), *The Techniques of Urban Economic Analysis* (West Trenton, N.J.: Chandler-Davis Publishing Co., 1960), in which the above article by Tiebout also appears.

ginal propensity to spend locally. Economic base studies usually show the multiplier as the ratio of total employment to basic employment. This is exactly the same. It can be shown in the following way:

$$\frac{1}{1-s} = \frac{1}{1 - \dfrac{\text{nonbasic employment}}{\text{total employment}}}$$

$$= \frac{1}{\dfrac{\text{basic employment}}{\text{total employment}}}$$

$$= \frac{\text{total employment}}{\text{basic employment}}$$

The economic base multiplier is then often used for forecasting the future growth of a region. The impact of the growth or decline of the basic (or exporting) industries on base employment is forecast. Then the change in basic employment is multiplied by the economic base multiplier to find out the future change in total employment. The implication of the procedure is that exports are basic to the growth of a region. Exports, however, are not the only way that regional income may be increased. This will be discussed in more detail in the next chapter. Furthermore, the whole rationale of the procedure is the short-run theory of income and trade. Thus, the multiplier is only useful for understanding the short-run impact of exports or other changes on the level of income and employment in a region. In the long run the variables held constant in the analysis may change and other kinds of changes in income and employment may take place.

Several other comments on economic base studies should also be made. In using employment instead of incomes or value added, several problems arise. Different occupations receive different wages. An expansion in a high-wage industry will have a greater secondary impact through the multiplier than expansion in a low-wage industry. Using employment figures neglects increases in output made possible by increases in productivity per worker. It also neglects property income, which may be high in some communities.

Conceptually, the multiplier is a short-run concept that takes time to work out its full effect. It depends upon the stability over time of the marginal propensity to consume and to import. From consumer studies we are sure that there is a fairly stable relation between consumption and income. But more is needed to use the multiplier for forecasting. The multiplier calculated above was based on the average propensity to consume. The marginal propensity is what is needed for these calculations. In fact the marginal propensity to spend locally tends to increase as the population and income of a region increase. The reason is that the marginal propensity to import decreases. Increases in employment and income increase the size of the market and make possible production of some items locally which were impossible before growth because the market was insufficient to support a minimum size plant.

Several statistical studies have indicated that the basic-nonbasic ratio is unstable over time and different between places, as would be expected from the above considerations.[4] Notice that this does not disprove the theory. It does cast doubt upon the empirical implementation of economic base studies for long-run forecasts.

IMPACT STUDIES

Although the economic base study has been found faulty and clearly unsuitable for long-run forecasting, its theoretical foundation is sound. Since the theory is short-run in concept, we may be able to utilize it for other kinds of studies. One of these studies is the analysis of the short-run impact of an event on the economy of a region. With suitable modification the economic base approach can be combined with an input-output framework to yield multipliers that will indicate the impact on a regional economy of a change in demand for a particular activity. What adjustments will be required, if the demand for coal decreases? What adjustments will need to take place, if a military base is moved from a town? What is the impact of introducing a major league professional baseball club into a community? These are a few of the questions for which short-run answers may be appropriate.

One framework for these kinds of analyses is the input-output framework used as an analytical tool, rather than as the descriptive framework previously presented. The major difficulty, as mentioned before, is collecting the data. A useful modification that requires less data is the intersectoral flows approach.[5]

The intersectoral flows approach begins with a survey to determine the percentage of each firm's sales to the same industry, other industries, domestic market sectors (such as households, investment, and local government), exports to the Federal Government, and other exports. These exports could also be classified by regions of destination. No sales figures are asked for—only estimates of the percentage distribution of

[4] Ralph Pfouts, "An Empirical Testing of the Economic Base Theory," *Journal of the American Institute of Planners*, vol. 23 (Spring, 1957), pp. 64–69; Ralph W. Pfouts and Erle T. Curtis, "Limitations of the Economic Base Analysis," *Social Forces*, vol. 36 (May, 1958), pp. 303–310. Both are reprinted in Pfouts, *op. cit.*, pp. 292–324.
[5] W. Lee Hansen and Charles M. Tiebout, "An Intersectoral Flows Analysis of the California Economy," *The Review of Economics and Statistics*, vol. 45 (November, 1963), pp. 409–418.

TABLE 7-1 DISTRIBUTION OF TOTAL EMPLOYMENT TO DEMAND SECTORS AND LOCAL INDUSTRIES, STATE OF CALIFORNIA, 1960* (Percentage distribution shown as the top entry; employment distribution in thousands enclosed in parentheses)

Demand sectors and industry groups to:

Industry groups from:	(1) Agriculture, forestry, fisheries, and mining	(2) Contract construction	(3) Transportation, communication, and public utilities	(4) Retail trade	(5) Finance, insurance, and real estate	(6) Services	(7) All manufacturing industries	(8) Primary metals	(9) Fabricated metals	(10) Nonelectrical machinery	(11) Electrical machinery	(12) Transportation equipment	(13) Instruments and ordnance	(14) Stone, clay, and glass	(15) Lumber products	(16) Furniture	(17) Miscellaneous manufactures
1. Durable manufactures	1.8 (16.4)	3.1 (28.2)	0.8 (7.7)	6.5 (59.6)	0.2 (1.8)	0.2 (1.8)	21.4 (195.9)	0.3 (3.0)	4.9 (44.4)	1.1 (9.6)	1.5 (13.7)	6.0 (55.3)	2.6 (24.1)	0.2 (1.4)	1.5 (13.3)	0.3 (3.1)	0.5 (4.6)
2. Primary metals		6.9 (3.5)	0.6 (0.6)	1.2 (0.6)			44.0 (25.1)	3.7 (1.9)	23.3 (11.9)	8.0 (4.1)	2.2 (1.1)	4.1 (2.1)	2.9 (1.5)			2.2 (1.1)	3.0 (2.9)
3. Fabricated metals	0.1 (0.1)	8.2 (7.8)	0.6 (0.6)	6.4 (6.1)		0.1 (0.1)	46.8 (44.5)	0.7 (0.7)	24.5 (23.2)	4.9 (4.1)	0.6 (0.6)	4.3 (4.1)	3.4 (3.2)	0.4 (0.4)	0.4 (0.4)	0.8 (0.8)	
4. Nonelectrical machinery	1.0	1.0	0.6 (0.5)	0.3 (0.3)			5.4 (4.8)			1.0 (0.9)	0.7 (0.6)	1.3 (1.2)	0.7 (0.6)				
5. Electrical machinery	0.9	0.7 (1.0)	0.1 (0.1)	4.0 (6.0)		0.1 (0.1)	11.8 (17.6)				4.5 (6.7)	4.8 (7.2)	2.4 (3.6)			0.1 (0.1)	0.1 (0.4)
6. Transportation equipment			1.8 (5.4)	4.4 (12.9)		0.4 (1.3)	18.0 (52.7)		2.8 (8.1)	1.2 (3.6)	0.2 (0.2)	9.2 (26.7)	4.7 (13.7)				
7. Instruments and ordnance			0.5 (0.5)	0.1 (0.1)		0.1 (0.1)	23.3 (17.5)				5.9 (4.4)		16.7 (12.5)				
8. Stone, clay, and glass	1.8 (0.8)	9.7 (4.3)	0.4	34.5 (15.2)		0.1 (0.1)	19.5 (8.6)	0.5 (0.2)	0.5 (0.2)					2.0 (0.9)			0.2 (0.1)
9. Lumber products	23.8 (14.3)	13.5 (8.1)		0.8 (0.5)			26.8 (15.4)	0.2 (0.1)	0.2 (0.1)			0.8 (0.5)	1.3 (0.8)	0.2 (0.1)	21.4 (12.8)		
10. Furniture and fixtures	0.3 (0.1)	5.1 (1.8)	1.1 (0.4)	43.6 (15.4)		0.3 (0.1)	5.6 (2.0)					2.5 (0.9)				3.1 (1.1)	
11. Miscellaneous manufactures	0.8 (0.2)	3.6 (0.8)	1.4 (0.3)	11.3 (2.5)		0.5 (0.1)	34.8 (7.7)	0.5 (0.1)				0.5 (0.1)	0.5 (0.1)		0.5 (0.1)		5.4 (1.2)
12. Nondurable manufactures	3.6 (16.0)	1.6	3.4 (15.0)	32.2 (142.5)	0.7 (3.3)	0.9 (4.0)	12.4 (54.0)	0.5 (2.3)	0.8 (3.5)	0.5 (2.0)	0.1 (0.3)	1.0 (4.6)	0.4 (1.9)	0.1 (0.3)	0.2 (0.2)	0.3 (1.2)	0.3 (1.2)
13. Apparel	1.1 (0.7)	0.2 (0.1)	0.3 (0.2)	45.2 (28.2)			1.1 (0.7)										
14. Textile-leather	0.8 (0.1)			58.3 (7.4)			1.6 (0.2)										
15. Paper	2.9 (0.8)	6.9 (1.9)	1.8 (0.5)	20.1 (5.5)	2.9 (0.8)	0.4 (0.1)	28.1 (7.7)				0.7 (0.2)	0.7 (0.2)					1.5 (0.4)

Demand sectors and industry groups to:

Industry groups from:	(18) Apparel	(19) Textile-leather	(20) Paper	(21) Printing	(22) Chemicals	(23) Petroleum	(24) Rubber	(25) Foods and beverages	(26) All industry groups	(27) Exports, private (X_p)	(28) Exports, government (X_g)	(29) Local consumption (C)	(30) Investment, business (I_B)	(31) Investment, housing (I_H)	(32) Government, current (G_c)	(33) Government Investment (G_I)	(34) Total employment
1. Durable manufactures			0.1 (0.6)	0.1 (0.6)	0.9 (8.5)	0.4 (3.2)	(0.4)	1.1 (10.1)	34.1 (311.6)	21.2 (194.0)	34.5 (315.1)	2.2 (19.9)	6.9 (62.7)		0.6 (5.4)	0.5 (4.8)	100.0 (913.5)
2. Primary metals			0.5 (0.3)			2.2 (1.1)			51.2 (29.2)	15.3	12.0 (6.1)	8.2 (4.2)	4.7 (2.4)		1.6	1.0	100.0
3. Fabricated metals			0.3 (0.3)		1.5 (1.4)	1.9 (1.8)	0.1 (0.1)	2.9 (3.7)	64.1 (61.0)	18.3 (17.3)	12.5	2.4 (2.3)	0.8 (0.8)		0.8 (1.4)	0.5 (0.5)	100.0 (57.0)
4. Nonelectrical machinery							0.7 (0.6)		(7.5)	53.4 (47.8)	10.7 (9.6)	0.3	26.2 (23.5)		(0.9)	(1.0)	100.0 (95.1)
5. Electrical machinery									16.5	26.2 (41.8)	26.2	0.3	14.5 (21.7)		(0.9)	0.7 (1.1)	100.0 (89.6)
6. Transportation equipment									24.8	10.8 (39.2)	61.7	0.2 (0.3)	2.5 (7.2)		0.2 (0.6)	0.1 (0.3)	100.0 (149.4)
7. Instruments and ordnance									24.7	61.7 (31.4)	62.4	0.2 (0.6)	7.2		0.1 (0.1)	0.1	100.0 (292.0)
8. Stone, clay, and glass					1.6 (0.7)	0.5 (0.3)	0.5 (0.2)	14.5 (6.4)	72.3	17.4 (180.2)	56.9 (42.7)	0.4 (0.3)	0.8 (0.6)		1.1	0.3	100.0 (75.0)
9. Lumber products					0.5 (0.3)		0.2 (0.1)		24.1 (18.1)	25.2 (13.0)	0.7	5.9 (2.6)	1.4 (0.6)		0.5 (0.1)	0.2	100.0 (44.1)
10. Furniture and fixtures									65.5 (28.9)	21.6 (11.1)	2.5 (1.5)	8.9 (5.3)	0.3 (0.2)		2.5 (1.5)	0.8 (0.2)	100.0 (59.8)
11. Miscellaneous manufactures					27.6 (6.1)				64.0 (38.3)	13.3 (12.9)	0.8 (0.3)	10.2 (3.6)	15.8 (5.6)		1.4	2.5 (0.9)	100.0 (35.4)
12. Nondurable manufactures	(0.2)	0.1 (0.3)	0.1 (0.6)	2.9 (12.8)	1.4 (6.0)	0.3 (1.5)	1.2 (5.2)	2.4 (10.6)	55.9 (19.8)	40.7 (4.7)	0.9 (0.1)	1.8 (0.4)	0.5 (0.1)		0.5	0.8 (0.2)	100.0 (22.1)
13. Apparel	0.8 (0.1)	0.1 (0.3)							52.5 (11.6)	25.5 (9.0)	3.1 (13.7)	14.3 (63.1)	0.7 (2.9)		2.7 (0.6)	0.7 (0.4)	100.0 (442.7)
14. Textile-leather	0.8 (0.1)								54.8 (242.8)	40.1 (112.5)	3.7 (2.3)	4.0 (2.5)			7.3		100.0 (62.4)
15. Paper				0.7 (0.2)	1.5 (0.4)	0.7 (0.3)		22.3 (6.1)	47.9 (29.9)	31.5 (4.0)	3.1 (0.4)	4.7 (0.6)	0.7 (0.2)		4.3 (2.7)	1.5 (0.4)	100.0 (12.7)
									60.6 (7.7)	31.8 (8.7)	0.4	2.2 (0.6)			2.2		100.0 (27.4)

TABLE 7-1 DISTRIBUTION OF TOTAL EMPLOYMENT TO DEMAND SECTORS AND LOCAL INDUSTRIES, STATE OF CALIFORNIA, 1960* (Percentage distribution shown as the top entry; employment distribution in thousands enclosed in parentheses) (Continued)

Demand sectors and industry groups to:

Industry groups from:	Agriculture, forestry, fisheries, and mining (1)	Contract construction (2)	Transportation, communication, and public utilities (3)	Retail trade (4)	Finance, insurance, and real estate (5)	Services (6)	All manufacturing industries (7)	Primary metals (8)	Fabricated metals (9)	Nonelectrical machinery (10)	Electrical machinery (11)	Transportation equipment (12)	Instruments and ordnance (13)	Stone, clay, and glass (14)	Lumber products (15)	Furniture (16)	Miscellaneous manufactures (17)
16. Printing	0.1 (0.1)	1.5 (1.1)	9.5 (7.0)	19.7 (14.4)	2.6 (1.9)	2.7 (2.0)	24.2 (17.8)	0.5 (0.4)	0.1 (0.1)	0.4 (0.3)	0.1 (0.1)	2.7 (2.0)	0.3 (0.2)	0.1 (0.1)	0.3 (0.2)	0.1 (0.1)	0.4 (0.3)
17. Chemicals		3.2	1.7 (0.7)	9.0			15.4 (6.3)	1.0 (0.4)	2.9 (1.2)	0.5 (0.2)		1.2 (0.5)	0.5 (0.2)	0.5 (0.2)			
18. Petroleum		1.3	20.2 (6.6)	31.1 (10.1)			18.4 (6.0)										
19. Rubber	2.6 (0.7)	1.8 (0.6)		5.2 (1.4)			31.5 (8.4)	4.6 (1.5)	4.6 (1.5)	4.6 (1.5)		4.1 (1.1)	5.6 (1.5)			4.1 (1.1)	1.9 (0.5)
20. Foods and beverages	8.2 (13.6)	8.6 (2.3)		43.1 (71.8)		5.2 (1.7)	4.6 (7.6)		2.6 (0.7)								
21. Total manufacturing	2.4 (32.4)	2.6 (35.5)	1.8 (22.7)	14.9 (202.1)	0.4 (0.6)	0.4 (5.8)	18.5 (250.6)	0.4 (5.3)	3.5 (47.9)	0.9 (11.6)	1.0 (14.0)	4.4 (59.9)	1.9 (26.0)	0.1 (1.7)	1.0 (13.5)	0.3 (4.3)	0.4 (5.8)
22. Agriculture, forestry, fisheries, and mining	6.5 (32.9)			12.0 (60.9)	0.4 (5.1)		51.6 (262.5)	0.3 (1.7)						1.9 (9.5)	0.1 (0.7)		
23. Contract construction																	
24. Transportation, communication, and public utilities	4.9 (18.2)	2.3 (8.4)	2.2 (8.3)	10.7 (40.7)	2.0 (7.3)	5.7 (21.1)	14.6 (54.4)	0.6 (2.1)	1.0 (3.8)	0.9 (3.5)	1.6 (6.0)	3.1 (11.7)	0.8 (3.1)	0.5 (1.8)	0.6 (2.4)	0.4 (1.4)	0.2 (0.8)
25. Wholesale trade	0.6 (1.8)	11.5 (37.1)	0.4 (1.3)	61.4 (197.1)	0.3 (1.1)	1.5 (4.7)	20.5 (65.7)	0.7 (2.2)	1.3 (4.0)	1.2 (3.7)	2.3 (7.3)	4.4 (14.1)	1.1 (3.4)	0.6 (1.9)	0.8 (2.5)	0.5 (1.5)	0.3 (0.9)
26. Retail trade	0.7 (6.7)	3.6 (33.8)	0.1 (1.0)				6.4 (16.7)										
27. Finance, insurance, and real estate	2.1 (6.7)	1.4 (3.7)	1.6 (4.3)	4.6 (12.1)	1.1 (2.7)	3.3 (8.7)		0.2 (0.6)	0.5 (1.3)	0.4 (1.1)	0.6 (1.7)	1.4 (3.6)	0.3 (0.7)	0.2 (0.6)	0.2 (0.6)	0.2 (0.4)	0.1 (0.2)
28. Services	0.5 (4.9)	0.4 (3.5)	0.7 (6.7)	4.8 (44.5)	1.3 (11.8)	2.2 (20.5)	6.0 (56.2)	0.2 (2.2)	0.4 (4.1)	0.4 (3.8)	0.7 (6.4)	1.1 (10.0)	0.3 (3.2)	0.2 (1.9)	0.3 (2.6)	0.2 (1.5)	0.1 (0.9)
29. Government																	
30. Total employment	1.7 (102.4)	2.1 (122.0)	0.8 (44.3)	9.5 (557.4)	0.5 (31.1)	1.2 (67.8)	12.5 (733.7)	0.3 (14.9)	1.1 (62.7)	0.4 (25.1)	0.6 (37.9)	1.8 (104.8)	0.6 (38.0)	0.3 (18.7)	0.4 (24.0)	0.2 (9.7)	0.2 (9.0)

Demand sectors and industry groups to:

Industry groups from:	Apparel (18)	Textile-leather (19)	Paper (20)	Printing (21)	Chemicals (22)	Petroleum (23)	Rubber (24)	Foods and beverages (25)	All industry groups (26)	Exports, private (X_P) (27)	Exports, government (X_g) (28)	Local consumption (C) (29)	Investment, business (I_B) (30)	Investment, housing (I_H) (31)	Government, current (G_c) (32)	Government investment (G_I) (33)	Total employment (34)
16. Printing	0.1 (0.1)	0.4 (0.3)	0.5 (0.4)	16.8 (12.4)	0.7 (0.5)	0.1 (0.1)	0.1 (0.1)	0.1 (0.1)	60.2 (44.3)	12.9 (9.4)	0.3 (0.4)	22.8 (16.7)	1.0 (0.7)		2.9 (2.1)		100.0 (73.6)
17. Chemicals			0.5 (0.5)	0.5 (0.2)	4.2 (1.7)	2.7 (1.1)	0.5 (0.2)	0.5 (0.2)	29.8 (12.2)	37.6 (15.4)	3.7 (1.5)	26.8 (11.0)	0.5 (0.2)		1.5 (0.6)		100.0 (40.9)
18. Petroleum							4.6 (1.5)	12.7 (3.4)	76.7 (25.0)	17.5 (5.7)	5.8 (1.9)						100.0 (32.6)
19. Rubber					2.0 (3.4)	0.4 (0.1)		2.5 (4.2)	47.9 (12.8)	32.3 (8.6)	12.4 (3.3)	0.4 (0.1)	6.7 (1.8)		0.4 (0.1)		100.0 (26.7)
20. Foods and beverages			0.1 (1.2)	1.0 (13.4)				1.5 (20.7)	56.3 (93.6)	21.5 (35.7)	2.3 (3.9)	19.0 (31.6)			1.0 (1.6)		100.0 (166.4)
21. Total manufacturing	(0.2)				1.1 (14.5)	0.3 (4.7)	0.4 (5.6)		41.0 (554.2)	22.6 (306.7)	24.2 (328.8)	6.1 (83.0)	4.8 (65.6)		0.9 (12.7)	0.4 (5.2)	100.0 (1356.2)
22. Agriculture, forestry, fisheries, and mining	(0.2)	(0.3)			0.5 (2.6)	4.2 (21.2)	0.4 (5.6)	44.5 (226.8)	70.0 (356.3)	28.6 (145.5)		1.4 (7.2)					100.0 (504.0)
23. Contract construction											1.6 (5.9)		25.3 (94.9)	51.1 (191.3)		22.0 (82.3)	100.0 (374.4)
24. Transportation, communication, and public utilities	0.7 (3.5)	0.2 (0.6)	0.3 (1.1)	0.8 (2.9)	0.4 (1.6)	0.4 (1.4)	0.3 (1.1)	1.8 (6.6)	42.4 (158.4)	19.9 (74.1)	2.1 (7.7)	32.4 (120.9)			2.3 (12.0)		100.0 (373.1)
25. Wholesale trade	0.8 (2.6)	0.2 (0.6)	0.4 (1.3)	1.2 (3.7)	0.6 (1.9)	0.5 (1.5)	0.3 (1.1)	3.6 (11.5)	96.5 (308.8)	2.0 (6.4)	0.5 (1.6)	0.9 (2.9)	0.1 (0.5)		0.1 (0.3)		100.0 (320.0)
26. Retail trade	0.1 (1.0)	0.1 (0.2)	0.1 (0.7)	0.1 (0.2)	0.1 (0.1)	0.1 (0.6)	0.4 (0.5)	0.5 (4.9)	8.4 (79.0)	0.3 (2.6)		90.2 (844.4)			1.0 (9.3)		100.0 (935.9)
27. Finance, insurance, and real estate	0.3 (0.9)	0.2 (0.3)	0.1 (0.7)	0.4 (1.0)	0.2 (0.6)	0.2 (0.4)	0.1 (0.3)	0.8 (2.2)	20.6 (53.9)	9.3 (24.7)	0.3 (0.9)	42.9 (112.1)	4.4 (11.5)	21.2 (55.3)	0.7 (1.9)	0.6 (1.5)	100.0 (261.8)
28. Services	0.3 (2.7)	0.1 (0.6)	0.1 (1.2)	0.4 (3.4)	0.2 (1.8)	0.2 (1.5)	0.1 (1.2)	0.8 (7.2)	15.9 (148.1)	6.6 (61.8)	0.6 (5.7)	71.3 (633.4)	1.1 (10.1)	3.7 (34.1)	0.8 (7.3)		100.0 (900.5)
29. Government											18.8 (156.7)				79.6 (661.6)	1.6 (13.3)	100.0 (831.6)
30. Total employment	0.8 (9.9)	(2.5)	0.1 (5.8)	0.4 (26.1)	0.4 (23.7)	0.5 (31.3)	0.2 (9.7)	4.7 (279.9)	28.1 (1658.7)	10.6 (621.8)	8.6 (507.4)	31.1 (1833.9)	3.1 (182.6)	4.8 (280.7)	12.0 (705.1)	1.7 (102.3)	100.0 (5892.5)

* Employment figures shown are for the year 1959, the latest available at the time of the study. The percentages applied were for 1960 sales. Percentage figures beyond the decimal point were included to avoid gross errors in rounding, but should not be considered significant.

SOURCE: Reprinted by permission of the publishers from W. Lee Hansen and Charles M. Tiebout, "An Intersectoral Flows Analysis of the California Economy," Review of Economics and Statistics, vol. 45, Cambridge, Mass.: Harvard University Press (November, 1963), pp. 412–413. Copyright 1963, by the President and Fellows of Harvard College.

sales. Each firm's total employment is then distributed among other industries and markets in proportion to the distribution of sales. The assumption is that employment is proportional to sales. The distributions of employment of all firms in the same industry are summed to form one row of an input-output table. Thus, the row shows how much employment in the row industry is generated by sales to each of the industries in the region and to each of the final markets. In Table 7-1, the employment distribution in each industry in each row is converted to a percentage distribution. The allocation of actual employment is shown in parentheses below the percentage.

From Table 7-1 it can be seen that 21.2 percent of employment in durable manufactures was generated from private exports. More, 34.5 percent was generated from exports to government. On the other hand, 34.1 percent of employment in the industry was generated by sales to other industries, such as agriculture, contract construction, retail trade, fabricated metals, electrical machinery, and transportation equipment. Thus, we can see that employment in durable goods is directly affected by changes in all the market sectors except housing investment. Nevertheless, 3.1 percent of sales in durable manufactures went to contract construction, and from row 23, we see that 51.1 percent of sales in contract construction went to the housing investment market. Therefore, changes in housing investment will indirectly affect durable manufacturing sales through their interindustry sales to contract construction. These sales from durable manufactures to contract construction would also be affected by the other markets and industries that contract construction sold to. By tracing each of the interindustry sales of each industry, all sales for an industry could be directly or indirectly attributed to one of the final market sectors.

The technique for tracing the interindustry sales is an iterative process and works in the following way. If 3.1 percent of durable manufactures goes to contract construction, 3.1 times 51.1 (percentage of contract construction sales to housing investment) yields 1.58 percent of sales from durable manufactures to housing investment. If 6 percent of durable manufactures is sold to transportation equipment, and 10.8 percent of transportation equipment goes for private exports, then 6 times 10.8 yields 0.6 percent of sales of durable manufactures that are indirectly attributable to private exports. But the transportation equipment industry also makes interindustry sales. Thus, 2.8 percent of transportation equipment sales goes to the fabricated metal industry, of which 18.3 percent goes to private exports. Therefore, 6 times 2.8 times 18.3 yields the 0.03 percent of sales from durable manufacturing that is also indirectly attributable to private exports through sales to the transport equipment and fabricated metals industries. One can see that carrying out all these types of calculations in the table could lead to assigning all the sales or employment in durable manufacturing either directly or indirectly to one of the final demand sectors. Table 7-2 shows the result in the Hansen-Tiebout study of California for durable manufactures and other industries.

Finally, all employment in all industries can be summed under the appropriate final market sector, as shown in row 30 of Table 7-2. This breakdown of employment is nothing more than a sophisticated economic base study. Instead of dividing employment arbitrarily into basic and nonbasic, or export and local service industries, Table 7-2 divides it into seven sectors. Moreover, the interindustry relationships have been taken into account.

From these data employment multipliers can be calculated that can be interpreted by the short-run theory of income and trade. In the previous analysis regional income was shown to be spent only on local purchases and imports. A more detailed analysis would show that local income was spent on consumption, investment in business, investment in housing, current local government expenditures, and government investment, while exports could be divided into private exports and exports to the Federal government.

In the short run, with the same assumption regarding wages, prices, etc., that was outlined previously, only consumption and imports of all of these categories would be assumed to be dependent on the level of income. The levels of investment and government expenditures are assumed to be not responsive to short-run changes in the level of regional income. Investment expenditures depend more on expectations and the interest rate. Government operations and investment would depend on contracted activities. Over a long period of time these expenditures would be responsive to the region's income. Thus, in the short run an increase in income from investment, government expenditures, or exports would increase local income. This increase in income would cause an increase in local consumption (the marginal propensity to consume), part of which would be spent locally.

In the same way as before, an increase in income would increase the equilibrium level of income by a multiple of the increase in exports, investment, or government expenditures, so long as the increase was continued in every time period. The multiplier would be as follows:

$$dY = \frac{1}{1 - s} dX$$

where dY is the change in the equilibrium level of income, s is the marginal propensity to consume locally, and dX is the change in exports, invest-

**TABLE 7-2 TOTAL DIRECT AND INDIRECT EMPLOYMENT TO
DEMAND SECTORS AND PERCENTAGES OF DIRECT TO
TOTAL EMPLOYMENT, STATE OF CALIFORNIA, 1960***
(Employment in thousands)

From industry groups	To demand sectors							
	X_P (1)	X_G (2)	C (3)	I_B (4)	I_H (5)	G_C (6)	G_I (7)	Total
1. Durable manufactures								
Direct	196.2	313.1	73.8	62.7	0	6.1	4.8	656.7
Indirect	66.4	84.2	50.7	20.2	22.2	2.9	10.2	256.8
Total	262.6	397.3	124.5	82.9	22.2	9.0	15.0	913.5
Direct percentage	74.7	78.8	59.2	75.6	0	67.8	32.0	71.9
2. Primary metals								
Direct	7.8	6.1	4.7	2.4	0	0.8	0.5	22.3
Indirect	8.3	7.8	4.5	3.4	2.9	0.4	1.4	28.7
Total	16.1	13.9	9.2	5.8	2.9	1.2	1.9	51.0
Direct percentage	48.4	43.9	51.6	41.3	0	67.1	26.1	43.8
3. Fabricated metals								
Direct	17.3	11.8	7.8	0.8	0	1.5	0.5	39.7
Indirect	14.7	13.4	12.5	4.5	6.5	0.9	2.9	55.4
Total	32.0	25.2	20.3	5.3	6.5	2.4	3.4	95.1
Direct percentage	54.1	46.9	38.3	15.2	0	61.5	14.8	41.7
4. Nonelectrical machinery								
Direct	47.8	9.6	0.6	23.5	0	0	0.9	82.4
Indirect	2.0	2.0	1.5	0.7	0.6	0.1	0.3	7.2
Total	49.8	11.6	2.1	24.2	0.6	0.1	1.2	89.6
Direct percentage	96.0	82.4	27.5	97.1	0	0	76.9	91.9
5. Electrical machinery								
Direct	39.2	62.4	5.7	21.7	0	0.1	1.1	130.2
Indirect	4.6	10.6	1.2	1.7	0.7	0	0.4	19.2
Total	43.8	73.0	6.9	23.4	0.7	0.1	1.5	149.4
Direct percentage	89.5	85.5	83.2	92.6	0	57.7	73.9	87.1
6. Transportation equipment								
Direct	33.4	178.2	12.3	7.2	0	0.1	0.3	231.5
Indirect	12.8	34.0	8.4	3.0	1.2	0.5	0.6	60.5
Total	46.2	212.2	20.7	10.2	1.2	0.6	0.9	292.0
Direct percentage	72.3	84.0	59.2	70.9	0	19.9	32.7	79.3
7. Instruments & ordnance								
Direct	13.0	42.7	0.4	0.6	0	0.1	0.2	57.0
Indirect	3.7	11.5	1.4	1.2	0.1	0	0.1	18.0
Total	16.7	54.2	1.8	1.8	0.1	0.1	0.3	75.0
Direct percentage	77.8	81.8	22.2	33.3	0	100.0	66.7	76.0
8. Stone, clay, and glass								
Direct	11.1	0.3	16.3	0.6	0	0.7	0.1	29.1
Indirect	3.1	0.7	5.7	1.4	2.7	0.2	1.2	15.0
Total	14.2	1.0	22.0	2.0	2.7	0.9	1.3	44.1
Direct percentage	77.9	31.3	74.0	29.9	0	80.2	7.9	66.0

**TABLE 7-2   TOTAL DIRECT AND INDIRECT EMPLOYMENT TO
DEMAND SECTORS AND PERCENTAGES OF DIRECT TO
TOTAL EMPLOYMENT, STATE OF CALIFORNIA, 1960***
(**Employment in thousands**) (*Continued*)

From industry groups	To demand sectors							
	X_P (1)	X_G (2)	C (3)	I_B (4)	I_H (5)	G_C (6)	G_I (7)	Total
9. Lumber products								
Direct	12.9	1.5	5.8	0.2	0	1.5	0.1	22.0
Indirect	12.8	2.6	10.9	3.0	5.5	0.6	2.4	37.8
Total	25.7	4.1	16.7	3.2	5.5	2.1	2.5	59.8
Direct percentage	50.2	36.5	34.6	6.3	0	70.7	4.0	36.7
10. Furniture								
Direct	4.7	0.3	17.5	5.6	0	0.7	0.9	29.7
Indirect	0.7	0.9	1.3	0.9	1.3	0	0.6	5.7
Total	5.4	1.2	18.8	6.5	1.3	0.7	1.5	35.4
Direct percentage	87.4	25.1	93.0	86.5	0	92.7	60.9	83.9
11. Miscellaneous manufactures								
Direct	9.0	0.2	2.7	0.1	0	0.6	0.2	12.8
Indirect	3.7	0.7	3.3	0.4	0.7	0.2	0.3	9.3
Total	12.7	0.9	6.0	0.5	0.7	0.8	0.5	22.1
Direct percentage	70.8	22.3	44.5	19.2	0	77.4	39.8	57.9
12. Nondurable manufactures								
Direct	112.9	13.7	191.8	2.9	0	8.6	0.4	330.3
Indirect	31.2	12.9	46.0	7.0	9.6	2.1	3.6	112.4
Total	144.1	26.6	237.8	9.9	9.6	10.7	4.0	442.7
Direct percentage	78.4	51.7	80.7	29.3	0	80.4	10.0	74.6
13. Apparel								
Direct	25.1	2.3	27.9	0	0	3.0	0	58.3
Indirect	0.9	0.8	1.1	0.4	0.6	0	0.3	4.1
Total	26.0	3.1	29.0	0.4	0.6	3.0	0.3	62.4
Direct percentage	96.6	73.9	96.3	3.8	0	98.8	0	93.5
14. Textile-leather								
Direct	4.0	0.4	7.3	0	0	0.1	0	11.8
Indirect	0.2	0.2	0.2	0.1	0.2	0	0	0.9
Total	4.2	0.6	7.5	0.1	0.2	0.1	0	12.7
Direct percentage	95.2	66.7	97.3	0	0	100.0	0	92.9
15. Paper								
Direct	8.7	0	5.6	0.2	0	0.2	0.4	15.1
Indirect	3.0	0.7	5.8	0.7	1.4	0.2	0.5	12.3
Total	11.7	0.7	11.4	0.9	1.4	0.4	0.9	27.4
Direct percentage	74.5	0	49.0	22.1	0	59.9	43.1	55.2
16. Printing								
Direct	9.5	0.4	29.7	0.7	0	2.2	0	42.5
Indirect	7.1	3.3	15.8	1.4	2.0	0.9	0.6	31.1
Total	16.6	3.7	45.5	2.1	2.0	3.1	0.6	73.6
Direct percentage	56.9	10.9	65.3	33.9	0	71.2	0	57.7

TABLE 7-2 TOTAL DIRECT AND INDIRECT EMPLOYMENT TO
DEMAND SECTORS AND PERCENTAGES OF DIRECT TO
TOTAL EMPLOYMENT, STATE OF CALIFORNIA, 1960*
(Employment in thousands) (Continued)

From industry groups	To demand sectors							
	X_P (1)	X_G (2)	C (3)	I_B (4)	I_H (5)	G_C (6)	G_I (7)	Total
17. Chemicals								
Direct	15.4	1.5	14.4	0.2	0	0.6	0	32.1
Indirect	2.4	1.4	2.7	0.7	1.0	0.2	0.4	8.8
Total	17.8	2.9	17.1	0.9	1.0	0.8	0.4	40.9
Direct percentage	86.4	51.3	84.3	22.3	0	82.0	0	78.5
18. Petroleum								
Direct	5.7	1.9	9.1	0	0	0.1	0	16.8
Indirect	4.6	2.0	6.1	1.3	1.0	0.4	0.4	15.8
Total	10.3	3.9	15.2	1.3	1.0	0.5	0.4	32.6
Direct percentage	55.4	48.9	60.1	0	0	21.9	0	51.7
19. Rubber								
Direct	8.6	3.3	1.4	1.8	0	0.1	0	15.2
Indirect	3.0	3.1	1.8	1.3	1.5	0.1	0.7	11.5
Total	11.6	6.4	3.2	3.1	1.5	0.2	0.7	26.7
Direct percentage	74.0	52.0	43.2	57.5	0	53.4	0	56.9
20. Foods and beverages								
Direct	35.9	3.9	96.4	0	0	2.3	0	138.5
Indirect	10.0	1.4	12.5	1.1	1.9	0.3	0.7	27.9
Total	45.9	5.3	108.9	1.1	1.9	2.6	0.7	166.4
Direct percentage	78.2	73.6	88.5	0	0	87.7	0	83.3
21. Total manufacturing								
Direct	309.1	326.8	265.6	65.6	0	14.7	5.2	987.0
Indirect	97.6	97.1	96.7	27.2	31.8	5.0	13.8	369.2
Total	406.7	423.9	362.3	92.8	31.8	19.7	19.0	1,356.2
Direct percentage	76.0	77.1	73.3	70.7	0	74.6	27.4	72.8
22. Agriculture, forestry, fisheries, and mining								
Direct	145.7	0	62.2	0	0	0.6	0	208.5
Indirect	90.4	12.0	181.6	4.0	5.6	4.6	2.3	300.5
Total	236.1	12.0	243.8	4.0	5.6	5.2	2.3	509.0
Direct percentage	61.7	0	25.5	0	0	11.7	0	41.0
23. Contract construction								
Direct	0	5.9	0	94.9	191.3	0	82.3	374.4
Indirect	0	0	0	0	0	0	0	0
Total	0	5.9	0	94.9	191.3	0	82.3	374.4
Direct percentage	0	100.0	0	100.0	100.0	0	100.0	100.0
24. Transportation, communication, and public utilities								
Direct	74.2	7.7	157.7	0	0	12.4	0	252.0
Indirect	30.6	19.3	49.6	7.4	9.4	1.6	3.2	121.1
Total	104.8	27.0	207.3	7.4	9.4	14.0	3.2	373.1
Direct percentage	70.8	28.5	76.1	0	0	88.6	0	67.5

TABLE 7-2 TOTAL DIRECT AND INDIRECT EMPLOYMENT TO
DEMAND SECTORS AND PERCENTAGES OF DIRECT TO
TOTAL EMPLOYMENT, STATE OF CALIFORNIA, 1960*
(**Employment in thousands**) (*Continued*)

From industry groups	To demand sectors							
	X_P (1)	X_G (2)	C (3)	I_B (4)	I_H (5)	G_C (6)	G_I (7)	Total
25. Wholesale trade								
Direct	7.0	1.6	180.7	0.1	0	2.3	0	191.7
Indirect	23.7	22.8	29.0	16.0	24.9	1.2	10.7	128.3
Total	30.7	24.4	209.7	16.1	24.9	3.5	10.7	320.0
Direct percentage	22.7	6.6	86.2	0.7	0	65.3	0	59.9
26. Retail trade								
Direct	2.6	0.1	844.4	0.5	0	9.3	0	856.9
Indirect	12.6	9.0	19.3	10.6	19.0	0.6	7.9	79.0
Total	15.2	9.1	863.7	11.1	19.0	9.9	7.9	935.9
Direct percentage	17.1	1.1	97.8	4.5	0	93.7	0	91.6
27. Finance, insurance, and real estate								
Direct	24.8	0.9	123.0	11.5	55.3	2.0	1.5	219.0
Indirect	10.1	6.0	18.5	2.6	3.7	0.6	1.3	42.8
Total	34.9	6.9	141.5	14.1	59.0	2.6	2.8	261.8
Direct percentage	70.9	13.2	86.9	81.4	93.7	77.3	54.3	83.6
28. Services								
Direct	61.9	5.7	703.6	10.1	34.1	7.8	0	823.2
Indirect	25.4	18.3	45.5	6.5	7.9	1.5	2.2	107.3
Total	87.3	24.0	749.1	16.6	42.0	9.3	2.2	930.5
Direct percentage	70.9	23.8	93.9	61.0	81.2	83.7	0	88.5
29. Government								
Direct	0	156.7	0	0	0	661.6	13.3	831.6
Indirect	0	0	0	0	0	0	0	0
Total	0	156.7	0	0	0	661.6	13.3	831.6
Direct percentage	0	100.0	0	0	0	100.0	100.0	100.0
30. Total employment								
Direct	625.3	505.4	2,337.2	182.7	280.7	710.7	102.3	4,744.3
Indirect	290.3	184.6	440.2	74.3	102.3	15.1	41.4	1,148.2
Total	915.6	690.0	2,777.4	257.0	383.0	725.8	143.7	5,892.5
Direct percentage	68.3	73.3	84.1	71.1	73.3	97.9	71.2	80.5

* Employment figures shown are for the year 1959, the latest available at the time of the
study. The percentages applied were for 1960 sales. Percentage figures beyond the decimal point were included to avoid gross errors in rounding, but should not be considered
significant.

SOURCE: Reprinted by permission of the publishers from W. Lee Hansen and Charles M.
Tiebout, "An Intersectoral Flows Analysis of the California Economy," *Review of Economics and Statistics*, vol. 45, Cambridge, Mass.: Harvard University Press (November, 1963),
pp. 412–413. Copyright 1963, by the President and Fellows of Harvard college.

ment, or government expenditures. The advantage of this formulation of the analysis over the previous simple model is that it takes account of the different direct effects of different sectors on income in the first round.[6]

If we allow a longer period of time, say a decade, instead of a year or two, so that investment and government expenditures are also dependent on the level of income, only exports would be independent. A change in exports would cause an increase in local income that would generate further increases in local income by increases in expenditures for consumption, investment, and government locally. Thus, the marginal propensity to spend locally, s, would be the sum of the marginal propensity to consume locally, the marginal propensity to invest locally, and the marginal propensity to spend on local government. The major difficulty with extending the length of time is that wages and prices will tend to vary, capital and labor may migrate, and the assumptions of the model would be denied. Thus, it is better adapted to the short-run impact studies.

Using the employment data in Table 7-2, a group of multipliers can be calculated. Assume that the average propensity to consume locally is the same as the marginal propensity to consume locally. Furthermore, assume

[6] Mathematically this model would be described as follows:

$$Y = C + I_B + I_H + I_G + G + X_P + X_F - M_c$$
$$C = a + bY$$
$$M_c = c + eC = c + ae + beY$$
$$I_B = \bar{I}_B \qquad G = \bar{G}$$
$$I_H = \bar{I}_H \qquad X_P = \bar{X}_P$$
$$I_G = \bar{I}_G \qquad X_F = \bar{X}_F$$

where
Y = net regional income
C = consumption
I_B = business investment
I_H = housing investment
I_G = local government investment
G = local government operational expenditures
X_P = private exports
X_F = exports to the Federal government
M_c = imports for consumption

Solving for Y:

$$Y = a + bY + \bar{I}_B + \bar{I}_H + \bar{I}_G + \bar{G} + \bar{X}_P + \bar{X}_F - c - ae - beY$$
$$Y = \frac{a + \bar{I}_B + \bar{I}_H + \bar{I}_G + \bar{G} + \bar{X}_P + \bar{X}_F - c - ae}{1 - b + be}$$

The changes in Y with respect to a $1 change in one of the parameters would be:

$$\frac{dY}{dX_P} = \frac{1}{1 - b(1 - e)}$$

$b(1 - e)$ is the marginal propensity to spend locally. It is the marginal propensity to consume b times the marginal propensity to spend locally out of consumption $(1 - e)$. e is the marginal propensity to import out of consumption, rather than from income as in the previous analysis.

employment is proportional to local income and consumption. Then s, the marginal propensity to spend locally, would be the total employment generated directly and indirectly from local consumption divided by total employment:[7]

$$C - M_c = sY$$

where

C = consumption
M_c = imports for consumption
s = marginal propensity to spend locally = average propensity
Y = income

$C - M_c$ generated 2,777.4 thousand jobs in 1960 in California. The total employment was 5,892.5 thousand.

Thus

$$2,777.4 = s5,892.5$$
$$s = \frac{2,777.4}{5,892.5} = 0.4713$$

Therefore, in 1960 the short-run multiplier for an increase in employment in any of these sectors—exports, government, or investment—was $1/(1 - 0.4713) = 1.89$.

The whole story, however, has not been told. A direct increase in one of these sectors causes an indirect increase through the interindustry linkages. Thus, a direct increase in employment from private exports, say in the transportation equipment industry, causes increases in employment and income in the supplying industries such as fabricated metals, nonelectrical machinery, and the instruments and ordnance industry. Every increase of one job in direct private export employment will cause an increase of 1.46 jobs in employment generated by exports, if the proportion of 625.3 thousand jobs in direct exports to 915.6 thousand in direct and indirect is constant for every level of employment.

Therefore, the overall multiplier for a change in employment in the private export sector would be as follows:

$$dY = \frac{1}{1 - 0.47} (1.46 \, dX) = 2.7594 \, dX$$

[7] Algebraically the marginal propensity to spend locally would be described as follows (using the definitions in footnote 6):

$$C = bY$$
$$M_c = eC = beY$$
$$C - M_c = bY - beY = b(1 - e)Y$$
$$\frac{C - M_c}{Y} = b(1 - e) = s$$

where dY is equal to change in total employment and dX is equal to change in direct private export employment.

In the short run the difficulties with the assumptions of the model are less likely to distort the estimated change caused by the impact of exports, investment, or government. Nevertheless, the criticisms leveled against the economic base studies are also relevant for this hybrid economic base and input-output analysis. In particular, this analysis uses employment data with its attendent difficulties, and average and marginal propensities are assumed equal.

BUSINESS CYCLES AND REGIONS

Another analysis that can utilize the short-run theory of income and trade is the study of how the income and employment of a region are affected by national business cycles. Is the character of the region such that national depressions, or recessions, cause widespread unemployment in the region, or is the character of the region such that national business cycles hardly cause a ripple in the flow of economic activity in the region? We can answer this question qualitatively using the following analysis based on the short-run income theory of the first sections of this chapter.[8]

Just as economists use the price elasticity of demand to measure the responsiveness of demand to changes in price, they can measure the responsiveness of a region's income to changes in incomes of other regions. The changes in income of other regions affect a region's income through the exports of that region. Thus, to find the responsiveness of regional income to business cycles we might calculate the percentage change in regional income divided by the percentage change in exports. We could express this in the following way:

$$\frac{dY/Y}{dX/X} = \frac{dY}{dX} \cdot \frac{X}{Y}$$

where X is the value of exports, Y is the income of the region, dX is the change in exports caused by changes in income in other regions, and dY is the change in this region's income caused by the change in exports.

For the ratio dY/dX we can substitute the multiplier that was derived in the first section of this chapter. It is $1/(1 - s)$ where s is the marginal propensity to spend locally and is equal to the marginal propensity to spend less the marginal propensity to import. Calling the marginal propensity to spend MPC and the marginal propensity to import MPI, the multiplier

[8] The following analysis is based on Rutledge Vining, "The Region as a Concept in Business-cycle Analysis," *Econometrica* (July, 1948), pp. 201–218.

can be expressed as the following ratio: $1/[1 - (MPC - MPI)]$. Similarly the ratio X/Y is exports divided by income. For X we can substitute $Y - E + M$, where Y is regional income; E is expenditure on consumption, government, and investment; and M is imports. We can do this because the definition of income at any level is the sum of expenditures and exports less imports. With these substitutions the expression for the responsiveness of income to changes in exports becomes as follows:

$$\frac{dY}{dX} \cdot \frac{X}{Y} = \frac{1}{1 - (MPC - MPI)} \cdot \frac{Y - E + M}{Y}$$
$$= \frac{1 - E/Y + M/Y}{1 - MPC + MPI}$$

This expression shows the percentage change in regional income with respect to the percentage change in exports to be equal to 1 minus the average propensity to spend plus the average propensity to import divided by 1 minus the marginal propensity to spend plus the marginal propensity to import.

Using this expression we can make three generalizations about the relative stability of income and employment in a region with respect to changes in income of other regions.

1. The greater the proportion of imports M/Y, holding MPC and MPI constant, the greater will be the percentage change in income with respect to a percentage change in exports. If the marginal propensities to consume and import were the same in two different places, the above expression for the place with the greater average imports would be greater. If there should be a reduction of exports from each community the multiplier impact would be the same in both communities. In the community with a greater share of its income going to imports, so long as these imports were tied not to exports but to local consumption, the percentage change in the equilibrium level of income would be greater because change in income from exports would represent a larger share of *local* income.

2. The less the short-run income elasticities of demand for imports, the smaller will be the marginal propensity to import.[9] The percentage change in income with respect to a percentage change in exports will be greater the less the short-run income elasticities of demand for imports, holding all the other terms constant. That is to say, the equilib-

---

[9] The income elasticity of demand for a product is the percentage change in expenditure for the product divided by the percentage change in income causing the change in expenditure. Thus, a 0 elasticity would indicate that there was no change in expenditures on the product with a change in income. An income elasticity of 1 would mean that expenditures on the item in question increased by the same percentage as income.

rium level of income in a community will fall more if its demand for imports stays about the same even though its income is falling because of a reduction in the demand for its own exports.
3. The greater the short-run income elasticities of demand for the exports of the region, the greater will be the change in exports of a region with a given change in the income of other regions. Therefore, a given change in national income will cause income in this region to fluctuate more.

We have previously indicated that the marginal propensity to import decreases as the size of a community increases. Does this mean that larger cities are sensitive to business cycles? Not necessarily. At the same time that the marginal propensity to import is falling, the total proportion of expenditures for imports falls. Both the proportion of exports and the proportion of imports of a region become smaller as the region becomes larger. There are no imports or exports if we consider the world as the economy under study. While statement 2 above would indicate that larger cities would be more susceptible to cycles, statement 1 indicates that this tendency is offset by the reduction in the average propensity to import.[10]

Although we do not have data to calculate the average and marginal propensities needed in the above expression, we do have notions and data about the income elasticities of demand for different products. Using these notions we can make qualitative statements about the percentage change in income of a region with respect to changes in national income. For example, Rutledge Vining compares the Fort Smith, Arkansas, trading area with that of Pine Bluff, Arkansas.[11] In Pine Bluff exports are cotton and lumber, which have high short-run income elasticities of demand. Furthermore, a high proportion of consumption is imported. Finally, imports consist of goods with low income elasticities of demand. Thus, this region is highly sensitive to change in national income. In fact this region experienced adverse flows of banking funds and even bank failures in the depressions of 1933 and earlier years.

In the Fort Smith area exports are agricultural, but include fruits, vegetables, poultry, livestock, eggs, and dairy products, many of which are processed in the region and for which the income elasticity of demand is low. Furthermore, much of the local production is consumed locally so that M/Y is lower than for the Pine Bluff area. Finally, imports consist of goods that have a relatively high income elasticity of demand so that the marginal propensity to import is high. Thus, the percentage change in income with

[10] Wilbur R. Thompson, *A Preface to Urban Economics* (Baltimore: The Johns Hopkins Press, 1965), pp. 141–147.
[11] Vining, *loc. cit.*

respect to a percentage change in exports is much lower for the Fort Smith area than for the Pine Bluff area. Fort Smith is a more stable area.

In Table 6-6 the amplitude of the decline in personal income in each region of the United States was compared with that of the nation. It was found that incomes in the Great Lakes, Plains, and Southwest Regions declined a greater percentage than in the nation. The income in the Rocky Mountain Region declined the same percentage as in the nation. The income in the other regions, New England, Mideast, Southeast, and Far West, declined by a smaller percentage than in the nation. If we had data on the average and marginal propensities to spend and to import, we might be able to explain these differences in amplitude of personal income clearly. If we had information on the income elasticities of the imports and exports of regions, we might also be able to make fairly definite statements. These, too, are unavailable, since we have only gross information on imports and exports.

Because of the difficulty in obtaining the data that fit the theoretical framework, alternative approaches to the analysis of the regional impact of business cycles have been tried. In particular, certain types of enterprise are known to be more responsive to business cycles than others. The sales of manufacturers of durable goods are known to fall off more severely than other business sales. The consumer can afford to put off the purchase of an automobile, washing machine, and other durable equipment if he becomes unemployed or if his income decreases, whereas he could not put off the purchase of food. Thus, studies have been made of the industrial structure of regions to see how this might affect the responsiveness of a region to cycles.[12] These studies, however, have not yielded convincing evidence that the industrial mix of a region will cause its cyclical responsiveness to be different. Obviously, a one-industry town in which the industry fluctuated sharply with national business cycles would be severely hit by national cycles. But in the case of larger areas, such as Detroit and Pittsburgh, the evidence is not so clear.

SUMMARY

In the short run, prices and wages can be assumed to be fixed. If this is the case the aggregate demand on a region's resources depends on income earned within the region and income earned in other regions. The demand can be divided into exports that depend on incomes in other regions, and

[12] A survey of these studies can be found in Walter Isard, *Methods of Regional Analysis* (Cambridge, Mass.: The M.I.T. Press, 1960), pp. 184–188. A recent study is George H. Borts, "Regional Cycles of Manufacturing Employment in the United States, 1914–1953," *Journal of the American Statistical Association* (March, 1960), pp. 151–211.

local expenditures that depend on incomes earned within the region being studied. In the short run an equilibrium level of income may be approached that is less than the full-employment level of income. With the assumptions relevant for a short-run analysis a change in the demand for a region's exports would cause the equilibrium level of income to change. The change would be a multiple of the change in exports. The multiplier is equal to $1/(1 - s)$.

The short-run theory of income and employment in a region is hard to implement because of the scarcity of data. Nevertheless, several techniques of urban and regional analysis are based on the theory, or can be shown to fit within the theory. One of these techniques is the economic base study. The economic base study approach has been to divide the employment of a region or community into jobs generated from exports and jobs generated from local expenditures. Export employment is forecast for the future. The change in employment generated by local expenditures resulting from the increase in exports is estimated by multiplying the estimated change in export employment by the multiplier. The change in total employment is the sum of the changes in export employment and local service employment.

The basic error in doing this is that it is the use of a short-run framework to handle a long-run problem. In the long run, prices and wages, population, technology, and the propensities to consume and import will change. Thus, it is a very gross projection.

Two other uses of the short-run theory are useful. One is a modified economic base study to analyze the short-run impact of a change in exports on a local economy. This is the intersectoral flows analysis. It is a modification of the input-output table and economic base studies. The employment multipliers estimated from the model are more refined than those of the economic base study. They take into account both the direct and the indirect effects of a change in employment in a given industry. Furthermore, more sectors are taken into account. Nevertheless, the problems of estimating the multiplier by using estimates of average rather than marginal propensities still exist.

The multiplier analysis is also useful in analyzing the impact of business cycles on a region. In particular it is useful to consider the percentage change in income resulting from a percentage change in the exports. By doing so, one does not confuse the size of the multiplier with the responsiveness of the region to cycles. One must take account of the percentage of the regional income spent on imports, the income elasticity of demand for imports and the marginal propensity to import, and the income elasticity of demand for the region's exports.

CHAPTER 8

In this chapter we turn to the long-run analysis of differences between regions in the rate of growth of total income and per capita income. The fundamental distinction between the long-run analysis of this chapter and the short-run analysis of the previous chapter is in the basic premises of analysis. In short-run analysis the basic question is about the use of the full capacity of the economy during a period in which that capacity does not change. Thus, prices, wages, income distribution, and technology are all held constant. In long-run analysis each region is assumed to reach its full-employment equilibrium income level. The basic question is how the full-employment equilibrium level of income can vary over time. While the potential level of regional income is given in short-run analysis, it is the variable to be determined in long-run analysis. In pursuing this question, the changes in the variables held constant in the short run (population, wages, prices, resources, technology, and the distribution of income) will be the key to understanding changes in the potential level of regional income.

To rely on the concept of potential full employment income as a measure of the growth of regions, however, is deceptive and can lead to incorrect decisions about pockets of poverty. Population may increase as fast as or faster than the potential level of regional income. Thus, the real welfare of a region's people in terms of each individual's spending power may not increase even though total income does. In order to relate population growth to income an additional measure of income will be used. Per capita income will be a measure of the changing welfare of a regional population. Notice, however, that this still does not measure another aspect of the welfare of the population: the distribution of income. Welfare in two different regions could be very different even though per capita incomes in the two regions were the same, if the distribution of income were different.

In this chapter we shall first outline a simple long-run model of an open economy. It is not really a rigorous model but a loose framework for relating the factors affecting the growth of a region within a country. We shall then discuss the reasons for the differences between regions in the growth rates of total income or product. A separate discussion of the comparative growth rates of per capita income will follow. This discussion will reveal the importance of resource migration in both per capita income growth and total income growth. The final section of the chapter will show why it is perfectly rational for migration of resources not to take place even though there might be differences in the rate of return on their use in different geographic places.

A SIMPLE LONG-RUN MODEL OF AN OPEN ECONOMY[1]

Once a region has been defined, the human and natural resources tallied, the technology accounted for, and the plant and equipment toted up, we can theoretically determine the potential output and income of the region. Output is still defined as net regional product. Allowance must be made for depreciation of current capital so that net product is reproducible (see Chapter 6). It is the level of income that could be maintained.[2] Consider a region that produces two things: a product for export and a local service. These are the two final market sectors of the regional economy. The sum of their production less imports is equal to net regional product.

Technically, there would be many combinations of amounts of exports and local services that could be provided with the given skills, resources, and economic organization. These possibilities can be shown in a production possibility curve.[3] In Figure 8-1, OA indicates the quantity of the export good that could be produced, given the resources of the economy, if nothing else were produced. OB indicates the quantity of local services that could be produced if no exports were produced. The curve AB traces the technical possibilities of producing various combinations of the two products.

Production is shifted from exports to local services or vice versa by shifting resources from the production of one to the other. The bowed-out shape of AB is due to the specialization of some factors of production. As more and more resources are shifted to either exports or local services, their productivity falls because they are better suited for production of the other product. Thus, when approaching B, along AB, a given shift in resources will reduce export production by more than it will increase production of local services. When approaching A, along AB, the same shift in resources

[1] In this section no one specific growth analysis has been relied upon. There is no single theory of growth or of regional growth. The following references, however, were instrumental in forming the discussion: George H. Borts and Jerome L. Stein, *Economic Growth in a Free Market* (New York: Columbia University Press, 1964); Richard H. Leftwich, *The Price System and Resource Allocation*, 3d ed. (New York: Holt, Rinehart and Winston, Inc., 1966), pp. 291–306; Douglass C. North, "Location Theory and Regional Economic Growth," *Journal of Political Economy*, vol. 63 (June, 1955), pp. 243–258; A. C. Pigou, *The Economics of Welfare*, 4th ed. (New York: The Macmillan Company, 1932), Part III, Chap. IX; T. W. Schultz, *The Economic Organization of Agriculture* (New York: McGraw-Hill Book Company, 1953), Chaps. 10, 17, 18; Charles M. Tiebout, "Exports and Regional Economic Growth," *Journal of Political Economy*, vol. 64 (April, 1956), pp. 160–169.
[2] There is, of course, the problem of depletion of natural resources. Depletion could cause a reduction in potential income that no depreciation allowance could prevent.
[3] Paul A. Samuelson, *Economics*, 6th ed. (New York: McGraw-Hill Book Company, 1964), pp. 17–27.

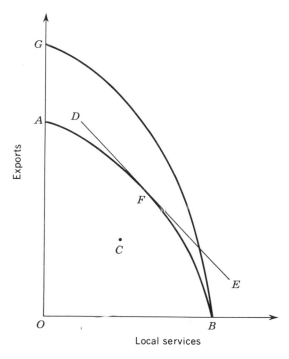

FIGURE 8-1

will reduce local services production by more than it will increase export production.

AB is a maximum boundary of production possibilities. Combinations of production inside the curve are possible, but they represent less than full employment in the economy. For example, an economy producing at point C in Figure 8-1 could be at a short-run equilibrium but producing at less than its full potential. The model for analyzing such a situation was described in the previous chapter. An increase in demand for the region's resources through exports or government expenditures could increase the short-run equilibrium level of income and production and so move the economy toward the production possibility curve.

Consider an economy producing at full employment. What determines the mix of its production? What determines the quantity of exports and local services produced? At what point along the curve AB is the economy producing? The answer is determined by relative prices. That combination will be produced at which the ratio of prices of the products equals the ratio of their marginal costs.

Assuming both industries are competitively organized, we have previously noted that each producer will maintain a rate of production such that price equals marginal cost. Moreover, the sum of the marginal cost curves of all firms in the industry is the supply curve for the industry. Thus, the supply curve of the industry traces out the cost to a community of increasing production of a commodity an additional unit. What is that cost? Yes, it is marginal cost, but it is also the value of other goods that cannot be produced when the resources of the community are shifted to the particular commodity. For transfers of resources from producing exports to producing local services the loss of production in exports is the cost of obtaining the increase in local services. The concept that the cost of obtaining resources to increase production in one good is the value of production of these same resources in other uses is called opportunity cost.

Resources will be bid away from the production of local services and used in the production of exports as long as the value of exports produced by those resources is greater than the value of local services produced by them. Of course, we could speak of it the other way round. Resources will be bid away from the production of exports and used in the production of local services as long as the value of local services produced by those resources is greater than the value of exports produced by them. This is saying the same thing as production in a particular commodity will increase as long as the price is greater than marginal cost.

We have previously pointed out that resources may not be equally productive in the production of exports and local services and that as the economy became more specialized in the production of one of the products, say exports, the increase in exports would be achieved by greater and greater reductions in the production of local services. As the economy becomes more specialized in the production of one of the goods, the opportunity cost of additional increases in production of that good increases. Thus, as resources are shifted, say from local services to exports, the value of production of these resources in local services is increasing. It is increasing not because the price of the product is increasing, but because the resources are more productive in local services than in exports with the increasing specialization. At the same time the value of production of these resources in exports is declining because the resources are not as productive in exports.

Resources will continue to be shifted from the production of one good to the production of the other until the value of production of an additional shift in resources is equal in either industry. At this particular point on the production possibility curve the shift of a small amount of resources from production in one industry to production in the other will cause a reduction in the quantity of one output equal in value to the increase in quantity of the other output achieved. That is,

$$p_x \cdot dq_x = p_1 \cdot dq_1$$

where

p_x = the price of exports

dq_x = the increase or decrease in the quantity of exports caused by a shift of resources

p_1 = the price of local services

dq_1 = the increase or decrease in the quantity of local services caused by the same shift of resources

Dividing both sides of the equation by p_x and dq_1, the equation can be expressed as follows:

$$\frac{dq_x}{dq_1} = \frac{p_1}{p_x}$$

The first ratio is the slope of a tangent to the production possibility curve showing the change in exports divided by the change in local services with a given shift of resources. This ratio is equal to the inverse of the ratio of the prices of the products at the point of the production possibility curve where a shift of resources is equally valuable. Thus, the point on the production possibility curve at which the economy will ultimately settle is where the slope of the tangent to the curve AB, such as DE in Figure 8-1, is equal to the inverse of the ratio of the prices of the products.[4]

Within this framework it is possible to discuss the ways that a region grows in total potential product and income. Any change that causes the production possibility curve to shift away from the origin causes an increase in the capacity of the economy to produce. An improvement in technology or productivity of the labor force would increase the potential income of the economy and cause the production possibility curve to shift outward. New skills or technology might not cover both products, but only one. Then the production possibility curve would shift along one axis only. For example, if the improvement occurred in the export sector, the production possibility curve would shift to GB. Increases in the labor force and in the stock of plant and equipment would also increase potential production and cause the production possibility curve to shift outward. New discoveries of natural resources or improved transportation making known resource deposits more accessible also will increase potential production. Another

[4] For a complete discussion of the conditions for the above analysis, see Paul A. Samuelson, *Foundations of Economic Analysis* (Cambridge, Mass.: Harvard University Press, 1963), pp. 230–236.

less obvious factor is economic organization. For example, a reorganization of farms into different sizes may affect productivity. Farms may be either too small or too large.[5]

It is interesting at this point to return to the export theory of regional growth.[6] The argument is that growth has essentially been a result of development of the export sector of the economy. How does this fit into the above framework? With no change in organization, technology, or resources, the only way that an increase in exports could be accomplished would be by reducing the production of local services. This would happen as the price for exports increased relative to that for local services. The increase in price would cause the ratio of exchange of exports for local services to fall. The preferred production choice would move from F toward A in Figure 8-1. Notice, however, that no growth has taken place.

For such a change to have any impact on growth the demand for exports must cause a change in one of the factors causing the expansion of the production possibilities curve. The transmission is through the demand for labor and capital. The demand for labor, capital, and other inputs is derived from the demand for the final product. All the inputs are related to the final product through the production function. If prices of the inputs are held constant, increases in the quantity of final product produced cause increases in all inputs used. That is, one moves along an expansion path in a diagram showing the isoquants and isocosts facing the firm.

The quantity of inputs demanded, however, would also vary with the price of the input. For example, consider the labor input. To see how the individual producer's demand for labor would change with price, we need to look at the isoquants showing the relation between the inputs and output and the isocost line showing the combinations of inputs that can be purchased at various outlays. If a producer is maximizing profits the rate of production will be at the quantity, such as Oq_1 in Figure 8-3, such that price will equal marginal cost. Furthermore the least-cost combination of labor and material, if they were the only two inputs, would be represented by point E in Figure 8-2. Line GH is the isocost line representing the least cost with which output q_1 can be produced, given the relative prices of labor and material. If the price of labor, the wage per man-hour, should decrease, the quantity of man-hours demanded by the producer would increase. The isocost line would shift to GI from GH, indicating the greater inputs that could be purchased with the same outlay. The unit costs of the firm decrease, since a greater output can be reached with the same outlay. Moreover, the new least-cost combination, such as F in

[5] Schultz, *op. cit.*, pp. 255–268.
[6] North, *loc. cit.;* and Tiebout, *loc. cit.*

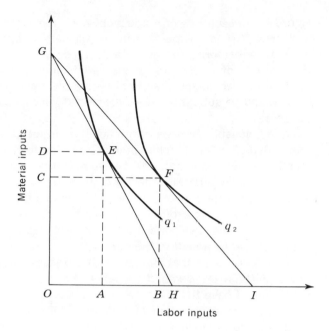

FIGURE 8-2

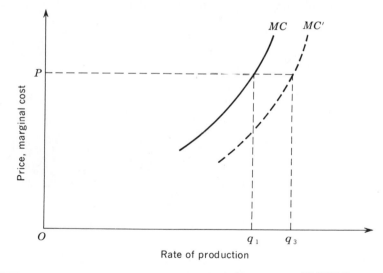

FIGURE 8-3

Figure 8-2, at each rate of production will require more man-hours per unit of output. The less expensive input will be substituted for the relatively more expensive one. Therefore, a decrease in the wage rate would cause the quantity of man-hours demanded to increase for two reasons: the total output would increase, increasing the demand for all inputs, and labor would be substituted for other inputs because it would be relatively cheaper.

The relationship between variations in input price and the quantity demanded of an input, holding the price of the final product and the prices of other inputs constant, can be illustrated in Figure 8-4. The line dd in Figure 8-4 is an illustrative demand curve for labor by an individual firm. As the price in the market for the final product increases, the rate of production that is most profitable also increases. Thus, even though there is no change in the wage rate, the demand for labor by the firm increases. This is shown by a shift in the demand for labor, such as the shift to $d'd'$ in Figure 8-4. Notice that changes in the prices of other inputs would also cause shifts in the demand for labor. An increase in the price of other inputs would have the same effect as a decrease in the wage rate. Labor would be relatively cheaper than the other inputs, and the demand curve would shift to $d'd'$ to indicate an increase in demand even though there was no change in the wage rate.

The industry demand for an input such as labor is the sum of the demands for labor of all of the firms in the industry, except that the price of the

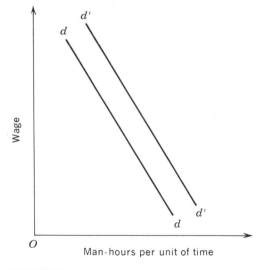

FIGURE 8-4

product is no longer constant. If the wage rate should fall, each firm would increase its production and the quantity of man-hours it would demand. But as every firm in the industry did this, the total quantity of the final product on the market would increase and force a decline in the price. The decline in the price of the final product would cause the demand for labor of each firm, dd, to shift downward to $d'd'$, as in Figure 8-5. Thus, a decline in the wage from w_1 to w_2 would cause the quantity of man-hours demanded by a firm to increase from OX to OY, and not to OZ. Demand curve DD traces out the demand for the input, taking into account the change in the price of the final product. It is the sum of all the DD curves that yields the aggregate industry demand for labor.

To analyze the impact of a change in the demand for exports on the change in the supply of inputs, such as labor or capital, we also need to show the determination of the wage rate in the export industry and other industries. To do this the supply curve of these inputs needs to be explicitly brought into the picture. The actual wage rate, interest rate, and prices of materials would be determined by the equilibrium of the quantity demanded and supplied. The response of input supply to a change in the input price depends on the time period considered. In a short period of time an increase of wages or the interest rate would cause an increase in the quantity of labor and capital offered. If the increase in price were maintained over a long period of time, the quantity supplied at the new

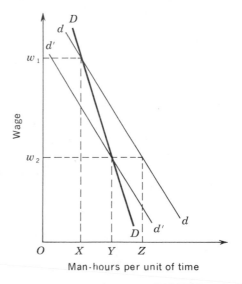

Man-hours per unit of time

FIGURE 8-5

higher input price would be even greater. In the short run, workers could shift occupations or employers in the same region without shifting their residence. There could also be an increase in hours worked. Employees would be willing to work overtime, if they were offered increased pay for doing so. Thus, in the short run the supply curve of inputs will be considered to be upward sloping. In the long run, however, there would be a much greater increase in the quantity of an input offered at the higher price. This would cause the short-run upward-sloping supply curve to shift to the right. A parallel analysis can be applied to a decrease in input prices in the short and long run. In this case the quantity supplied would be reduced, but the reduction would be greater in the long run than in the short run. Graphically, this is done by showing short-run changes in the quantity supplied along a supply curve and by showing long-run changes by a shift in the short-run supply curve.

After this long digression to show the link between production of exports and local services on the one hand and the input markets on the other, we shall return to how the increase in demand for exports could increase resources and the potential production of a region. The increase in demand for exports caused the price of exports to rise relative to local services. The relative rise in export price caused a shift of resources from producing local services to producing exports by causing an upward shift in the demand for labor and capital in the export industry and a downward shift in the demand for labor and capital in the local services industry. Illustrations of these shifts for the labor market in the export industry and the local services industry are shown in Figures 8-6 and 8-7. The change in relative prices of the final products causes the original demand curve DD to shift to $D'D'$. In the export industry it is an outward shift, and in the local services industry it is an inward shift. If the economy was in equilibrium before the change in exports, the wage rate would have been the same in both markets, w. In the short run the changes in demand cause the wage in the local services labor market to fall and the wage in the export market to rise.

Furthermore, in a competitive world in which labor and capital were freely mobile, wages and interest rates on capital would have been equal in these two markets and would also have been equal to the prevailing wage and interest rates in markets in other regions. The real wages and interest rates, that is, would have been equalized. We have already noted that the nominal wages might be different in order to take account of differences in the cost of living, amenities, and other preferences of people. Thus, the shift in the demand for labor in the export labor market of the region will also raise the wage above the prevailing wages in other regions.

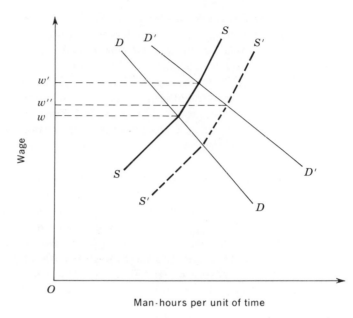

FIGURE 8-6

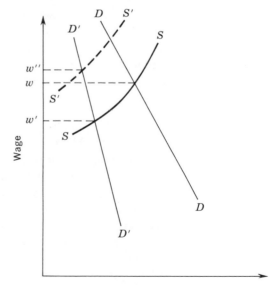

FIGURE 8-7

The higher real wage in the labor market for the export industry would cause workers to migrate from the labor market for the local services industry and from labor markets in other regions. In the long run the transfer of workers into the export labor market would cause the market's supply curve to shift to the right. The labor supply curve might shift to $S'S'$ as in Figure 8-6. In the other markets from which the workers migrated the labor supply curves would shift to the left. Fewer man-hours would be offered at each wage rate, since fewer workers would be in each market. Thus, in these markets the labor supply curve might shift to $S'S'$ as in Figure 8-7.

The migration of the workers would continue until the supply curve in the export labor market had shifted so far out that the equilibrium real wage in that market was equal to the equilibrium wage in all other markets. Simultaneously, the supply curve in all other labor markets would be shifting inward, causing the real wage in these markets to increase. The shift inward would continue until the wages in these markets were equal to the wages in the export labor market. The migration would continue until the real wage rates in all labor markets were equal. This would be wage w'' in Figures 8-6 and 8-7.

The same analysis would apply to the capital markets. Investment funds would shift from other markets to the export investment market until the rate of return on investments in all markets was once again equal.

To the extent that workers and investment funds come from outside the region, the resources of the region would have been increased and the production possibility curve would shift outward. There would not only be a relative shift from local services to export production, but it would be possible that the production of both local services and exports could be increased.

DIFFERENTIAL GROWTH RATES BETWEEN REGIONS
IN THE VOLUME OF PRODUCTION

To understand differential regional growth the events causing shifts in the location of the factors of production and capacity of particular regions to produce need to be analyzed. The factors causing change may come from many sources, as we have indicated. A change in the demand for an exported product could, as we have seen, cause a region to grow or decline. An alternative might be that a region is no longer the most profitable location for the production of the exported good. Changes in transportation costs, discoveries of new raw material deposits, or changes in relative factor costs in other regions may make other regions more profitable locations for production of the product. In this case a region's production of the export product declines with the same subsequent effects as a general shift in the demand for the product. A decline in the profitability of a region as a location for a particular good causes a downward shift in the demand for the production of the good from the particular region.

Growth of a region's income, of course, may be caused by changes in productivity, technology, or known resources within a region. The change might come from the local service sector of the economy. Nominal wages do not necessarily have to be equalized—only real wages. Some regions have lower costs of living or more agreeable living conditions. Changes in either of these factors may result in the attraction of industry or of retired persons who do not have to be employed. Either of these events would support increased employment in the local services sector.

When we speak of the shift in production of a particular product from one place to another, it does not necessarily mean that the actual production facilities are shifted. Production capacity for a given product in one region may be increasing, while that in other regions is the same, declining through attrition of firms as they go out of existence, or growing at a slower rate of growth.

As production and income in a national economy increase, there is a systematic impact on the relative demand for different kinds of goods and services. The income elasticities of demand for goods and services differ. As incomes rise, the consumption of some items rises more than proportionately with income and the consumption of other items rises less than proportionately with income. Thus, as national income rises, the demand for some items will not rise as rapidly as others. Because the income elasticity of demand for food is among the lowest, the agricultural sectors of the economy have been the slowest growing sectors of the economy.[7]

As an illustration of the different rates of growth of different industries, Table 8-1 is constructed to show the amount that participation income increased above or below the national average in different industries. Participation income is the sum of wages and salaries, other labor income, and proprietors' income.[8] The sum of the differences in Table 8-1 equals 0. Negative signs imply, not actual absolute declines in income, but the amount by which the increase in a particular industry was less than it would have been if the industry had grown at the average rate for the nation. For example, participation income from agriculture was −$23,358 million, indicating that participation income from agriculture rose $23,358 million less than it would have if it had increased at the same rate as the

[7] Harvey S. Perloff et al., *Regions, Resources, and Economic Growth* (Baltimore: The Johns Hopkins Press, 1960), pp. 335–340.
[8] Robert E. Graham, Jr., "Factors Underlying Changes in the Geographic Distribution of Income," *Survey of Current Business* (April, 1964), p. 20.

TABLE 8-1 INDUSTRIAL BREAKDOWN OF INCOME
CHANGE DUE TO INDUSTRY-MIX EFFECTS,
1948–1962 (In millions of dollars)

Industry	Relative income change
Agriculture	$ − 23,358
Trade	− 5,524
Transportation	− 4,504
Textiles	− 3,368
Bituminous coal	− 2,289
Lumber and furniture	− 1,535
Apparel	− 1,326
Food	− 1,081
Leather	− 600
Anthracite coal	− 499
Petroleum refining	− 469
Motor vehicles and equipment	− 166
Metal mining	− 136
Crude petroleum mining	− 67
Tobacco	− 44
Machinery except electrical	− 10
Other	− 1,655
Nonmetallic mining	55
Stone, clay, and glass	84
Rubber	123
Instruments and miscellaneous	392
Printing	419
Paper	640
Ordnance, primary and fabricated metals	855
Chemicals	1,202
Communication and public utilities	1,433
Nonautomotive transportation equipment	2,572
Military payroll, Federal government	2,741
Civilian payroll, Federal government	2,799
Construction	2,914
Electrical machinery	3,322
Finance	5,693
Services	9,067
State and local government	11,990
Other	112

SOURCE: Robert E. Graham, Jr., "Factors Underlying Changes in the
Geographic Distribution of Income," *Survey of Current Business* (April,
1964), pp. 26, 27.

average of all industries. This has been caused by the lower income elasticity of demand for agricultural goods than for other goods in the economy, by the decline in agriculture's share of United States exports, and by competition from synthetic and natural substitutes from nonagricultural sectors.[9]

Services tend to high income elasticities of demand and this is reflected in the greatest increases being among the service industry group: finance, services, and government. Income elasticities, however, are not the whole story. In addition there are substitution effects between industries. Oil and gas have been expanding at the expense of coal. New materials have been expanding at the expense of lumber. Historically, industries differ in improvements in technology and in changes in consumer demand caused by changes in taste. Anything that causes shifts in the national demand and supply for each commodity will effect change in the earnings from each industry.

This does not mean, however, that we can calculate the national growth rate of each industry in a region, and from this directly estimate the growth of income in that region. Nor does it mean that the historical differences between regions in the growth of income can be explained solely by differences in the national growth rate of industries located in each region. As noted in the discussion of the location of industry and the equilibrium patterns that might arise, the conditions that make a site optimum during one point in time may change so that in later periods other sites are better for the location of an industry. As new sites become more profitable for the production of a particular good, production tends to increase in that place relative to previous sites because that place can offer the product at lower prices.

A comparison of the actual growth rate in eight regions of the United States with the growth rate that would have occurred if each region's growth rate had been the weighted average of the national growth rates of industries located in the region will illustrate the point. In Table 8-2, column 1 shows the change from 1948 to 1962 in participation income in each region that would have occurred if each industry in each region had grown at the same rate as that industry grew in the nation. Column 2 shows the actual change in participation income in each of the regions from 1948 to 1962. Taking the error in forecasting the actual change as a percentage of the level of participation income in 1962 shows that the errors would have varied from 1 to 13 percent. If states had been the basis for estimation rather than regions, the error would have been even larger. Thus, changes

[9] Perloff et al., *loc. cit.*

in the relative locational characteristics of each region are an important aspect of any analysis of differential regional growth.

Several studies have taken advantage of the notion of dividing the reasons for differential regional growth into industrial-mix reasons and regional share reasons to analyze regional growth in the United States.[10] A calculation similar to the one in Table 8-2 is made. That is, the growth of income or employment that would have occurred in a region if each industry had grown at the national rate of growth of that industry is determined. The difference between this hypothetical growth and the actual growth of income or employment, as shown in column 3 of Table 8-2, is attributable to changes in a region's share of production caused by changes in the relative locational characteristics of the region. The same estimates could be reached by first calculating how much income or employment in each

[10] Perloff et al., *op. cit.*, part 4; and Graham, *op. cit.*, pp. 15–32. The latter study divides growth in income into three components: that which would have occurred if the region had grown at the national rate of growth, the difference between the latter and the change that would have occurred if each industry had increased at the national rate of growth (industry-mix effect), and the difference between the sum of the latter two components and the actual change in growth which shows the component change caused by industry in the region growing at a different rate than its national average (regional share effect). In Table 8-2 the national growth and industry-mix effects are combined into the industry-mix effect.

TABLE 8-2 A COMPARISON OF HYPOTHETICAL GROWTH BASED ON INDUSTRIAL-MIX AND ACTUAL GROWTH BETWEEN UNITED STATES REGIONS, 1948–1962 (In millions of dollars)

Regions*	Income change due to industrial mix (1)	Actual income change (2)	Error (column 1 minus column 2)	Participation income, 1962	Error as percentage of income, 1962
New England	$12,304	$ 10,602	$+1,702	$ 28,456	05.9
Mideast˙	49,999	40,151	+9,848	108,445	09.0
Great Lakes	41,834	33,744	+8,090	92,731	08.7
Plains	12,085	11,817	+ 268	35,383	00.7
Southeast	22,609	29,778	−7,169	69,998	10.2
Southwest	10,000	13,531	−3,531	30,049	11.7
Rocky Mountain	3,174	4,454	−1,280	10,245	12.4
Far West	21,614	29,591	−7,977	62,105	12.8
United States		173,667			

* For definitions of these regions, see Figure 6-2.

SOURCE: Calculated from Robert E. Graham, Jr., "Factors Underlying Changes in the Geographic Distribution of Income," *Survey of Current Business* (April, 1964), p. 24.

industry in each region increased above or below the national average for that industry. The sum of these differences would be the change in income or employment due to the regional share effect. The difference between the actual growth and the regional share effect would be the industry-mix effect previously calculated. This approach is in no way a theory of regional growth. It is a way of separating the data in order to determine how much of the difference in a region's growth is attributable to industry-mix or location factors.

Nevertheless, if factor markets functioned so that real returns to inputs were equalized within and between regions, there would be little concern for differential regional growth. Changes in the total volume of income and employment would be irrelevant. Labor and capital would migrate from low-return to high-return areas until real returns were equalized. These markets do not always function this way, and it is therefore important to analyze differences in total regional economic growth.

DIFFERENTIAL GROWTH RATES BETWEEN REGIONS IN THE LEVEL OF PER CAPITA INCOME

As mentioned in Chapter 6, per capita income is a measure of the welfare of people in a region. Table 6-5 shows the relative changes in per capita income from 1840 to 1960 in the United States. The purpose of this section is to indicate why differences between regions in per capita income exist and how relative changes in per capita income could have taken place.

The theory in the previous section indicating that real earnings would tend to equalize between regions does not refer to per capita income. Even if real earnings were equalized between regions, substantial differences between regions in per capita income could exist. For example, we know that on the average whites earn more than nonwhite persons, that males earn more than females, that wages in the city are higher than in rural areas, and that wages in occupations of different skills are different. If different proportions of these characteristics of the population were located in each region, per capita income levels would be different even though wages for the same skill were equal. Furthermore, there might be differences in the labor participation rate (the proportion of the population in the labor force). This rate may differ between regions because of the age distribution of the population. Age can enter another way. Workers at different ages in the same occupation earn different earnings, so that age distribution differences between regions could cause differences in the per capita income. Finally, property ownership may be unevenly distributed between geographic regions, causing per capita income to differ. Even after taking account of many of these factors, a recent study found that differentials in earnings per worker still exist between regions in the United States.[11]

A true test of the equalizing influence of migration would be an analysis of real returns to labor and capital in the same uses in different places. For unless it can be shown that the market is not operating to equalize such real returns there can be differences between regions in the volume of production and in per capita income without there being any differences in consumer welfare. Several attempts have been made to show the differences between regions in money wages for different industries. Tables 8-3 and 8-4 show attempts to indicate the differences between regions in nominal earnings in different industries. They cannot be converted to real earnings because we do not have an index of the differences in the cost of living between regions. Comparisons of the rate of return on capital between regions have almost never been made. One such attempt is shown in Table 8-5. This table shows the difference between New England and the United States in the marginal rate of return on gross investment in several industries. Since industry definitions in all these comparisons are fairly broad, differences between regions in the proportion of sectors within the

[11] Perloff et al., *op. cit.*, Chaps. 27–30.

TABLE 8-3 OUTPUT PER WORKER IN AGRICULTURE BY REGION, 1950

Region*	Output per worker
New England	$3,652
Middle Atlantic	3,832
Great Lakes	3,222
Southeast	1,568
Plains	3,935
Southwest	3,851
Mountain	4,658
Far West	4,412

* For definitions of these regions, see Fig. 6-2. The Middle Atlantic Region is the same as the Mideast Region.

SOURCE: Reprinted by permission from Harvey S. Perloff et al., *Regions, Resources, and Economic Growth*, published for Resources for the Future, Inc. (Baltimore: The Johns Hopkins Press, 1960), p. 557.

TABLE 8-4 AVERAGE HOURLY EARNINGS OF MANUFACTURING PRODUCTION WORKERS BY REGION, BY INDUSTRY, 1947

Industry	New England	Middle Atlantic	Great Lakes	Southeast	Plains	Southwest	Mountain	Far West
Food	$1.00	$1.07	$1.14	$ .80	$1.08	$ .89	$1.05	$1.22
Textiles	1.14	1.14	1.09	.92	.96	.85	.82	1.20
Apparel	.92	1.05	.99	.75	.85	.73	.80	1.11
Lumber	.96	.98	1.03	.60	.95	.94	1.20	1.55
Furniture	1.00	1.16	1.18	.83	1.08	.88	1.07	1.35
Paper	1.15	1.17	1.22	1.11	1.09	1.11	—	1.44
Printing	1.24	1.49	1.47	1.21	1.21	1.32	1.30	1.71
Chemicals	1.08	1.29	1.30	1.04	1.22	1.22	1.24	1.41
Petroleum and coal	1.41	1.60	1.51	1.30	1.29	1.57	1.65	1.55
Leather	.97	1.11	1.06	.88	.92	.82	.94	1.20
Stone, clay, and glass	1.18	1.14	1.23	.94	1.05	1.02	1.13	1.32
Primary metals	1.23	1.44	1.50	1.14	1.31	1.20	1.40	1.48
Fabricated metals	1.14	1.26	1.33	1.05	1.15	1.22	1.27	1.49
Machinery except electrical	1.29	1.37	1.43	1.06	1.17	1.14	1.23	1.54
Electrical machinery	1.14	1.33	1.30	1.08	1.09	1.07	.85	1.34
Transportation equipment	1.28	1.45	1.51	1.20	1.26	1.31	1.18	1.58
Instruments	1.14	1.33	1.23	1.15	1.12	1.08	1.05	—

* For definitions of these regions, see Fig. 6-2. The Middle Atlantic Region is the same as the Mideast Region.

SOURCE: Reprinted by permission from Harvey S. Perloff et al., *Regions, Resources, and Economic Growth*, published for Resources for the Future, Inc. (Baltimore: The Johns Hopkins Press, 1960), p. 577.

broad industry groups could cause differences even though returns in the same occupation or in the same subindustry were equalized.

In 1950 the highest per capita income was in the Far West, and the lowest was in the Southeast. The ranking was Far West, Mideast, Great Lakes, New England, Rocky Mountain, Plains, Southwest, and Southeast. The earnings figures although not exactly fitting this ranking do tend to follow it. Thus, we might use per capita income, in the absence of earnings per hour for early decades, as an indicator of high and low wage areas. It is

TABLE 8-5 COMPARISON OF THE MARGINAL RATE OF RETURN
ON CAPITAL BETWEEN NEW ENGLAND AND THE REST OF THE
UNITED STATES FOR THE MACHINERY AND CHEMICAL
INDUSTRIES, 1939–1947 AND 1947–1954

Industry	$m_{ne} - m_{us}$,* 1939–1947	$m_{ne} - m_{us}$,* 1947–1954
Machine tools	−0.7915	+0.2192
Metalworking machinery	−0.6814	−0.3546
Cutting tools, jigs, fixtures	−0.1364	−0.0963
Food products machinery	−2.1809	+2.1445
Textile machinery	−0.2939	−0.1279
Woodworking machinery	+3.2852	+3.2234
Paper industries machinery	−0.0570	−0.1190
Printing trades machinery	+0.3506	+0.0137
Special industry machinery	−0.3582	+0.6324
Pumps and compressors	+1.5394	+0.6889
Elevators, escalators, conveyors	+0.9202	+0.3298
Power transmission equipment	−0.2800	+0.1565
General industry machinery	+0.4815	−0.0759
Typewriters	+0.4223	−0.2737
Sewing machines	−0.2279	+0.1015
Refrigeration machinery	−0.3007	+0.4544
Valves and fittings	−0.9565	+0.0364
Ball and roller bearings	+0.2905	−0.1663
Machine shops	+0.9485	+0.1211
Toilet preparations		+1.46
Pharmaceutical preparations†		+1.38
Compressed and liquefied gases†		+0.92
Soap and glycerin		+7.00
Glue and gelatin		−1.38
Paints and varnishes		+1.34
Fertilizers		+4.83
Plastics materials		+1.53
Alkalies and chlorine†		+0.70
Cleaning and polishing preparations		+0.37
Insecticides and fungicides		+0.22
Printing ink		+0.89
Chemical products not elsewhere classified		−0.22

* m_{ne} is the marginal rate of return on capital in New England. m_{us} is the marginal rate of
return on capital in the United States. The marginal rate of return is calculated by dividing
the change in proprietary income in 1939–1947 or 1947–1954 by the total investment during
the same period. Proprietary income is value added less wages and salaries. It includes
profits, interest, rent, and taxes. m is the marginal rate of return on gross investment, since
the investment data include depreciation expenditures.
† Calculated for the New England and Middle Atlantic Regions because data were unavailable for the New England Region only.

SOURCE: By permission from George H. Borts and Jerome L. Stein, *Economic Growth in a
Free Market* (New York: Columbia University Press, 1964), pp. 177–178; and Jerome L.
Stein, *Economic Factors in the Location of Industry: Part One: The Chemical Industries*,
mimeographed report (Providence, R.I., Brown University, College Community Research
Program, December, 1957), p. 35.

important to note that per capita income is only a tentative indicator of wages. There is no theoretical reason for the two to be the same, or even to be in the same rank order.

Nevertheless, using per capita income from 1840 to 1960 (Table 6-5) for an indicator of return to labor by regions, we then have something with which to compare actual migration statistics. The comparison should indicate whether the net migratory flows of people are in the direction suggested by theory. Table 8-6 shows the net migration per 1,000 average population from 1870 to 1950. Unfortunately, we do not have historical information on interregional capital flows.[12]

Over the entire period there has been a large net immigration to the Far West and a large net emigration from the Southeast, as one would expect since the Far West has always had the highest per capita income, and the Southeast during this period has always had the lowest per capita income. From 1880 to 1950 one would also have expected migration from the Southwest. In fact there has been strong net immigration into the region until 1930–50. Since personal income per capita in the Plains states was less than the national average in 1880 and from 1920 to 1950, a net emigration

[12] Nevertheless, evidence on capital flows for 1953 and 1957 indicates that shifts in regional demand for capital and concentrations of property owners in particular regions are the major determinants of capital flows. See J. Thomas Romans, *Capital Exports and Growth Among U.S. Regions* (Middletown, Conn.: Wesleyan University Press, 1965).

TABLE 8-6   NET REGIONAL MIGRATION PER 1,000 AVERAGE POPULATION, 1870–1950

Region*	1870–1880	1880–1890	1890–1900	1900–1910	1910–1920	1920–1930	1930–1940	1940–1950
Northeast	42	102	107	91	48	4	−6	−1
Middle Atlantic	14	75	82	113	47	54	12	5
Great Lakes	3	37	46	33	72	55	−4	13
Southeast	−18	−26	−39	−33	−47	−64	−23	−58
Plains	210	170	−10	−9	−26	−56	−46	−73
Southwest	311	98	249	176	41	27	−39	−10
Mountain	695	548	196	289	96	−74	−11	−13
Far West	282	396	160	481	220	307	145	284

* For definitions of these regions, see Fig. 6-2. The Middle Atlantic Region is the same as the Mideast Region.

SOURCE: Reprinted by permission from Harvey S. Perloff et al., *Regions, Resources, and Economic Growth*, published for Resources for the Future, Inc. (Baltimore: The Johns Hopkins Press, 1960), p. 593; and from Everett S. Lee et al., *Population Redistribution and Economic Growth, United States, 1870–1950* (Philadelphia: American Philosophical Society, 1957), table P-1, pp. 107–231.

from the area at those times would be expected. In fact there has been a net emigration from the Plains Region since 1890. The income data would also suggest migration from the Rocky Mountain Region from 1930 to 1950. There has in fact been a net emigration from this region since 1920. Finally, from 1930 to 1940 in the Great Lakes and from 1930 to 1950 in New England there was a net emigration, when in fact the income data would indicate a net immigration. This may be a result of the inadequacy of the data on per capita income, or it may reflect property components in per capita income.

These statistics only give an indication of what is happening. For a true test of the equilibration of the market mechanism, we would need specific rates of return to labor of given skills in different places and specific rates of return to capital in different places, and we could then compare actual migration to these earnings figures. These figures are unavailable. Nevertheless, there have been several studies indicating dissatisfaction with the equalization of returns from migration. We would not have seen the differences in earnings that exist today and have persisted over time, if migration had caused an equalization of returns.[13]

COSTS AND RETURNS TO LABOR AND CAPITAL MIGRATION

The persistent differences between regions in the returns to labor and capital can be explained by the return to investment in migration and may have nothing to do with imperfections in market operations, such as the lack of information about new opportunities.[14] In order to analyze the problem we need to understand how choices between actions involving time are made. Thus, in this section the first discussion will be about selecting between choices involving time and risk. Then the analysis will be applied to the worker's choice between migrating and not migrating, and to the investor's choice of lending or risking capital nearby or in a new, more distant location. The analysis will show why it is possible in theory for there to be differences between regions in the return to factors of equal productivity and for no equalizing migration of labor to take place.

To evaluate an action or investment that yields costs and returns over a period of time, the stream of incomes and costs must be discounted to a

[13] George Borts, "Returns Equalization and Regional Growth," *American Economic Review* (June, 1960), pp. 319–347; T. W. Schultz, *The Economic Organization of Agriculture* (New York: McGraw-Hill Book Company, 1953), chap. 18; and Dale E. Hathaway, "Migration from Agriculture: The Historical Record and Its Meaning," *American Economic Review* (May, 1960), pp. 379–391.

[14] This section is based on the analysis of labor migration in Larry A. Sjaastad, "The Costs and Returns of Human Migration," *Journal of Political Economy*, special supplement (October, 1962), pp. 80–93. For development of the concept of expected income, see Burton Weisbrod, "An Expected-income Measure of Economic Welfare," *Journal of Political Economy* (August, 1962), pp. 355–367.

present value. The income stream must be capitalized. To find out the worth of an income of a certain amount, say $100, in each of the next ten years, we must calculate how much it would cost to obtain a bond that would yield the same income. The question is how much it would cost to buy a bond that would yield $100 in each of the next ten years. The cost of the bond depends upon the interest rate, and the interest rate must be known to make the calculation. The present value of the first year's $100 is found by solving for P in the following equation:

$$P(1 + r) = \$100$$

That is, what sum plus the interest on it for one year will equal $100? If the interest rate is 0.05, the value of P is $100/1.05, which is $95.05. The present value of the income received in the second year is found by the following formula:

$$P(1 + r)(1 + r) = \$100$$

That is, what sum P, plus the interest on it for the first year, plus the interest from the first to the second year on the sum of P, plus the first year interest will equal $100? If the interest rate is 0.05, the solution is as follows:

$$P = \frac{\$100}{(1.05)^2}$$

If I can get an annual yield of 5 percent on a bond in alternative investments, then the $100 from this particular activity coming in two years must pay off the equivalent.

By now you should expect the present value of the $100 in the third through tenth years to be solved by using the following equation:

$$Pn = \frac{\$100}{(1 + r)^n}$$

where

Pn is the present value of the $100 received in the nth year

n is the year of receipt of the $100

r is the interest rate

The total present value of the income stream of $100 in each of the next ten years is the sum of the present values of the income received in each of the ten years. This can be expressed in the following way:

$$P = \frac{\$100}{(1.05)} + \frac{\$100}{(1.05)^2} + \frac{\$100}{(1.05)^3} + \cdots + \frac{\$100}{(1.05)^{10}}$$

Suppose that the analysis was of the income from a machine that would be worth nothing at the end of the ten years. If alternative opportunities to invest money would yield a 5 percent rate of return per year, then the investor would not spend more than $772.10, the present value of the income stream, for the machine. An alternative way to look at the problem is to solve the following equation for the interest rate:

$$C = \frac{\$100}{(1+r)} + \frac{\$100}{(1+r)^2} + \frac{\$100}{(1+r)^3} + \cdots + \frac{\$100}{(1+r)^{10}}$$

Given the cost of the machine, C, the interest rate that equates the present value of the income stream with the cost of the machine is the productivity of the machine. The investment is worthwhile if the rate of return is greater than the rate of return that could be earned in alternative investments.

If, under the first approach, the cost is greater than the present value, or if under the second approach the rate of return is less than that which could be earned in alternative investments, the investment would not be undertaken.

To apply this approach to a worker's decision on whether he should migrate we need to estimate the costs of migration, the returns (which are the increase in earnings), and the appropriate interest rate. The costs of migration include the following costs: the moving costs above the ordinary living expenditures, the earnings foregone while in transit, the cost of retraining for a new job if required, and the psychic costs of leaving familiar surroundings. For the family man another cost may have to be added to those listed above. The move applies to his whole family. If the new place does not provide opportunities for his wife to work but the current location does, the present value of the foregone earnings of the wife would have to be counted as costs of migration.

The returns to investment in migration include the following gains: the present value of the increase in earnings, the psychic values if there are any in the new place, and the opportunity for other members of the family to work where none exist in the current location. The earnings in the new place do not necessarily have to be in the same occupation. Earnings in occupations utilizing similar skills may also be appropriate. The uncertainty of getting a new job quickly may be handled by applying a probability to the increase in earnings rather than treating the increase as a sure thing. Another possibility would be to raise the interest rate used to discount earnings in the new place. The rate of return should be the return that the potential migrant might receive in alternative investment if he did not spend it on migrating.

What, then, are the implications of this investment approach for generalizations about migration? First, migration is less likely for men who are older. The life span over which the increased income might be earned is lower than for young men. Furthermore, it is less likely that the increase will be as great for older as for younger workers. Seniority yields increases in pay, but if the worker moves to another place, and in particular if he changes occupations, he may lose the pay gain of seniority so that he would not receive the same wage as men of comparable age and skill in the new place. He would be starting all over again. Thus, migration is more likely to be profitable for the young. Second, the cost of migration is less the closer is the new alternative. This cost will increase with distance. The move of jobs is easiest to carry out when no move of residence is required.

Even if migration is profitable, there may be further hindrances to the migration. People cannot borrow money without collateral. Thus, even if the investment would be profitable, the move might not be made because the worker could not borrow the necessary money. During a period when windfall gains were received, workers and farmers might conceive it as a good omen for next year's crops and stay put longer. On the other hand, it might just provide the funds to make the move. When workers have been unemployed some time, it is unlikely that they will have the necessary cash to make the move, or that they will have the collateral to borrow the necessary funds.

To apply the approach to the movement of capital from one place to another we need to elaborate the costs and returns from the shift. For a lender in a financial institution—banks, life insurance companies, and savings and loan associations—the costs of lending in another place are the additional costs of handling the loan once it is made. For an entrepreneur the cost of transferring capital or property wealth is more difficult. Suppose that market and supply conditions have changed since the initial location of the establishment. Whereas the establishment was optimally located initially, assume that the site is no longer optimal for the particular product. What is the cost of shifting resources? The plant and equipment cannot be moved. The entrepreneur can sell them and use the funds to move to a new site. The cost of shifting capital will be the actual transportation cost, a small amount, plus the loss on his investment. If he should continue to operate the plant in the old suboptimal site, profits would not be maximized. If the sale of plant and equipment should be less than the present value of earnings from the plant at the suboptimal site, the loss is a cost of moving the capital. In particular, retail and manufacturing plants in a declining area are locked in. They cannot find buyers for their present establishments because investment returns in the same activity are greater elsewhere. If the place should become an optimum location for another activity, the establishment might be sold for closer to its present value, or the entrepreneur could shift to a new product while in the same location. If the plant and equipment are torn down and abandoned, the cost of moving capital is the demolition cost plus the loss of the present value of the enterprise if it had remained in operation at the old site.

The returns from moving to a new site are the increase in earnings per invested dollar in the new site. The interest rate used to calculate the present value of the increased earnings is the rate of return that it is possible to receive by investing the money in financial institutions or other companies.

The implications of the analysis for the mobility of capital are that the shifting of capital from one place to another is not the costless proposition often assumed in economic analysis. In particular, investments in retail enterprises and in manufacturing plant and equipment are extremely difficult to shift out of when located in declining areas. The formation of loanable funds in undeveloped or partially developed areas lags behind that of the more developed areas. In the United States there is a tendency toward a surplus of loanable funds in the Northeast and a deficiency of funds in the South and West. The problem of investing or shifting these funds is not costless. In particular a greater risk factor is included the farther away the funds will be invested. The cost of shifting the location of an enterprise will decrease as its remaining life shrinks. The lower the present value of an enterprise the less the cost of selling out and shifting its location.

SUMMARY

For the total level of potential income and employment in a region to increase there must be an increase in available inputs or an increase in the productivity of the inputs. An increase in the demand for exports of a region may in the long run facilitate growth because it causes an increase in the returns to labor and capital to produce the export good that attracts workers and investment funds from other sectors of the same region and from other regions. The immigration of capital and labor would increase the level of potential income and employment in the region. There are, of course, other ways that the amount and productivity of inputs might increase.

Nevertheless, differences between regions in the growth of income and employment would be unimportant if the wages and return to capital were equalized between input markets within and between regions. One measure of the extent to which these returns are not equalized is the level of per capita income. Differences between regions in the proportion of several population characteristics could cause differences in per capita incomes even though returns to inputs in the same use in each region were equalized. Although there has been some tendency for the percentage differences between regions in per capita income to narrow and although migration has tended to flow from low per capita income regions to high per capita income regions, differences between regions in earnings after population characteristics have been taken into account do exist and have persisted for long periods of time.

The reason for the persistence of incomes to be different in different regions is not necessarily a result of imperfections in the marketplace, such as the lack of information about new opportunities. The reason why migration of labor and capital may not continue until wages and return on capital are equalized is that investment in migration is not profitable. For older workers and for job changes requiring a change of residence the present value of net returns will probably not be sufficient to cover the cost of migration.

CHAPTER 9

THE IMPACT
OF GROWTH
ON REGIONAL
STRUCTURE

In the first section of this book the principles behind the location of industry were explained. Once this was covered, the theory of location was used to explain the spatial structure of regions. A jump was then made to investigate the behavior of the aggregate level of income and employment during the short run and the long run between regions. In this chapter we return almost full circle to investigate the impact of changes in population, income, and technology on regional structure. Our procedure will be to return to the land use model of Chapter 5 and the simple model of systems of cities in Chapter 3. First we shall allow a given change in population, holding all other growth variables constant, and see what changes would occur in the models. Then changes in income and technology will be taken up in turn to see their impact on the spatial structure of the regional economy. Finally, we shall make some comments on the relation between economic development and cities. The models are still very fragmentary and only give clues about directions of change.

POPULATION GROWTH

As the population of a region increases, the simple model of a system of cities would predict that the number of cities would increase and that new hierarchies would arise. As a result, the size of the largest place would also increase.

For each market area an increase in population would cause the demand curve to shift to the right, allowing excess profits. New firms would enter the market and cause the geographic area necessary for a threshold-size market to shrink. Thus, the first-order places serving a rural hinterland and the town itself with convenience-type goods will increase in number. It will take more of them to cover the region completely, and the places will be closer together. Since second- and higher-order places are determined by the number of satellites, s, for each higher-order city, there will also be an increase in the number of higher-order places. If the number of satellites in the system is three, an increase in the number of first-order places would create new second-order places—one for every three new first-order places. One new third-order place would be created for every three new second-order places, and so on. One hypothetical system of such places was described in Table 3-1. If, as in that table, the original system had six hierarchical orders of places, if the proportion of population in a place were one-half the population served, if the number of satellite places were three, and if the population of the system more than tripled, a seventh-order place would arise to serve three sixth-order places.

Consider the problem of an increase in population less than triple its original size. If the population should only double, there would arise twice as many cities in each rank order, but there would be an insufficient market for a seventh-order place. Suppose, however, that the population grew to a level somewhere between two and three times the original population. There would be an insufficient market to create a third complete hierarchy of six orders of cities. It would appear that some lower-order places will not be served by higher-order places. One or the other or both of the sixth-order places will serve a larger population than indicated by the system. Their populations would thus rise proportionately.

A more appropriate model for analyzing the impact of an increase in population on the number, size, and spacing of cities would be the continuous distribution of city sizes based on the random variation of the multiplier in the previous model. That is, the model with fixed orders of places in which each place has the same population as other places in the same order and is a fixed multiple of places in the next lower order is changed so that the multiplier is a random variable causing city sizes to be continuous rather than six discrete jumps (when there are six orders). Under the assumption that the proportion of the population of the market area residing in the central place is small, close to 0, the population of each place times its rank will be a constant. Using this model an increase in population would increase the number of places, reduce the distance between them, and increase the size of the largest place.

As in the previous model, the increase in population would cause the demand curve in each market to shift to the right, allowing excess profits. New firms would enter the market and cause the geographic area necessary for a threshold size market to shrink. Equating each central place to the center of each market size, the geographic area of each hinterland would shrink. The population served in the lowest-order place would remain the same as before, but the area would change. New places would arise between older ones. If the model is to hold, the new distribution of city sizes and number of cities must be such that the product of the rank and size of the city equals a constant. If, indeed, the populations of the places, or cities, are proportional to the population served, the largest place serving the entire region would increase in population. Thus, there would be more places, they would be closer together, and the number of cities would increase.

To understand the impact of population change in a central place upon land use we must look at its impact upon the demand for goods and services. An increase in the number of people in a central place will shift to the right the demand curves for goods and services in that place. At current prices an excess demand for goods and services would exist. Thus, market prices would be bid up and the rent gradients for land for each use would be shifted upward in order to make sufficient land available to produce the goods demanded. Depending upon the size of the increased population, there would be increased demands for housing, urban services, manufacturing products (but perhaps not from this city and its hinterland), and agricultural products (also partially from this city-region and partially from others). To the extent that the increased demands are upon this city-region, the hinterland will increase in diameter. Furthermore, the urbanized area will expand. The increased price for land should cause more intense use of land at given distances from the market center. Houses near the urban core will be turned into offices or rooming houses, and farmland at the fringe of the city will be converted to residential use.[1]

Population changes can have their impact not only through increases or decreases in the aggregate population, but also through shifts in the composition of the population. "Shifts in the composition of population" means shifts in the cultural groups making up the population, shifts in the occupational structure of the population, shifts in the geographic location of the population, and shifts in the income distribution of the population.

We can associate shifts in the cultural groups making up the population with changes in taste patterns that cause change in demand for specific products. For example, some cultural groups enjoy neighborhood bakeries. A shift increasing the proportion of this group in the population would cause more land to be devoted to these establishments. Cultural groups may have different diets causing changes in agricultural production with shifts in the proportion of certain cultural groups in the population. Land for some products would diminish, while land for other more favored products would increase in extent.

Shifts in the geographic distribution of the population might occur through shifts of population from the rural hinterland to the central places, in which case the impact would be the same as an increase in population in the central place. The shift might also occur through a shift in population from one central place to another. In this case there would be a shrinkage in the supply area and the urbanized area of the place with declining population,

[1] This section on the impact of population growth on land use relies on the following two works: Edgar S. Dunn, Jr., *The Location of Agricultural Production* (Gainesville, Fla.: University of Florida Press, 1954), chap. 6; and Richard F. Muth, "Economic Change and Rural-Urban Land Conversions," *Econometrica*, vol. 29, no. 1 (January, 1961), pp. 1–23.

and extension of the supply area of the place receiving population. The central place receiving population would also expand and its land would be more intensively used with the increase in its rent gradient.

Shifts in the occupational structure and income distribution of the population are easily handled as changes in the income of the population. This leads us into the next section, an investigation of how an increase in per capita income will affect systems of cities and land use.

INCREASES IN PER CAPITA INCOME

As the per capita income of a region increases, the simple model of a system of cities would predict that the number of cities would increase and thus that the distance between cities would decrease, that the size of cities in low orders would increase, and that there would be fewer orders of cities given no change in population or total rural population.

For each market area an increase in per capita income would cause the demand curve to shift to the right, allowing excess profits. These excess profits would appear to attract new firms. As before, equate each central place to the center of each market. The rural population served in the lowest-order place would decrease. Since each person is buying more, fewer persons are needed to make up the threshold-size market. The increase in per capita income has not decreased the number of persons required to serve the threshold-size market. Just as many people are needed to produce the same quantity as before, but that quantity is purchased by fewer customers. Thus, the ratio between the serving population and the population in the market has increased. With no change in the total population in farming, more first-order places would be required. The change in per capita income would not appear to change the number of satellite places for each center above the first order. Thus, the second-order places would include three of the lower-order places. The population of the second-order place, however, depends upon how many people are required to serve the trading area. Following the simple model assumptions, the population of a place in each order is the same proportion of the population served as in every other order. Therefore, the change in population of the second-order place will depend upon whether the total population served was reduced by a greater or lesser proportion than the increase in the proportion between the population of a center and the population served. In any case, since the number of first-order places has increased, the number of places in each order will increase. Thus, with the total population held constant, fewer orders of places will fit into the system than before. Nonetheless, there will be more places altogether.

In the terminology of the simple model of Chapter 3 and Table 3-1, the increase in per capita income causes the proportion k to increase and the rural population served by the first-order central place to decrease, while the total population of the system and the number of satellites, s, remain unchanged. For example, suppose that the system of cities before a change in per capita income is that described in Table 3-1 in which the rural population served by the lowest-order place is 1,000; the proportion of population in the central place, k, is one-half the total population served; each central place above the first-order place has three satellites; and the population of that system remains the same, 15,552,000.

Consider a change in per capita income that causes per capita consumption in the first-order trading area to increase so that 1,000 people could serve 1,600 instead of 2,000 people. Thus, each first-order place would serve itself and 600 rural people after the income change. This would make k equal to five-eighths instead of one-half. In Table 3-1 there were 243 first-order places serving the rural population as well as themselves. If there were no change in the number of rural people in agriculture, there would still be 243,000 rural people on the land. If each first-order place would now serve only 600 of them, there would have to be 405 first-order places to serve the same area and population. If there were three first-order places for each second-order place, there would be 135 second-order places. Each second-order place would serve 4,800 people in three first-order places plus its own population. The ratio between its own population and the population served would be the same as for the first-order place, five to eight. Thus, the population of the second-order place would be 8,000 and the population served would be 12,800. Table 9-1 illustrates the system of cities that would result. Although there would be only four orders of places after the income change, each order place above the first would have a larger population than previously. The total population of the system in the table would be only 12,288,000, which is less than before the income change. To add another order would require a population of over thirty million. In effect, then, some fifth-order places would exist and would serve more than three satellites.

In the case of the continuous distribution model in which the rank of a place times its size is equal to a constant, an increase in per capita income would have a similar effect. The largest place would have to be around five-eighths of the total population, since it serves the entire region. This is larger than the largest city before the income change. Before the income change the largest city would have contained about one-half of the total population. The continuous distribution of city sizes is generated by the random variation of the multiplier that increases the city size of each order

TABLE 9-1   HYPOTHETICAL SYSTEM OF CITIES*

Order	Population of centers in order	Population served by each center	Number of centers in each order
1	1,000	1,600	405
2	8,000	12,800	135
3	64,000	102,400	45
4	512,000	819,200	15

* This table is based on Table 3-1. It assumes the same total population in the region, 15,552,000. The number of satellites is the same, three. The proportion, k, that the population of a central place is of the total population served is greater, five-eighths. The rural population served by the first-order place is less than in Table 3-1; it is 600 instead of 1,000. The direction of change in the size and number of places from Table 3-1 to Table 9-1 is indicative of change caused by an increase in per capita income in a region.

from the next lower order. Before the income change the multiplier would have randomly varied around 6. The multiplier is $s/(1 - k)$. After the income change the multiplier randomly varies around 8. Holding total population constant, the number of orders (or multiplications by the multiplier) has to decrease as k increases. Thus, the income change will cause k to increase, the number of cities to increase, and the population of cities in each order to increase.

If per capita income increases even though population structure remains the same, or if per capita income increases because of a shift in the occupational structure or income distribution of the population, there will be a relative increase in demand for many products, and thus a relative increase in the supply areas necessary to produce them. As mentioned before, the income elasticity of demand for agricultural products tends to be low. But not all agricultural products have low income elasticities of demand. The demand for fresh vegetables and fruits tends to increase more than proportionately as income increases. The agricultural products that have the greater income elasticities of demand are "protective" foods. The agricultural products with the lower income elasticities of demand are "energy-producing" foods.[2] The amount of land required per calorie of protective food is greater than the amount of land required per calorie of energy-producing food. Thus, as income increases the demand for farmland increases more than proportionately to the increase in demand for agricultural products.[3]

Equally important, however, is the comparison of the income elasticity of demand for agricultural products relative to housing and other urban

[2] Dunn, op. cit., pp. 74–75.
[3] Ibid.

services. If the income elasticity of demand for housing is unity or greater, and the demand for agricultural products from the adjacent hinterland is less than 1, an increase in per capita income will increase the demand for housing by more than the demand for food, and the urban land uses will encroach on the agricultural hinterland.[4]

TECHNOLOGICAL CHANGE

The impact of technological change on the size and spacing of cities and on land use will depend upon the nature of the change. In the following discussion we will investigate the impact of a reduction in transportation costs because of change in technology, the impact of changes in the minimum threshold size of firms because of changes in economies of mass production, the impact of increases in yield per acre and decreases in agricultural average costs because of improvements in technology, and the impact of a decrease in average costs without changes in yield per acre. Although the changes in yield per acre are expressed in terms of agricultural production, the changes apply also to other land uses in which the change would be expressed in output per square foot.

We shall first investigate the impact of a change in transport cost on the size, number, and spacing of cities. Once again assume the simple model of a system of cities. In the model resources are ubiquitous. Thus, transportation cost changes only affect demand. With a reduction in transportation costs customers adjacent to the plant do not change the quantity of the product that they demand because they originally paid no transportation costs. As transportation costs are reduced, customers some distance away from the plant will find that the price they pay for the product is reduced. They pay the price at the plant plus transportation cost. Thus, with no change in the plant price, the demand schedule for each customer at distances from the plant will shift to the right. Summing all the demand curves for each customer over the whole market of a plant, the aggregate demand for the firm's product shifts to the right. Since we begin from a situation of equilibrium in which the demand curve was tangent to the average cost curve, the shift to the right of the demand curve causes excess profits. If these are large enough, new firms will enter the market and reduce the number of persons in each market, until the demand curves of each firm are once again tangent to their average cost schedules.

The impact of these changes on the size, number, and spacing of cities is the same as the impact of an increase in per capita income. The simple model of a system of cities would predict that the number of cities would

[4] Muth, *loc. cit.*

increase, the distance between them would decrease, and the cities above the first order would increase in size. The mechanism is exactly the same. Since average cost has not changed, the number of people required for a given quantity of output is the same as before the change in transportation cost. The new equilibrium of each firm may not be at the exact same output as before the change, but it will be approximately the same. The number of persons served in the market has decreased because each person is consuming more than he previously did because the delivered price is less. The ratio of persons in the center to persons served by a center has increased. In the same way as in the case of an increase in per capita income this increases k, the proportion of the served population in the market center. Holding population constant, the impact on the simple model of a system of cities would be the same as described in Table 9-1. The analysis of the continuous distribution model would also be the same.
' If at the same time that transportation costs are reduced by changes in technology, there is also a change in economies of scale so that very large plants can produce at lower average and marginal costs than smaller plants, then city size would decrease instead of increase. The change in scale means that the geographic area that could be served by one large firm would encompass the areas served by several small firms. The larger firm as a result of technological change could sell in other markets for less than the smaller firms could in spite of the greater distance from the plant site. Therefore, if transport costs were reduced and economies of scale were increased, the aggregate demand for one firm's product would shift to the right. Not only is each person buying more because of the reduced delivered price, but the extent of the market has increased. Would not all firms be competing everywhere because of the technological knowledge available to everyone? Yes, but the minimum size market that would be necessary for each firm to survive would now be bigger than before. Fewer firms would be able to survive. Eventually the demand curve facing each firm would be just tangent to the average cost curve. Each firm would still be a partially monopolistic firm because of our assumptions that delivered prices determine market areas and that new firms will crowd into the region until the demand curve for each firm is forced to tangency with its average cost. Thus, fewer firms will be needed to serve the same region than were needed before the changes.

The impact of these two changes in transport cost and economies of scale on the size, number, and spacing of cities is to reduce the number of places, to increase the distance between them, and to decrease their size. To keep population constant, however, the number of cities would have to increase through an increase in area. This time the rural population served by the lowest-order place would increase. Nothing would seem to cause s, the number of satellites, to change, but k, the proportion of population in the center of a trading area necessary for serving the area, would decrease if the labor input per unit of output decreased because of the shift in the average cost curve. Assume that the city system before the changes was the same as described in Table 3-1. Consider that the change causes the rural population served by the lowest-order place to increase from 1,000 to 3,000 and k to change from $\frac{1}{2}$ to $\frac{1}{4}$.

The smallest place would now have 1,000 persons and would serve 3,000 rural persons instead of 1,000. The multiplier would now be 4 instead of 6. Only 81 first-order places would fit into the same region that held 243 first-order places before the changes. Within the constraints of the multiplier the largest city would be reached by the fifth order, and it would serve only 1,024,000 people, about one-fifteenth of the original population. The only way to maintain the same population and allow the parameters to change as assumed is to allow the geographic area of the region to expand. It has to expand sufficiently to allow 729 first-order places to arise, each serving 3,000 rural people. This would allow seven orders of places to exist, the largest of which would serve 16,384,000, about 800,000 more than the original population. The largest city would have a population of only 4,096,000 instead of the 7,776,000 in the largest city before the change. Use of the continuous distribution model would yield no different results.

So far we have assumed that resources were ubiquitously located. If we dropped this assumption, input prices would vary with different locations. Average cost curves would shift up or down from place to place depending upon the relationship of a place with respect to its input sources. The uniform distribution of places would then be distorted by those places that could attract firms from the center of their markets because costs were so low that they offset the maximizing of receipts at the center of markets. Under these circumstances a reduction of transportation costs could cause a concentration of market centers with the same functions instead of a dispersal of centers. This would occur if the reduction in transportation costs caused the delivered price from the lower-average-cost production center to be lower than the average cost of higher-average-cost producers at their centers. The higher-cost centers would be eliminated from competition, and the market areas of the low-cost centers would be larger. The same impact would occur, and it would be more likely to occur, if there were a simultaneous increase in the economies of scale through a shift down and to the right in the average-cost schedule.

Several studies tend to support this analysis. They have observed that production centers have tended to be more concentrated after the improvement of some mode of transportation. Isard summarizes them in this way: "Historically we find that reduced transport rates have tended (1) to transform a scattered, ubiquitous pattern of production into an increasingly concentrated one, and (2) to effect progressive differentiation and selection between sites with superior and inferior resources and trade routes."[5] On a plain in which resources were uniformly distributed, however, a reduction in transportation costs would cause decentralization, as we have seen. The observed historical relationship could only have occurred on such a plain if changes in economies of scale and reduction in transportation rates occurred simultaneously.[6]

It is now time to investigate the impact of technological change on land use.[7] If technological change induced a general reduction in transportation costs, the slope of the rent bid curve for each activity would be less. There would be no effect on the ceiling rent each use would pay for land at the market center, since its calculation does not require any transportation cost. The result would be an expansion of all land use, and an expansion in the amount of land for each use. Thus, with no change in market prices for products, the reduction of transportation costs increases the amount of land devoted to producing each good and causes an increase in supply. This is reflected in a shift to the right of the supply curve in each market. There will be an excess supply of each commodity and the price will be forced down. As the price decreases, the rent bid curve for each use will also shift down, reducing the amount of land devoted to the use. Whether more or less land is devoted to a particular use after the change in transportation cost depends upon the price elasticity of demand for the product.

If the demand for the product is perfectly inelastic, that is, if there will be no change in the quantity demanded in the market with a change in price, the price of the product will continue to fall, causing the rent bid curve to continue to fall until the same amount of land as before the change is devoted to producing the product in question. Of course, if any change in land productivity resulted because of the new rent levels, then more or less land would be required to achieve the same production as before depend-

[5] Walter Isard, *Location and Space-economy* (Cambridge, Mass.: The M.I.T. Press, 1956), p. 87. Isard cites the following studies: W. H. Dean, Jr., *The Theory of the Geographic Location of Economic Activities* (Ann Arbor, Mich.: Edwards Brothers, Inc., 1938), chap. 3; E. M. Hoover, *Location Theory and the Shoe and Leather Industries* (Cambridge, Mass.: Harvard University Press, 1937), chap. 3; and H. Ritschl, "Reine und historische Dynamik des Standortes der Erzeugungszweige," *Schmollers Jahrbuch*, vol. 51 (1927), pp. 813–870.
[6] August Lösch, *The Economics of Location* (New Haven, Conn.: Yale University Press, 1954), pp.174–178. Lösch, however, would not agree that the impact of a change in technology on production centers and trading areas would have a further impact on the geographic distribution of towns; it would only change their economic functions. The simplified model used in Chap. 3 of this book, however, does show an impact because not all possible trading-area sizes are always used. Each function with the same size trading area would be affected the same way by the change in transport costs. A new set of all possible trading-area sizes would be used.
[7] This analysis relies on the following studies: Dunn, *op. cit.*, chap. 6; and Earl R. Swanson, "Technological Change and the Location of Agricultural Production," *Modern Land Policy* (Urbana, Ill.: The University of Illinois Press, 1962), pp. 113–119.

ing on whether productivity decreased or increased. If rent paid were less, land would be substituted for nonland resources, and productivity per acre would fall. More land would be required after the change in transportation cost. Less land would be required after the change if more rent were paid, and nonland factors would be substituted for land resources.

As long as the market demand curves for the final products are downward sloping (have some price elasticity of demand) the change in transport cost will cause a decrease in price that in turn will cause an increase in the quantity of the product demanded as the supply curve shifts to the right. Thus, price decreases and causes the rent bid curves to fall until once again the amount of land in a particular use produces the quantity demanded in the market that firms are willing to supply at the market price. But now the quantity is greater than before the change in transportation cost. Thus, the new equilibrium will require more land. For those goods for which the price elasticity of demand is greater than 0 land use will expand. It will expand more for those goods with greater elasticities of demand. A reduction in transportation cost without a change in income or population would cause the urban areas to encroach upon rural areas as long as the price elasticity of demand for urban services, such as housing, had a greater price elasticity of demand than agricultural products.

Now consider a change in technology that increases production per acre of land. With no change in input or output prices such a change in technology would mean that a firm could increase its rate of production with no change in outlay. That is the same as a reduction in total cost at each rate of production. The productivity change would mean that at each location rent could be increased until the total cost and total revenue curves were once again tangent. Therefore, the rent bid curve for each activity with the change in technology would shift upward. It would not, however, be a parallel upward shift. At the same time that the rent bid curve shifted upward the slope would become steeper. From Chapter 5, you will remember that two uses with the same price but different productivities per acre would have different rent bid curves. The use with the greater productivity would have a higher and steeper rent bid curve.

It would be unusual for all productive activities to experience the same productivity benefits at the same point in time. Therefore, we shall investigate the impact of a technological change causing the product per acre for one crop or for one use to increase, while no changes occur in the production function of other products. For illustrative purposes consider a market center at which two products are sold. Before the change in technology spatial equilibrium exists. The rent bid curves might be as shown in Figure 9-1. AB and CD are the rent bid curves for two uses: I

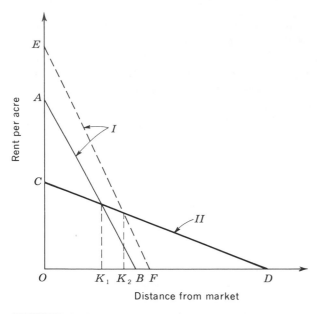

FIGURE 9-1

and II. As a result of the improvement in technology in the production of product I, the rent bid curve shifts to EF. Therefore, there would initially be an increase in land devoted to the production of I. The radius of the land use zone would increase from OK_1 to OK_2.

In the long run, however, the rent bid curve EF would shift back toward the origin. The increase in land devoted to use I would increase the supply without any change in input or output prices. Thus, it causes a shift to the right of the supply of product I. There is then an excess supply in the market and the market price is forced down. If the demand for I were perfectly inelastic, EF would shift parallel downward so that it would intersect CD inside OK_1. Less land will be devoted to production of I because the same quantity is demanded as before but the productivity of land is greater. Notice that even if there is a slight price elasticity of demand, the amount of land devoted to I will still decrease. If the elasticity of demand for I were large, the amount of land devoted to I would increase.

So far the analysis has assumed that nothing has occurred to change the rent bid curve for product II. If, however, land for production of I encroaches upon land formerly used for II, or if land for production of I shrinks so that land formerly used for I now is used for II, there will be a shift in the market supply of product II. If more land is devoted to II than before, the supply curve will shift to the right, there will be an excess supply, the market price will decrease, and the rent bid function will shift down until the amount of land produces a quantity that is demanded at the market price. If less land is devoted to II than before, the supply curve will shift to the left, there will be an excess demand, the market price will increase, and the rent bid curve will shift up until the amount of land produces a quantity that is demanded at the market price.

Finally, consider a technological change that allows the average nonland cost per unit of output to decrease but does not change the output per acre. Once again suppose that the technological change affects product I, but not product II. In this case the initial impact is an upward parallel shift in the rent bid curve AB. Unlike EF in Figure 9-1, the new rent bid curve in this case would have the same slope as AB. Neither the productivity per acre nor the transport cost of the product has changed so that the slope remains unchanged. At each location, however, the ceiling rent is higher because total cost has been reduced and more rent can be offered before the total cost curve is tangent to the total revenue curve.

Initially, the increase in the rent bid curve will cause an increase in the amount of land devoted to product I. Land will be taken from production of II. This will cause a shift to the right in the market supply curve for product I. There will be an excess supply at the current market price, causing that price to decrease. The decrease in the market price will cause the rent bid curve EF to shift back down. The new boundary will be farther from the market than the old as long as the price elasticity of demand for product I is greater than 0. Since land for the production of II will be reduced, some adjustment in the rent bid function for product II will also be required. The final equilibrium, however, will find the amount of land devoted to product I increased so long as the price elasticity of demand is greater than 0.

ECONOMIC DEVELOPMENT AND URBANIZATION

We have now indicated the way in which those variables usually associated with economic growth—population growth, increases in per capita income, and technological change—might affect the spatial structure of the economy. We have tried to isolate deductively the impact of each variable on the size, number, and spacing of cities, and on the land use pattern in each city. Since there is no common impact from each change, the actual change in the spatial structure of an economy will depend upon the particular mix of changes in population, per capita income, and technological change taking place.

Some writers, however, have argued that the causal relation between economic development and cities does not just flow from development to structure, but in the reverse direction as well. Their argument is that economic growth proceeds more rapidly near urban industrial centers called growth poles.[8] There appear to be three main reasons for more rapid development near these centers. The first reason is that agglomeration economies attract plants from other sites that are equally attractive locationally except for the agglomeration economies of the urban center. Thus, the agglomeration economies described in Chapter 4 that were used in that static context to explain the congregation of many activities in one place are also used to explain why old firms and new firms just starting may be attracted to developed urban centers rather than to smaller places or the hinterland. The second reason is that the input markets operate more efficiently in and near these centers. In and near these urban centers there are fewer impediments to factor price equalization. Workers easily shift to better-paying jobs, and capital easily shifts to investments with better payoffs. The information about new opportunities is more complete, the distance between workers and opportunities is less, and the distance between surplus capital and investment opportunities is less. The third reason is that the urban atmosphere is more conducive to innovation and technological change. It is hard to pin this down. It is partly because of the "energy" of urban people and partly because of the ease of communication between so many people in the same place—which would appear indistinguishable from agglomeration economies.

While a few empirical studies have tended to verify the proposition that urbanization causes more rapid progress, other studies have not. The evidence is not clear. On the one hand Tang has found that input markets in agriculture operate more efficiently near urban centers than at locations farther away.[9] On the other hand, Berry has found that one aspect of the growth pole thesis that a highly integrated system of cities should be associated with economic development does not hold. Dividing systems of cities into primate systems and rank-size systems, where "primate" indicates one large city or a few large cities dominating many small villages with intermediate size places missing and where "rank-size" indicates systems conforming to the rank-size rule, Berry could find no association between indices of economic development and type of city size distribution

[8] See T. W. Schultz, *The Economic Organization of Agriculture* (New York: McGraw-Hill Book Company, 1953), pp. 146–171, 283–320; Eric E. Lampard, "The History of Cities in the Economically Advanced Areas," *Economic Development and Cultural Change*, vol. 3 (January, 1955), pp. 81–102; and John R. P. Friedmann, "Locational Aspects of Economic Development," *Land Economics* (August, 1956), pp. 213–227.
[9] Anthony M. Tang, *Economic Development in the Southern Piedmont, 1860–1950* (Chapel Hill, N.C.: The University of North Carolina Press, 1958).

in a comparison of ninety-five countries.[10] Although Berry found no association between urbanization (index based on percentage of population in cities over 20,000) and type of city size distribution, he did find a strong association between urbanization and economic development.

Two further comments need to be made on economic development and cities. The first is that changes in transportation technology cause changes in transportation routes as well as costs. Such a change can cause a change in a city's hierarchical rank in a region. For example, before the railroad, St. Louis was the largest center in the Upper Midwest. It served as a distribution and exporting point for trade between the Upper Midwest and the rest of the world. Agricultural products were collected at St. Louis and shipped to Europe and New York via New Orleans. Manufactured products from New England were distributed to the region from St. Louis after being shipped up the Mississippi River from New Orleans. Even the Erie Canal did not make Chicago a better transshipment point to the East because there was no good transport link between Chicago and the entire Upper Midwest. The river system was St. Louis's great advantage. The development and construction of railroads provided a way for Chicago to develop a transport link with the Upper Midwest Region. In the 1850s the construction of railroads connecting Chicago to Missouri, Illinois, Iowa, Minnesota, Wisconsin, Indiana, Ohio, and the South, as well as with New York made Chicago the cheapest trade route for exports from and imports to the Upper Midwest Region. By 1870 population statistics confirmed the fact that Chicago was the largest and most dominant city of the region.[11]

The second further comment is that the impact of development on cities described in this chapter is a comparative-statics analysis. The analysis began with an equilibrium situation, changes were introduced, and the new optimum spatial equilibrium was found. The impact of the introduced change was in the form of the change in equilibrium size, number, and spacing of cities, and the change in land use within cities. The shift from one optimum spatial organization to another will take time, and may never be accomplished. Nevertheless, the direction of change will be as indicated by the shift. Change in the geographic distribution of economic activity would be accomplished by migration of resources. Even though there are differences between places in the returns to resources of a given quality, the indicated migration may never take place. The reason lies in the analysis of the costs and returns to migration discussed in the previous chapter.

[10] Brian J. L. Berry, "City Size Distributions and Economic Development," *Economic Development and Cultural Change*, vol. 9 (July, 1961), pp. 573–587.
[11] Wyatt Winton Belcher, *The Economic Rivalry between St. Louis and Chicago, 1850–1880* (New York: Columbia University Press, 1947); Lewis F. Thomas, "Decline of St. Louis as Midwest Metropolis," *Economic Geography* (April, 1949), pp. 118–127; W. H. Bishop, "St. Louis," *Harpers New Monthly Magazine* (1884), p. 501.

SUMMARY

We have shown that in a plain with uniform resource distribution an increase in population would tend to cause an increase in the number and size of cities and a decrease in the distance between them. It would tend to increase the amount of land used for urban uses. An increase in per capita income would tend to cause the number of cities to increase, the size of cities to increase, and the distance between them to decrease. It would tend to cause the amount of land devoted to agricultural uses to decrease relative to urban uses, and to cause population to shift from rural to urban areas.

Technological change resulting in reduced transportation costs would tend to cause an increase in the size of cities, a decrease in the distance between them, and an increase in the number of places. It would tend to increase the amount of land devoted to the production of items the price elasticity of demand for which is greater than 0. Technological change resulting in reduced transportation costs and increased economies of scale would tend to reduce the number of places, increase the distance between them, and decrease the size of cities. The impact of technological change upon the amount of land devoted to the production of particular goods and services depends upon whether the improvement changes the output per acre of land and whether the price elasticity of demand is greater than 0. Land for the production of a good with a small price elasticity of demand may be reduced if technological change increases the output per acre. Technological change causing no increase in the output per acre will tend to cause an increase in the amount of land devoted to a product so long as the price elasticity of demand is greater than 0.

Nevertheless, we have also shown that the reduction of transportation costs on a plain in which resources were unevenly distributed would tend to cause concentration of production places rather than the decentralization shown to occur on the plain with ubiquitous resources.

Although it is obvious that economic development will cause changes in the spatial structure of the economy, that same structure may also influence economic development. There is some evidence to indicate that economic development progresses more rapidly near urban industrial centers.

The changes in size, spacing, and number of cities caused by technological change in transportation may cause individual cities to change their rank in the hierarchy of cities.

All the changes will require time to work themselves out, and they may in fact never do so because the costs and returns to the migration of resources may not be profitable.

With a few exceptions we have studied the structure, stability, and growth of regions as they would be without government action or interference. Households and businessmen acting independently in their own self-interest have determined the spatial order of the economy. We have, however, already noted the impact of political boundaries on market areas and systems of cities. We have also mentioned the impact of Federal expenditures on different regions. In this chapter we shall treat these matters in a systematic fashion. First, we shall determine the functions of government in a competitive economy. Second, we shall investigate the special problems of overlapping government jurisdictions to see what can be said about what level of government should carry out various functions. Third, we shall investigate the role of government in solving the problems of depressed areas and urban blight. These three topics will be discussed within the special framework of the spatial organization of the economy previously developed. The goal of public policy throughout will be assumed to be to maximize the value of resources at the national level rather than to maximize the value of a particular region's resources possibly at the expense of other regions.

THE ROLE OF GOVERNMENT[1]

As noted in Chapter 8, resources in a competitively organized economy would be allocated to the production of goods and services in such a way and in such locations that their value would be maximized. Value depends upon the price of each product, which is itself determined by equilibrium in the product markets. This equilibrium is the situation in which the quantity people demand is equal to the quantity businesses are willing to supply at the current price. This price reflects the value that people place on the last unit of product received, and it also reflects the marginal cost of producing the good or service. Production will shift from goods and services that are valued less on the margin by consumers than their marginal cost to goods and services that consumers find more valuable on the margin than their marginal cost. Goods, services, and resources are allocated in

[1] See Richard A. Musgrave, *The Theory of Public Finance* (New York: McGraw-Hill Book Company, 1959), chap. 1. A less advanced discussion may be found in Francis M. Bator, *The Question of Government Spending* (New York: Collier Books, a division of Crowell-Collier Publishing Co., 1962), chaps. 6, 7. A similar discussion in the urban setting is in Vincent Ostrom, Charles M. Tiebout, and Robert Warren, "The Organization of Government in Metropolitan Areas: A Theoretical Inquiry," *American Political Science Review*, vol. 55 (December, 1961), pp. 831–842.

such a way that each man's welfare is maximized, since each individual is free to purchase whatever he chooses within his income.

Nevertheless, there are several circumstances in which the free market will break down and not provide the goods and services desired by individuals. Furthermore, the marketplace maximizes welfare, given the income distribution of families in the economy. This distribution may not be considered equitable. Finally, the economy may be unable to reach full employment during short periods of time. Each of these situations requires the interference of government and is the basis for an economic role of government.

Because the last two functions are more easily discussed, they will be taken up first. In Chapter 7 it was shown that in the short run an economy may tend toward an equilibrium level of income that represents less than full employment of resources. There is nothing within the system that causes full employment to be reached, except over a long period of time. Therefore, the first government function is to stabilize the economy at full employment.

The price of goods and services—their value to households at the margin and their cost to the economy at the margin—depends upon who has income. If everyone had the same income there would be a different demand for goods and services than if 1 percent of the families had 99 percent of the income and the other 99 percent of the families had 1 percent of total income. Income is the sum of wages and salaries, rent, interest, dividends, and profits of proprietors. Each component of income is a return for the use of a resource. Wages and salaries are the return for human resources; rents are the return for land, real estate, and property rights; interest payments are the return for money lent; and dividends and profits are the return for risk. With the exception of profits and dividends the rate of return to each resource is equal to the value of product produced by the resource on the margin during a particular time period. Nevertheless, because individuals differ in their skills and abilities and in their holdings of property, income is not equally distributed to every individual or family. The community may consider the resulting distribution inequitable. In a democratic society the determination of taxation and subsidization is made through the elected legislature by majority vote. The second government function, then, is to reapportion income toward the distribution considered equitable by society.

Even if incomes were considered equitably distributed and the resources of the economy were fully employed, there would be another reason for government interference in the market economy. Some goods would not be produced in the market even though individuals and families wanted them and could afford to pay for them. These goods and services would not be produced in the market because they are not subject to the exclusion principle. This means that a seller could not exclude consumers from the benefits of the product if the consumer did not pay. Good examples are national defense and a police force for internal security. If a private army were to provide this service to citizens of an area, they might try to charge each individual a price that would cover the total cost of the service. If, however, an individual decided not to pay the price, he would still benefit from the services of the army. He could not be excluded from the benefits because he did not pay, except by forcible removal from the region. The latter action is outside voluntary market action. Individuals would then have incentive to avoid payment, the cost of the service would not be covered, and the service would not be provided in the marketplace. Thus, the government, as the agent for the collective society, can step in and see that the good or service is provided. The decision is made through the legislature, which in turn provides the funds through taxation.

Some goods are produced in the market in greater or lesser amounts than if marginal benefits and costs were equated. The value of the product to the consumer and the marginal cost of providing the product have not been equated. They may not be equated because externalities exist. The firm attempting to maximize profits makes its decisions on the basis of the costs it incurs and the revenues it receives. In some cases not all the costs incurred by the economy because of a firm's activity are incurred by the firm itself. These are called social costs. Sometimes not all the benefits generated by a firm's activity yield revenues for the firm. These are called social benefits.

The classical case of social cost is air pollution. A firm may pollute the air or streams with emissions from its production process. The pollution will cost others in the economy, and these costs will not be reflected in the operating costs of the firm. Air pollution increases the maintenance cost of buildings on surrounding lots and increases medical costs of individuals. Water pollution may increase the costs of treating drinking water for downstream cities and may kill wildlife. These social costs are not borne by the acting firm. In such cases government intervention is justified in order to internalize the social costs. Since measurement of the social costs is extremely difficult, the usual action has been to prohibit pollution. One example is the smoke control ordinance that exists in many cities.

An example of social benefits arises from public housing and water resource investments. The economic justification for government water resource expenditures for dams and river improvements and for government expenditures on public housing is often based on social benefits.

Private enterprise does not and would not build water resource projects or public housing because the receipts would not be sufficient to cover the costs of construction. Nevertheless, the projects are said to be profitable because of their benefits to people not directly involved in the transactions. For example, public housing would benefit the whole community rather than just the occupants of the housing, it is argued, because the construction of such good housing for the poor and elimination of slums would reduce fire hazards, welfare payments, and crime.[2] In the same way the benefits of river improvements could not be captured through receipts by a private firm because the river is a public thoroughfare. People could benefit from the improvements without paying the enterprise that constructed the improvements. Thus, externalities can justify the government provision of some goods and services in the economy.

The market process also breaks down in the case of decreasing cost industries. These industries have been called natural monopolies. They arise because large fixed costs are required to enter the activity and because marginal costs are small. Over the relevant range of production,

[2] Sometimes these claims are unjustified. See Hugh O. Nourse, "The Effect of Public Housing on Property Values in St. Louis," *Land Economics* (November, 1963), pp. 433–441.

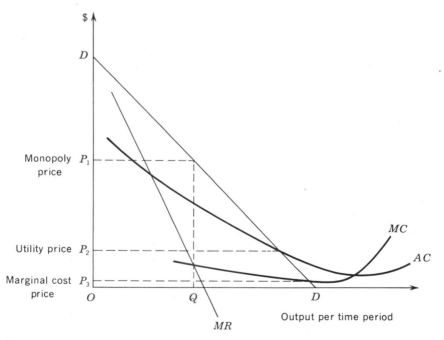

FIGURE 10-1

marginal cost is always less than average cost. Thus, the output of such industries cannot be priced at the socially desirable equality with marginal costs without incurring losses. The situation can be described in a graph, such as Figure 10-1. The market demand for the industry's product is DD. Average cost AC declines over the relevant range of output. Marginal cost is low throughout this range and is less than average cost. Figure 10-1 characterizes the cost and demand situation for most public utilities, such as water, electric, gas, telephone, bridge, and railroad companies.

Without government interference these services would be provided, but at monopoly prices. Competition would be unstable and would fail because the first firm in the business, or the one with the most financial backing, could continue lowering prices until other firms were run out of business. From the economist's point of view the result is unsatisfactory because resources are misallocated. The price that would maximize profits for the monopolist, P_1, is much greater than the marginal cost of producing the good or service. People value the last unit higher than its cost to the community. The community would be better off if resources were used to increase the production of the utility, since the value of resources in the production of other products is less. Therefore, some kind of government intervention would be necessary to prevent the misallocation of resources resulting from the free-market monopoly price in natural monopolies.

We can summarize the last three cases for government interference as the argument for the third economic function of government. This last function is correction of misallocations of resources resulting from externalities or monopolies, or because goods are not subject to the exclusion principle.

GOVERNMENT AND THE SPATIAL ORGANIZATION
OF THE ECONOMY[3]

The regional or spatial problems of government may now be posed. We begin by pointing out that the decisions for government action in a democratic society are made in a legislature by majority rule. Ideally the area affected by an action of government would be coterminous with the area that people in the decision-making body represent. In reality, of course, the ideal seldom occurs, and herein lie many of the regional problems of public policy.

The legislative decisions of the Federal government are made by representatives of the entire geographic area of the United States. Many of

[3] On this section see Ostrom, Tiebout, and Warren, *loc. cit.*

these decisions affect all the people of the country, but some have regional impacts. For example, the income tax does not fall equally on all regions. If in fact the cost of living is different in different regions of the country, income taxes are a greater burden on people in the regions where the cost of living is higher. We have seen in Chapter 6 that per capita income is low in some regions and high in others. Federal income taxes will come more than in proportion to population from high per capita income regions. This is not to judge the equity of the tax flow, only that it exists.

Federal expenditures will not necessarily be spent in areas where tax receipts are greatest. Notice that it is unnecessary for the government to have a conscious regional policy to affect regional development. During the 1950s the Defense Department changed from buying tanks and other hardware to buying missiles. This caused a substantial shift in Federal military expenditures from the Great Lakes Region to the Southwest and the Far West.[4] All other things remaining equal, this kind of situation causes a reduction of employment in the Great Lakes Region and an increase in the Far West, and requires a locational adjustment of production or employment or both.

The Federal government had an important influence in regional development in the United States through its control of territorial land. Railroads were built by private companies with the aid of the right-of-way land given to them as a subsidy by the government. Areas connected by rail had greater access to markets and materials and were in better competitive positions than other regions without railroads.

The Federal government can affect the growth of a region through its tariff policy. If it chooses to tax imports of material that are required in industry z, then cost of industry z will rise and it will be less competitive in world competition. Those regions in which industry z would find its optimum location might suffer a reduction in exports, income, and employment. Price supports on such products as cotton have had the same result. The increase in cotton prices may make it extremely difficult for the United States textile industry, which you will note from Table 4-1 is concentrated in only a few regions, to be competitive in world markets. In fact the situation is worse in the case of cotton. Cotton is sold on the world market at lower prices than to domestic textile producers.

At the state and local level the regional policy problem is different. Although there are some similar problems when states receive taxes from the whole state while spending in particular parts, there is also the different problem of a political unit's taking action which affects an area greater

[4] Robert E. Graham, Jr., "Factors Underlying Changes in the Geographic Distribution of Income," *Survey of Current Business* (April, 1964), p. 23.

than the jurisdiction of the governmental unit. These external benefits or costs to individuals in areas outside the area of the political decision making organization will be called spillovers. Spillovers are a particular problem in metropolitan areas with fragmented government units. The metropolitan area is often composed of a central city with its own government and several rings of suburban communities, each with its own government. There are over 100 such governments in the St. Louis Metropolitan Area.[5]

Each political unit makes decisions regarding the goods and services that it should provide for itself. For example, one community may build a library, provide roads, set aside land for a park, maintain full-time police and fire departments, and maintain a school system. Another community in the same area may establish a school, good roads, a police department, and a voluntary fire department. Even though the second community does not provide a park, the individuals of that community may benefit from the park of the first community. It is difficult to exclude a nontaxpayer from such a park because the very reason for providing the park is that it provides social benefits. Besides, there might be families in the community with the park who would not have tax receipts because they rent their house space rather than own it. This would be a particular problem if the only tax in the community were a property tax.

An even better example of the spillover effect is the road system. Each community takes care of its own roads, including the posting of traffic control signs and speed limits. Good roads benefit all the inhabitants of a metropolitan region. Poor roads, those that are not kept in good repair, or those that are narrower in one community than in others along the same route, cause traffic bottlenecks as well as increased costs in time and automobile wear and tear for all the inhabitants of the metropolitan area. Since these spillover costs and benefits are not incurred by the decision-making political organization, they are not used in the organization's calculations on spending. Thus, some communities underspend for roads because so many of the benefits accrue to other communities.

As in the case of the regional impact of Federal policies, inequality of average income between areas within the metropolitan area complicates and creates many of the so-called urban problems thought to require consolidated or metropolitan government action. In the post World War II era the development of the automobile, the federal subsidy of freeways, and the Federal Housing Administration Insurance program, coupled with the income tax benefits of home ownership, have encouraged the expansion of single-family housing on the periphery of the city. Young families demand

[5] John C. Bollens, *Exploring the Metropolitan Community* (Berkeley, Calif.: University of California Press, 1964), p. 35.

space for children and good schools. These new middle-class suburbs encroached on the older suburbs that had been built in an earlier era. The suburbs formed new political subdivisions rather than joining the political organization of the central city. In this way a multitude of suburban governments was established to respond to the needs of these constituents. Nevertheless, the central city was often left with a concentration of households in the lower end of the income distribution. Neighborhoods have always been relatively homogeneous with respect to income, ethnic group, and tastes for community living. But the new situation brought these neighborhoods into their own political decision-making groups. Furthermore, not all the suburbs that developed were well off. Some were made up of poor minority group families. Thus, municipal governments in the same metropolitan area often reflect different income groups.

The establishment of communities within the metropolitan area based on income reinforces the problem of the spillover impact of each community upon the other. Many of the central metropolitan services that would not be provided by the market, because of either externalities or exception to the exclusion principle, had been first established by the central city. These might include an extensive park system, libraries, museums, zoo, roads, sewer system, water system, and police and fire protection. The benefits from these services spill over to the new residents who are outside the taxing jurisdiction of the central city with the result that central cities have had to support institutions even when the persons who benefited from the institutions could have helped to support them if they could have been reached.

URBAN AND REGIONAL PROBLEMS

It is now time to tie these various strands of thought together and take a brief—all too brief—look at some of the main urban and regional "problems" and their proposed solutions in order to evaluate whether there might not be alternative and better policies available. The list of problems could and does fill many books, but the essential features can be brought out by describing a few of the more important problems. At the regional level we have "depressed areas." At the urban level we have "urban blight."

Beginning first with the regional setting, we find that there are at least two definitions of a depressed area that do not necessarily cover the same situation. *Depressed areas* have often been defined as those areas in which per capita income, or some other measure of welfare such as family income, is very much below the national average. These areas are poverty areas and may or may not have a problem of unemployment. But chronic unemployment above the national average has been used as a definition by several Federal Acts providing funds to help depressed areas.

Either of these situations could be the result of inadequate locational adjustment. Unemployment would be a short-run problem, low per capita income a long-run problem. As previously indicated, these might occur because workers and capital did not shift to new employment opportunities in other regions. The migration might not have taken place because information about new opportunities was not communicated. Another reason, however, that migration might not have taken place is that it was not a profitable investment to undertake. Finally, even if it were a profitable investment to undertake, workers might not have been able to make the move because they had no capital or collateral to use for borrowing the required funds.

The role of government in this situation within the framework set forth at the beginning of this chapter could be one of several. First, there would be the option to redistribute income in favor of low-income persons. A standard of living might be established below which persons would not be taxed, but below which they would receive a transfer of income from the government to bring their income up to the standard.[6] Such a policy would reach the depressed areas and increase the income of the inhabitants to an adequate standard of living. Second, the government might eliminate its own policies obstructing the mobility of resources, or might promote the flow of information about new opportunities. In particular, the minimum wage law may obstruct the adjustment of wages necessary for the market to reallocate employment. Third, the government might provide goods and services such as a transportation system and water resource investments that have not been provided by the market because their benefits are social benefits. A benefit-cost study would be necessary to show whether the social benefits existed to justify the investment. The public investment might increase the accessibility of the region to make it profitable for new investment. New employment opportunities could increase employment and wages in the region. Fourth, the government might subsidize the migration of individuals willing to move, or subsidize their retraining. Notice, however, that the national product would be reduced if individuals who were unwilling to move even if moving and retraining costs were paid were forced to migrate.

There is no justification for subsidizing investment in an area if it would be unable to stand on its own feet without aid. Such a subsidy would only further misallocate resources in the economy and reduce potential national

---

[6] Milton Friedman, *Capitalism and Freedom* (Chicago: The University of Chicago Press, 1962), pp. 190–195.

product. Moes, however, has suggested that this is precisely the policy that should be undertaken. He suggests that workers in depressed areas be taxed to provide subsidies to attract firms to their places so that the workers will not have to migrate to obtain new job opportunities.[7] A subsidy great enough to attract industry may also be great enough through the reduction of real wages in the local area to induce further migration. If the subsidy did work, the lower real wages, even taking account of lower costs of living, might be less desirable than the other forms of government interference that increase worker productivity.[8]

If these are the actions government may take, which level of government should undertake them? From our earlier considerations of the ideal political framework in which decisions were made by the collective action of all the people in the area impacted by an action, it would appear that the Federal government would have to be responsible for action to alleviate depressed areas. The reason is that many of the benefits are spillover benefits, such as retraining that accrues to individuals who leave an area. On the other hand, it behooves a local area to inform businesses about the advantages of their locale. Nevertheless, subsidy by the local government to attract firms from other areas may merely shift business from one place to another and not contribute to total national product. In fact it may reduce the potential by attracting production to less than optimum sites.

Now let us take up the problem of urban blight. The market does not eliminate slums or blighted areas of the city because externalities exist. If there were a new use for slum property, and if the present value of the new use were greater than the cost of buying and demolishing the slum building, property owners or buyers would still be unwilling to convert the land to the new use. The reason is that the rest of the neighborhood would still be in slum use. As soon as the new building or structure were put in place, its value would be diminished by the impact of the general neighborhood conditions. A solution would be for a developer to buy up all the land in a neighborhood and develop the entire neighborhood. In an already developed area of a city, however, several current landholders who heard of the deal could raise their price so high to the developer that the developer could make no profit from the project.[9] Thus, there is a need for the government to intervene.

[7] J. E. Moes, *Local Subsidies for Industry* (Chapel Hill, N.C.: The University of North Carolina Press, 1962).
[8] George Borts and Jerome Stein, *Economic Growth in a Free Market* (New York: Columbia University Press, 1964), pp. 200–201.
[9] Otto A. Davis and Andrew B. Whinston, "The Economics of Urban Renewal," *Law and Contemporary Problems* (Winter, 1961), p. 105.

If, in fact, this is the reason for the existence of blight, the only role that government would be required to take would be to aid in condemnation of land to eliminate the monopoly profits of holdouts. In the United States, however, the law does not allow condemnation of land for private purposes. Therefore, it may be that the Urban Renewal Act is the only way to get things done. An agency of the local government buys the slum land, clears it, and sells it to the highest bidder. The private buyer develops the land. If the new development is profitable to the builder, the government should make neither a profit nor a loss. The private developer should be willing and able to pay for the cost of the old buildings plus their demolition. Under these conditions there is no need for Federal intervention in urban affairs. The municipal government can handle the problem of blight.

Nevertheless, Federal legislation has also provided for subsidies. Under the Urban Renewal section of the Housing Act, local agencies buy, clear, and sell the areas of the city that they designate as blighted. There are provisions for relocating the occupants of the blighted area. But beyond this the Federal government provides to the local agency a subsidy equal to the difference between the receipts from sale of the cleared land and the costs of acquiring and clearing the blighted property. The justification for the subsidy was that the housing to be rebuilt would be for the low-income families occupying slum houses. The Urban Renewal program was intended to provide a decent home for every American.[10] The subsidies have been paid out, but most reuse of urban renewal land has been for commercial or industrial property, or to house higher-income families.

The justification for subsidies was to house poor people. In fact, however, the use of the subsidy has been to redevelop urban land, the justification for which would be based on externalities. In that case, though, the subsidy is not justified, only the condemnation action.

Blighted areas are occupied by poor families. The incomes of these families are too low to enable them to purchase or rent "standard" housing. Nevertheless, substandard housing is just one symptom of poverty. Another symptom is inadequate schools in municipalities occupied by the poor. Another is inadequate nutrition. In such a situation government policy would be to redistribute income. The argument against the redistribution of income has been that the poor would not spend their income on better housing, education, etc., but on big cars and television sets. If, however, we are to base policy on the optimality of market solutions, the income transfer would be the correct solution. Each individual or family is assumed to know what choices of expenditure from their income will

<hr />

[10] On this point, and in reference to this section in general, see Hugh O. Nourse, "The Economics of Urban Renewal," *Land Economics* (February, 1966), pp. 65–74.

maximize their welfare. Others cannot make this choice. The disturbing questions to ask are the following ones: Who determines what is good for the poor? When do the poor become able to determine how they should spend their income? Do they become capable when they take on the same middle-class standards as the people who are attempting to determine how the poor should spend their income?

For a policy of redistribution of income, action is required at the Federal level. If it were attempted by communities, the rich would migrate to their own municipalities where income transfers would not be voted. Only at the Federal level through majority action could the redistribution function be fulfilled.

The economic justification for zoning is also based on the resource reallocation function of government. The most profitable site for a soap factory or other use of land does not take account of the social benefits or costs that might be incurred. Some uses of land, such as putting a soap factory in the middle of a residential neighborhood, would cause the surrounding property to suffer losses in value. The social costs are difficult to measure and so have not been internalized by taxation. Land use controls have been used to prevent incompatible uses from causing social costs.

SUMMARY

Except under certain specified conditions the market organization of the economy will efficiently allocate resources. Government intervention is required to redistribute income when necessary; to stabilize employment; and to reallocate resources in those cases in which externalities exist, in which the exclusion principle does not hold, and in which natural monopolies exist. The spatial organization of the economy and government may create an additional externality. Benefits or costs from action by one governmental unit may spill over to individuals of other governmental units. Within this framework it was found that the economic role of government in solving the problem of depressed areas would be to subsidize migration, redistribute income, eliminate obstructions to migration, and provide public investments that would be justified on the basis of benefit-cost analyses. To solve the problem of urban "blight" it was found that the economic role of government would be to provide the mechanism by which externalities could be circumvented. To the extent that the problem was considered one of poverty, the economic role of government would once again be redistribution of income.

BOOKS

Alonso, William: *Location and Land Use* (Cambridge, Mass.: Harvard University Press, 1964).

Artle, Roland G.: *The Structure of the Stockholm Economy* (Ithaca, N.Y.: Cornell University Press, 1965).

Berry, Brian J. L., and **Pred, Allen:** *Central Place Studies, A Bibliography of Theory and Applications,* Bibliography Series no. 1 with supplement (Philadelphia: Regional Science Research Institute, 1965).

Borts, George H., and **Stein, Jerome L.:** *Economic Growth in a Free Market* (New York: Columbia University Press, 1964).

Chenery, Hollis B., and **Clark, Paul G.:** *Interindustry Economics* (New York: John Wiley & Sons, Inc., 1962).

Chisholm, M. D. I.: *Rural Settlement and Land Use: An Essay in Location* (London: Hutchinson University Press, 1962).

Dean, W. H., Jr.: *The Theory of the Geographic Location of Economic Activities* (Ann Arbor, Mich.: Edwards Brothers, Inc., 1938).

Duncan, Otis Dudley, et al.: *Metropolis and Region* (Baltimore: The Johns Hopkins Press, 1960).

Dunn, Edgar S., Jr.: *The Location of Agricultural Production* (Gainesville, Fla.: University of Florida Press, 1954).

Greenhut, Melvin: *Plant Location in Theory and in Practice* (Chapel Hill, N.C.: The University of North Carolina Press, 1956).

Haggett, Peter: *Locational Analysis in Human Geography* (New York: St. Martin's Press, Inc., 1966).

Hoover, Edgar M.: *The Location of Economic Activity* (New York: McGraw-Hill Book Company, 1948).

———: *Location Theory and the Shoe and Leather Industries,* Harvard Economic Studies, vol. LV (Cambridge, Mass.: Harvard University Press, 1937).

———, and **Vernon, Raymond:** *Anatomy of a Metropolis* (Cambridge, Mass.: Harvard University Press, 1959).

Ingram, James C.: *Regional Payments Mechanisms: The Case of Puerto Rico* (Chapel Hill, N.C.: The University of North Carolina Press, 1962).

Isard, Walter: *Location and Space-economy* (Cambridge, Mass.: The M.I.T. Press, 1956).

———: *Methods of Regional Analysis: An Introduction to Regional Science* (Cambridge, Mass.: The M.I.T. Press, 1960).

Lösch, August: *The Economics of Location* (New Haven, Conn.: Yale University Press, 1954).

Miernyk, William: *The Elements of Input-Output Analysis* (New York: Random House, Inc., 1965).

Moes, J. E.: *Local Subsidies for Industry* (Chapel Hill, N.C.: The University of North Carolina Press, 1962).

Mueller, Eva, Wilken, Arnold, and **Wood, Margaret:** *Location Decisions and Industrial Mobility in Michigan, 1961* (Ann Arbor, Mich.: Institute of Social Research, The University of Michigan, 1961).

National Bureau of Economic Research: *Trends in the American Economy in the Nineteenth Century,* Studies in Income and Wealth, vol. 24 (New York: National Bureau of Economic Research, 1960).

————: *Regional Income,* Studies in Income and Wealth, vol. 21 (Princeton: Princeton University Press, 1957).

Ohlin, Bertil: *Interregional and International Trade* (Cambridge, Mass.: Harvard University Press, 1957).

Perloff, Harvey S., et al.: *Regions, Resources, and Economic Growth* (Baltimore: The Johns Hopkins Press, 1960).

Pfouts, Ralph (ed.): *The Techniques of Urban Economic Analysis* (West Trenton, N.J.: Chandler-Davis Publishing Co., 1960).

Romans, J. Thomas: *Capital Exports and Growth among U.S. Regions* (Middletown, Conn.: Wesleyan University Press, 1965).

Schultz, T. W.: *The Economic Organization of Agriculture* (New York: McGraw-Hill Book Company, 1953).

Schwartz, Charles F., and **Graham, Robert E., Jr.:** *Personal Income by States since 1929* (Washington, D.C.: U.S. Government Printing Office, 1956).

Tang, Anthony M.: *Economic Development in the Southern Piedmont, 1860–1950* (Chapel Hill, N.C.: The University of North Carolina Press, 1958).

Thompson, Wilbur: *A Preface to Urban Economics* (Baltimore: The Johns Hopkins Press, 1965).

Tiebout, Charles M.: *The Community Economic Base Study,* Supplementary Paper no. 16 (Committee for Economic Development, 1962).

U.S. National Resources Planning Board: *Industrial Location and National Resources* (1943).

Vernon, Raymond: *Metropolis 1985* (Cambridge, Mass.: Harvard University Press, 1959).

Weber, Alfred: *Theory of the Location of Industry,* translated by C. Friedrich (Chicago: University of Chicago Press, 1929).

ARTICLES

Airov, Joseph: "The Construction of Interregional Business Cycle Models," *Journal of Regional Science,* vol. 5 (Summer, 1963), pp. 1–20.

Allen, G. R.: "The 'Courbe des Populations,' A Further Analysis," *Bulletin of the Oxford University Institute of Statistics,* vol. 16 (May and June, 1954), pp. 179–189.

Beckmann, Martin J.: "City Hierarchies and the Distribution of City Size," *Economic Development and Cultural Change,* vol. 6 (April, 1958), pp. 243–248.

Berry, Brian J. L.: "City Size Distributions and Economic Development," *Economic Development and Cultural Change,* vol. 9 (July, 1961), pp. 573–587.

Borts, George H.: "Regional Cycles of Manufacturing Employment in the United States, 1914–1953," *Journal of the American Statistical Association* (March, 1960), pp. 151–211.

————: "Returns Equalization and Regional Growth," *American Economic Review,* vol. 50 (June, 1960), pp. 319–347.

Burton, Edith T.: "Quarterly Estimates of State Personal Income: A New Series," *Survey of Current Business* (December, 1966), pp. 13–15.

Chinitz, Benjamin: "Contrasts in Agglomeration: New York and Pittsburgh," *American Economic Review,* vol. 51, no. 2 (May, 1961), pp. 279–289.

Davis, Otto A., and **Whinston, Andrew B.:** "The Economics of Urban Renewal," *Law and Contemporary Problems* (Winter, 1961), pp. 100–110.

Due, John F.: "Studies of State-Local Tax Influence on Location of Industry," *National Tax Journal* (June, 1961), pp. 163–173.

Fox, Karl A., and **Kumar, T. Krishna:** "The Functional Economic Area: Delineation and Implications for Economic Analysis and Policy," *Papers and Proceedings of the Regional Science Association,* vol. 15 (1965), pp. 57–85.

Friedmann, John R. P.: "Locational Aspects of Economic Development," *Land Economics,* vol. 32 (August, 1956), pp. 213–227.

Graham, Robert E., Jr.: "Factors Underlying Changes in the Geographic Distribution of Income," *Survey of Current Business* (April, 1964), pp. 15–32.

Guthrie, J. A.: "Economies of Scale and Regional Development," *Papers and Proceedings of the Regional Science Association,* vol. 1 (1955), pp. J1–J10.

Hansen, W. Lee, and **Tiebout, Charles M.:** "An Intersectoral Flows Analysis of the California Economy," *The Review of Economics and Statistics,* vol. 45 (November, 1963), pp. 409–418.

Harris, Chauncy D.: "The Market as a Factor in the Localization of Industry in the United States," *Annals of the Association of American Geographers,* vol. 44 (1954), pp. 315–348.

Hathaway, Dale E.: "The Migration from Agriculture: The Historical Record and Its Meaning," *American Economic Review,* vol. 50 (May, 1960), pp. 379–391.

Hirsch, Werner Z.: "Interindustry Relations of a Metropolitan Area," *The Review of Economics and Statistics,* vol. 51 (August, 1959), pp. 360–369.

Lampard, Eric E.: "The History of Cities in the Economically Advanced Areas," *Economic Development and Cultural Change,* vol. 3 (January, 1955), pp. 81–102.

Metzler, Lloyd: "A Multiple-region Theory of Income and Trade," *Econometrica,* vol. 18 (October, 1950), pp. 329–354.

Mills, E. S., and **Lav, Michael R.:** "A Model of Market Areas with Free Entry," *Journal of Political Economy,* vol. 72, no. 3 (June, 1964), pp. 278–288.

Moses, Leon: "Location and the Theory of Production," *Quarterly Journal of Economics* (May, 1958), pp. 259–272.

Muth, Richard F.: "Economic Change and Rural-Urban Land Conversions," *Econometrica,* vol. 29 (January, 1961), pp. 1–23.

————: "The Spatial Structure of the Housing Market," *Papers and Proceedings of the Regional Science Association,* vol. 7 (1961), pp. 207–220.

North, Douglass C.: "Location Theory and Regional Economic Growth," *Journal of Political Economy,* vol. 63, no. 3 (June, 1955), pp. 243–258.

Ostrom, Vincent, Tiebout, Charles M., and **Warren, Robert:** "The Organization of Government in Metropolitan Areas: A Theoretical Inquiry," *American Political Science Review,* vol. 55 (December, 1961), pp. 831–842.

Singer, H. W.: "The 'Courbe des Populations,' A Parallel to Pareto's Law," *Economic Journal,* vol. 46 (June, 1936), pp. 254–263.

Sjaastad, Larry A.: "The Costs and Returns of Human Migration," *Journal of Political Economy,* vol. 70, Special Supplement (October, 1962), pp. 80–93.

Stigler, George J.: "The Division of Labor Is Limited by the Extent of the Market," *Journal of Political Economy,* vol. 59, no. 3 (June, 1951), pp. 185–193.

Swanson, Earl R.: "Technological Change and the Location of Agricultural Production," *Modern Land Policy* (Urbana, Ill.: University of Illinois Press, 1962), pp. 113–119.

Tiebout, Charles M.: "Exports and Regional Economic Growth," *Journal of Political Economy,* vol. 64, no. 2 (April, 1956), pp. 160–169.

————: "Location Theory, Empirical Evidence, and Economic Evolution," *Papers and Proceedings of the Regional Science Association,* vol. 3 (1957), pp. 75–82.

————: "The Urban Economic Base Reconsidered," *Land Economics,* vol. 32 (February, 1956), pp. 95–99.

Vining, Rutledge: "Delimitation of Economic Areas: Statistical Concepts in the Study of Spatial Structure of an Economic System," *Journal of the American Statistical Association* (March, 1953), pp. 44–64.

————: "The Region as a Concept in Business Cycle Analysis," *Econometrica,* vol. 16 (July, 1948), pp. 201–218.

Weisbrod, Burton: "An Expected-income Measure of Economic Welfare," *Journal of Political Economy,* vol. 70, no. 4 (August, 1962), pp. 355–367.

INDEX